For Solomon Morris Sandler
1914-2013

"By one of those dark pathways behind the official consciousness, the old man's death has affected me deeply."

Sigmund Freud, writing about the death of his father in 1896.

Table of Contents

Tea with Freud

An Imaginary Conversation
about
How Psychotherapy Really Works

Steven B. Sandler

Preface

I first decided to write this book because I wanted to explain psychotherapy to the general reading public. I had already written a book for clinicians, and I wanted to spread the word. When I decided to write for a wider audience, it occurred to me that in order for this book to hold the attention of readers who are not psychotherapists, the style of it would need to be something more than the straightforward expository writing of my first book. I therefore hit upon the idea of presenting the information as a series of imaginary conversations with Sigmund Freud. To that end, I have written chapters that alternate between his office in Vienna and my office at Albany Medical Center in upstate New York. In the Albany chapters, I present psychotherapy by using actual verbatim language (with minor alterations in the service of clarity and confidentiality) taken from videotapes of sessions. In the Vienna chapters, I discuss the sessions with Professor Freud, the most famous pioneer of modern "talk therapy."

Psychoanalysis has evolved since Freud, of course, and the approach I wish to describe is a particular offshoot of Freud's work that is not called psychoanalysis at all. It is known as Short-Term Dynamic Psychotherapy; the term *dynamic* refers to the dynamic struggle between, on the one hand, unconscious thoughts, feelings, and memories, and, on the other hand, the defenses against them. This is typically a briefer treatment than analysis, one that involves more active interventions on the part of the therapist. There is a growing body of research to support its efficacy, and I have found it to be a powerful method to help people get to the root of their problems. I hope to convince the reader that this therapy works, and I would like to share some ideas about *how* it works.

Toward the end of the book, I explain my own attempts at making innovations to dynamic psychotherapy. Even though dynamic psychotherapy can be impressively effective, I have found that some patients seem to relapse and return with the same symptoms that brought them to treatment in the first place. Eventually, I realized that for the last century, we therapists have spent a lot of time working with our patients' negative memories, but rarely in any theory is there a rationale for working with *positive* memories. By adding a systematic approach to dealing with early memories of positive experiences, I have seen better, more durable results in the office. I also argue that a focus on positive memories can provide a platform for spiritual growth. I came to these ideas via both personal experiences and sessions with patients, and I explain all this in my imaginary discussions with Freud.

During the process of the writing, a few unexpected things happened. First, I found myself telling the history of how psychoanalysis originally developed. This is a story that I have always found interesting and inspirational; it is a part of our cultural and intellectual heritage. Second, bits and pieces of autobiography seemed to slip into the writing and insist that they have a logical place there, until I finally relented and let them stay. Third, a psychological conflict started to develop between my imaginary Freud and me. As I started writing, a friend counseled that every story needs a good central conflict, so I decided to let it evolve as it would. When it became a struggle between master and disciple, I tinkered a bit with my own identity; I shaved years off my actual age so that I would be the younger therapist who tries, very hesitantly, to debate the older master.

In order to protect the privacy of my patients, I have employed the usual tricks of the trade. I have changed some basic identifying data (age, occupation, family composition, etc.) to disguise the patient. In addition, I have used composites of more than one patient in a given chapter. In doing so, I hope I have accomplished the goal of presenting psychotherapy as it actually happens without jeopardizing the confidentiality of my patients who were brave enough to allow videotaping in the office.

Obviously, my original plan of explaining psychotherapy has been broadened to accommodate the additional goal of telling stories. There is the story of psychoanalysis, beginning with young Freud's trip to Paris to listen to the lectures of a famous neurologist. There is also the story of a conflict between master and disciple, the relationship between my imaginary Freud and me, as well as the *real* relationship between us, my fluctuating assessment of what his work has meant to me over the years. There are the stories of my patients: the sad stories of painful disappointments and traumatic experiences in childhood, as well as the heroic stories of how they faced the emotional meaning of their lives and struggled to overcome the past. Finally, I suppose I have also written a psychoanalytic parable (albeit highly exaggerated and fictionalized) about my relationship with my own father. The book became an unintended bit of self-analysis, written as my father was finally dying after ninety-eight years of giving everybody a piece of his mind.

I hope this book can be useful not only to the "general" readers interested in how our minds work and what can happen in a psychotherapy office—and who doesn't have a secret interest in analyzing family and friends?—but also to the students of psychology, whether undergraduate college students or graduate trainees who are working toward a career in the profession. I hope I can pique their curiosity about modern dynamic therapy.

Sigmund Freud

The Consulting Room

A sample of Freud's collection

1. Where Did the Roses Go?

*B*y the time I reach the apartment building at Berggasse 19, it is nearly two in the afternoon. The sky over Vienna is increasingly cloudy, and the first drops of rain are starting to fall. A young couple walking arm in arm look up at the sky in unison and pick up their pace a bit. Given my destination, it would be fitting to have strident discharges of lightning and thunder, signifying an elemental conflict between earth and sky. Mother Nature is not so inclined today. This is merely a soft spring rain, and I have arrived just in time to avoid getting too wet. I enter by the main door of the building and walk up a long flight of stairs bordered by a wrought iron banister. At the top of the stairs, the door to the apartment suite has his name on it in bold lettering. The door opens, and I am greeted by a maid, a petite young woman who smiles politely but says nothing. I assume that she speaks no English, and I have never studied German. She shyly motions to me to follow her into a waiting room. When we get to a closed set of double doors, she knocks softly and disappears without a word.

"Good afternoon, please come in." I am not sure what I was expecting, but I am immediately surprised that he is not taller. After all, this is Sigmund Freud. I am standing before one of the intellectual giants of the Western world, and I am not prepared to meet a man of rather average height. He is very handsomely dressed, of course; his three-piece suit is accompanied by a bowtie that is partly hidden, tucked beneath the collar of a clean white shirt. His whole demeanor is professional and confident, but his unremarkable height is not what I have anticipated. I suppose I have traveled to Vienna with some sort of childlike notion of a man who is larger than life, a father figure staring down at me—at all of us—from an Olympian peak. Instead, I find myself eye to eye with Freud, a man no bigger than myself.

"It is an honor to meet you, Professor Freud. Thank you so much for agreeing to speak with me. I know how busy you must be."

"It is my pleasure." He is just the age at which I always imagine him. He is neither the forty-year-old with the thick, dark beard and relentless ambition, nor the frail eighty-year-old who is struggling with oral cancer and packing his belongings to escape the Nazis. Someplace in his late fifties, perhaps sixty or so, this is the Freud who has clearly established himself as a major thinker. He is still strong and healthy, and still capable of producing more important work.

I am at least twenty years his junior, still in my thirties; curiously, I feel even younger standing before him. For a brief moment, I glimpse a memory of myself sitting in the library of the Capital District Psychiatric Center in Albany. I can see myself as a psychiatry resident, sitting at a small desk with a volume of Freud's work open in front of me. There was something in those pages that confirmed for me that my decision to switch from pediatrics into psychiatry was the right move. Freud was trying to go beyond the classification of symptoms and diseases, beyond the typical treatments of his day (water baths, massage, and rest cures), beyond giving the patient suggestions under hypnosis—You *can* move your arm!—to arrive at an understanding of the root of the problem. He wanted to comprehend the mysteries of the psyche. I remember sitting in that library, paging through his book, feeling like I was being initiated into a very selective secret society whose membership was limited to intrepid explorers of the mind.

Now I am standing before him, and he looks at me directly for a long moment, as if he is already engaged in a psychological calculus of my character. Naturally, I am taking a measure of him as well, trying to read what I can in his eyes. Although he is a man of ordinary height, there is nothing ordinary about his gaze. He looks at me with the eyes of someone with an immense capacity for concentrating on one object at a time, and presently that object is me. There is obvious intelligence in those eyes, of course, and a look of relentless curiosity. Here is a man who can ponder a question for years: *What is anxiety?* He can wrestle with such a question tirelessly, and he can continually revise his understanding of it. He has a very direct gaze, a look of someone who is neither afraid to see nor afraid to be seen. For a brief moment, I think back and puzzle over something I once read about him. In one of his books, he wrote that he sat to the side of the couch, out of the patient's view, because he could not stand to have people staring at him all day long. After one long moment of meeting his gaze, I have trouble believing this.

I can imagine that his eyes might be unnerving to some people, but there is warmth in them, too, and it would not be hard to imagine him breaking into laughter and making a joke. I find myself wondering why the photographs of him always show such a stern expression. He is not smiling or laughing at the moment, but there is nothing severe about his gaze. Something in his look makes me feel welcomed as well as analyzed. I wonder for a moment what I convey to my own patients when I look at them sitting across from me in my office back in Albany.

"Come take a seat, and we will have a nice chat. You have traveled far. New York State, yes?" His English is quite good. Accented, but good. My first impression of his consulting room is that it reminds me of a museum, or perhaps the back office of the museum curator—a cigar-smoking curator, to be sure, as the air is permeated with the smell of cigar smoke. The walls are crowded with framed artwork depicting ancient civilizations and their myths. To my left, there is a painting of Pan, the half-man and half-goat of Greek mythology who caused *panic* in mortals when they encountered him in the forest. In addition to the paintings, there is Freud's famous collection of miniature antique statues, sitting on a ledge, on a desk, in glass display cases, or wherever there is a bit of space. These are the little artifacts from around the world that he had acquired over time, and there are legions of them. On one table, I see Egyptian figures standing erect, a large camel, and a couple of sitting Buddha figures among rows of other assorted pieces. One would think, judging by the cluttered profusion of antiquities, that the resident of this place is someone who is far more interested in archeology than psychology.

There are bookshelves, of course, filled with hardcover volumes. On one of the shelves, I notice a photo of a woman. She has a penetrating gaze the equal of his. Surrounded by the collections of weighty books and dead little statues, the woman in the photo looks intensely alive and alert. One of his relatives, perhaps? A sister? But he had several sisters, so it would make no sense to have a photo of only one of them.

"Yes, I live in Albany." The couch is directly in front of me as I enter, and to the left of the couch, there is a wide green upholstered chair for him to sit in while listening to the "associations" of his patients. Why do I keep looking at the couch? In order to answer my own question, I look once more, and then I allow myself the visceral reaction taking shape within me: *This is it! I am looking at Sigmund Freud's couch!* This is the couch that has symbolized, for well over a century, a guided journey into the center of the human psyche. This couch was the epicenter of some of the greatest psychological discoveries my profession has ever known. I have to take in every detail of it. There is a large Oriental rug thrown over it, a second rug hanging on the wall behind it, and a third larger one beneath our feet. Of the many colors in the rugs, the reddish browns stand out most to me, giving a very warm feeling to the room. There are large pillows on the couch for the patients to use, as well as a blanket in case of cold drafts in the room. I can barely believe my good fortune at being here.

"Gretchen will bring us tea in a moment. She is a nice young lady, but not very fast." Freud's eyes are smiling now. "So tell me, where is Albany?"

"We are due north from New York City. And just straight west of Clark University in Massachusetts, where you lectured."

"Ah, yes, Clark. I gave five lectures there in 1909. And I lectured in German, with no translator. In those days, serious American students studied German."

For a moment, I wonder if this is meant as a criticism. I have heard that he does not have a particularly good opinion of Americans in general. His eyes are still kindly, though, as if he is just expressing a reminiscence of his own life rather than a judgment upon mine.

"So you wrote to me about a new approach to psychoanalysis, yes?" he asks.

"Yes, I did. Not exactly psychoanalysis, though. There are still people who identify themselves as psychoanalysts, but I practice a newer model of psychotherapy that is nonetheless based on your original work. It involves a number of changes in both theory and technique, which is why we no longer call it psychoanalysis, even though it follows your most important concepts. Anyway, I thought you might be interested in hearing about it. I have often wondered what you would think of it, and I would love to have your opinion." These are the words I speak, but as I say them, the word *approval* drifts into consciousness. Where does that come from? *I would love to have your approval.* Is that why I really came here today? Am I seeking his approval? I have been practicing psychotherapy for some years now, so why would I care what anyone thinks? Yet there it is: the word *approval*.

"And I would be very interested to hear about these modern changes," he says. "Where would you like to begin?" There is a soft knock on the door, and the maid Gretchen enters with a tray. She serves us both tea with sugar from a large serving tray. There are no tea bags, of course, just a pot of hot water with loose tea brewing inside. She places a tea strainer over my cup and pours the tea while the strainer catches the tea leaves. She serves Freud, and then they speak for a minute or two, but I understand nothing except when he tells her *Danke.* As she leaves the room, I decide I should really study German one day. I wonder if his work would mean something different to me if it traveled to my brain in the rail car of the original German, without changing trains at the station of a translator.

"Please," he adds with Old World charm and modesty, "educate me about these new ideas, and I will be your humble student."

"Yes, all right, then. I will begin." And then I draw a blank. My mind is empty and my tongue is struck dumb. Where should I begin? How did I even presume to come here and tell him about what has transpired since he completed his monumental work? In the psychotherapy approach that I follow, so much of his theory has been rejected or simply discarded, like unnecessary baggage dropped over the side of a ship.

I know that my psychoanalytic contemporaries would object, but I find no use for some of his famous concepts. The oral, anal, and phallic stages of development: gone. The central role of the Oedipal conflict in therapy: gone. Penis envy, the libido theory, the death instinct: gone, gone, gone. Even his beloved *Interpretation of Dreams* has lost some of its importance. But I have to start someplace. I drop a cube of sugar into my cup and stir it around to give myself an extra few seconds to think.

"Well," I begin, "things have taken a turn that you might not have foreseen. You see, many psychotherapists—I myself am not one of them—left psychoanalytic thinking entirely, after your time was over. Many other types of therapy were developed without psychoanalysis as a basis."

"Oh yes, I can imagine. There was always resistance to my work, and the struggle is not over yet, I am quite sure." I can see in his eyes a brief flicker of defiance; there is a readiness to fight.

"Well, some of these other approaches to therapy are not really a resistance to your work; they are just other ways of thinking. And those therapists are definitely helping people. But among those who remained interested in your work—even though we don't call ourselves psychoanalysts—there has been a kind of revival, along with the development of newer techniques. Actually, part of the newer approach stems from your first psychological publication, the book you wrote with Dr. Breuer."

"Ah, yes, Breuer. Josef Breuer. He made a very important contribution to psychoanalysis. In fact, he was one of the two greatest influences upon me."

As he offers this praise of Breuer, I get a conflicting message from his body language. The animated defiance that was in his eyes a moment ago is replaced by a look of coldness. He folds his arms across his chest. His lips are pressed tightly together. The overall impression is that he has withdrawn to another room and closed the door behind him. Clearly, I have blundered already. I should have known that mentioning Breuer would be a mistake, based on what I have read about their relationship.

Josef Breuer

Breuer, also a Viennese physician, was a friend, colleague, and mentor to Freud for years. In fact, it was a case of Breuer's—the case of Anna O.—that influenced Freud to begin the work that would later become psychoanalysis. I remember a photograph of Dr. Breuer in a library book. The camera recorded a man with kindly eyes and a long beard, the perfect image of the grandfather in a children's storybook, or perhaps the neighborhood rabbi. It is not a face that broadcasts acrimony or ill will, but somehow things fell apart after he and Freud collaborated on a book. The friendship turned to animosity—on Freud's part—and my mentioning of Breuer has already chilled the atmosphere. I can see that I will be navigating through rocky waters. I remind myself that the unhappy ending with Breuer also happened with others who were close to Freud: his teacher Meynert, his friend Fliess, his disciple Jung. I will have to steer more carefully.

"You see, Professor, some of us have emphasized a return to your ideas, even your early ideas published in that book, *Studies on Hysteria.* We look for negative experiences in childhood that might be responsible for the current symptoms. For example, we look for childhood losses or separations, divorce, child abuse, rejection by a parent, and so on. We encourage the patient to remember those events and situations. And they not only must remember them but also must *remember with emotion.* They have to get in touch with the buried emotions. As you said in the book, remembering without emotion usually produces no result. So we have gone back to your earliest work, added some newer techniques, and we are seeing wonderful results." I pause, and there is a long silence. I cannot read his reaction at the moment, although he looks less distant now. Perhaps I have distracted him from my Breuer gaff and got him thinking about his early work. Still, he does not look pleased. I half expect him to end the visit and dismiss me from his consulting room. I take a pre-emptive step by adding one more thought. "We are in the minority of therapists now, but we are convincing more of our colleagues to consider this approach and see its value." I have read of his struggles with the physicians of his day, and how he often felt isolated and unaccepted by his peers. Maybe I can win him over by getting him to view me and my colleagues as allies who are fighting the same battles that he had fought.

There is only silence. I can hear the ticking of a clock on the wall. At first, I assume that the continuing silence means that he has finished with the discussion. Then I remember that this is Freud, the original analyst, a man who sat quietly to one side of a couch all day listening to people talk. He must have trained himself to listen carefully without interrupting. Besides, I am probably too accustomed to the rapid chatter of my era. Now I am in his world, a slower, more leisurely world. If he could join me in a few of the fast-paced conversations of my typical day, he would probably think we are all quite mad.

"Yes, yes, that was our earliest work," he finally says. "That was the 'cathartic method,' as Breuer called it. We thought that the patient must have an emotional catharsis as part of the treatment. He should remember the distressing events of the past, and release all the pent-up emotion. But that did not always work so well. In the development of psychoanalysis, I moved on from there and developed more refined methods. The patient was taught to *free associate*—to say whatever comes to mind—while the analyst was taught to make interpretations. That is how we make the unconscious conscious. *That* is psychoanalysis."

"Well, of course, that is true psychoanalysis," I say. This is not what I want to say, but I cannot say what I really think. *No, what my colleagues and I do today is also psychoanalysis, even though we don't call it that, and we are getting better results.* "I mean no disrespect to psychoanalysis, Professor, but many analysts began to feel discouraged with the results of that approach. After your time had passed, they started looking for ways to alter the technique, while still maintaining the theoretical basis of the work."

"In other words, you and your colleagues have abandoned the pure gold of psychoanalysis for some kind of alloy."

"Well, no, I don't see it that way at all. What we do is still faithful to the essential psychoanalytic theories you put forth. Really, it is still psychoanalysis, in a sense."

"You have changed it entirely, and you still use my term for your alloy?" He is clearly offended now.

"No, we don't call it psychoanalysis. We call it dynamic psychotherapy, after your term *psychodynamic*. There is still the dynamic struggle: on the one side, there are the impulses, thoughts, and feelings trying to emerge, and on the other side, the defense mechanisms trying to keep things in check. Many of us call our work short-term dynamic psychotherapy, because it is shorter than traditional psychoanalysis."

"So you just want a short treatment?"

"No, sir, it is not always short." I can feel myself getting a little irritated with him. *If you don't want to listen to anything I have to say, then why did you agree to a meeting in the first place?* "But what is wrong with a brief treatment? You treated the composer Gustav Mahler in one long walk around town. Your original cases were sometimes short in length. We are trying to recapture the best ideas of your work, and those early days of your thinking were filled with pure gold. Surely, you must have felt that at the time."

Freud breaks eye contact and gazes off to one side, as people tend to do when they are gazing into their own memories to retrieve something long since stored away. Again, I have to adjust to the pacing of his culture and stop myself from saying ten more things that rush to my mind. I have to give him a little space. The clock ticks. He sips tea. I wait.

"Those were interesting times," he says, suddenly softening his look and becoming more reflective. "We knew so little, but there were those who were looking for answers. Here and there, a few people were willing to ignore the officially accepted nonsense of the past and look deeper. Breuer told me about his fascinating case, of course, but he was not the only one." He glances at a painting on his wall; in the painting, a group of men are gathered for some kind of meeting. "I went to study with Charcot, you know. The other important influence on my work. There was Breuer and his remarkable case of Anna O. And there was Charcot, the great French neurologist. You have heard of him, yes?"

"Yes, of course. We learned about Charcot joints in medical school."

A Lesson with Dr. Charcot at the Salpêtrière by Brouillet

"Jean-Martin Charcot," he continues. "He was brilliant, absolutely brilliant. He taught his students to correlate the signs and symptoms of the living patient with the pathological findings on the autopsy. He clarified the nature of several neurological diseases: multiple sclerosis, amyotropic lateral sclerosis, Charcot-Marie-Tooth disease. Brilliant.

"I went to see him in Paris when I was young. I was twenty-nine years old, and I was a neuropathologist back then. I was already quite taken with Breuer's account of his case, and I became quite curious about the whole topic of hysteria. I knew that Charcot had also taken an interest in hysteria, and I was eager to hear what he had to say about it. Many of the patients on his hospital ward were women, and they were such fascinating patients. They had dramatic physical symptoms, but there was never any clear evidence of a physical ailment. They would complain of a paralyzed arm or an inability to walk; they had amnesia, or they had convulsions. In some cases, there was temporary blindness or deafness. The physical exam was always normal."

"Yes," I say, "I read about these patients in my residency. In current psychiatric terms, we would probably say that they had a mix of diagnoses, including conversion disorder, post-traumatic stress disorder, and borderline personality disorder." I explain the terms to him. "And a few of them probably suffered from multiple personality disorder."

"But you have so many names for one thing! Such a patient did not have five different illnesses, sir. She had one illness, call it what you may. We called it *hysteria*."

"Well, I would have to admit that our current system of classification leaves much to be desired."

"Indeed!" he huffs. "Where is the effort to integrate the symptoms into one coherent construct? In your modern system, we will be lost in multiple diagnoses with no clear plan of treatment."

I do not know what to say to him. I have an impulse to defend our modern terminology, but I see his point. No matter; he clearly is not waiting for a reply. He is quick to return to his story.

"In previous generations, physicians were convinced of the age-old myth: hysteria was supposedly due to a problem of the uterus. The uterus had somehow broken loose from its moorings and was wandering around the abdomen. Absurd!" He laughs. "The uterus! And men could not have hysteria, of course, because they had no uterus!" We both laugh, and I am relieved that we seem to be moving away from an argument about diagnostic terms. "Charcot was one of the brave souls who challenged this nonsense."

"So he saw the problem as a psychological one?" I ask.

"Not exactly. Charcot thought that hysteria occurred in people who had a hereditary weakness, an element of *degeneracy*. However, once the patient had that hereditary weakness, the symptoms were triggered by ideas, triggered by the mind. For example, a common type of hysteria was traumatic hysteria. A physical or psychological trauma had occurred, and the residual ideas set the symptoms in motion. You see, he was talking about the mind, not the uterus. He was speaking about *traumatic memories*. And how grandly he spoke!"

He goes on to describe Charcot's lectures. One morning a week, Jean-Martin Charcot, the greatest neurologist in Europe, would speak to a packed auditorium. Physicians and students eagerly attended, and even writers and other interested people with no medical training would come to hear him talk. He was a celebrity in Paris and throughout Europe. Patients came to him from all over the world.

"*Les Leçons du Mardi*," he says. "The Tuesday Lessons, we called them. And each one was a gem. It was more than just a lecture. It was like nothing you have ever heard." Freud sits back and settles into his topic. Charcot would start to describe his subject for the day. He was a gifted speaker, but he also used visual aids—he was an accomplished painter—to make his point clearer to his listeners. Sometimes he would illustrate with drawings on a chalkboard. Photography was becoming more popular and accessible, and he used that too as a means to help the audience see the dramatic problems of his hysterical patients. But this was only the beginning of the performance. Charcot would actually imitate the behaviors of the hysterical patient: the tremors, the posturing, the convulsive shaking. He went beyond medical education; this was theatre, and the highest quality of theatre.

Freud goes from story to story, sharing with me his memories of the Salpêtrière Hospital of Paris in 1885. The time passes quite pleasantly in this manner, and I can easily imagine this passionate Frenchman captivating his audience with the bewildering symptoms of his patients and his animated style of teaching. I can understand Freud's early excitement, and I feel like I am sitting in nineteenth-century Paris among the best physicians of the day, sitting beside Freud himself and basking in Charcot's authoritative eloquence.

"He was the Master. Can you imagine the great Charcot imitating for us the puzzling symptoms of the hysteric?" Freud stands up, and for a moment I think he is going to recreate Charcot's performances, but he only steps over to a desk and picks up a cigar box. "In celebration of Charcot!" he exclaims. I decline his offer, and he picks out a cigar for himself and continues his reminiscences.

After the introductory lecture, illustrated with drawings, photographs, and his imitations of the symptoms, Charcot would bring out the actual patient, often a woman from his hospital wards. He had already described the symptoms that she suffered with, and she now exhibited those exact symptoms.

"It was the most brilliant teaching I have ever seen. One would leave the auditorium with that lecture resonating in one's mind for the rest of the day." He lights the cigar and pauses, but only for a moment.

"There was more. That was just the lecture and the demonstration of symptoms. It was fascinating just to see the symptoms of these patients, of course, but Charcot wanted to learn something more about what caused them. He had studied hypnosis, and he used it as a tool to understand the pathology of hysteria. In fact, hypnosis was the key to discovering the unconscious. Let me explain.

"When a patient was hypnotized, she generally could not remember the discussion that transpired under hypnosis once the session was over. Suppose, shall we say, that Charcot speaks to a hypnotized patient who loves to grow flowers. Suppose he speaks with her about planting a beautiful rose garden. When she comes out of the hypnotic state, she remembers nothing about their conversation, nothing about discussing roses. Nothing at all. But when she is hypnotized a second time, she can indeed remember the entire discussion, including the rose garden. So why did she have no memory of it when she was in the normal waking state? Where did the roses go? They were concealed in some hidden part of the mind! The conversation about roses was inscribed in a part of the mind that was inaccessible to her in her normal state of consciousness. It was in the *unconscious.*

"You see, I did not discover the unconscious. It was known to the hypnotists, and probably known to poets and sages for centuries. I merely explored the contents of the unconscious and demonstrated its many manifestations in our lives—in neurotic symptoms, in dreams, jokes, slips of the tongue, religious views. The unconscious is everywhere one looks. And when we look, we find not only buried memories, but more often we find thoughts, wishes, and emotions that have been hidden from view."

I open my mouth to comment, but Freud is steadily gaining momentum.

"And listen to what Charcot did next. After inducing a hypnotic state in a patient, he actually created hysterical symptoms, right in front of us! He told a young woman that she would not be able to move her arm, and when she emerged from the hypnotic state, she had a paralyzed arm. It was quite impressive. He had created the symptom just by putting the idea into her mind." Freud is passionate now, reliving the glorious time of his early introduction to the workings of the mind.

"So the trip to Charcot came after you had already heard about the case of Anna O." I avoid using Breuer's name, even though Freud has mentioned it.

"Breuer's case. Yes, he had told me about it." I guess we are past that danger now; he seems ready to talk about it. "Breuer had told me about the case that he later published as the case of Anna O. The treatment concluded in 1882, several years before I was awarded a grant to study with Charcot. The case made a great impression on me. He and I would speak of it again upon my return from Charcot's hospital in Paris. Breuer's patient had many serious symptoms of hysteria, and he had cured her by talking. The patient herself called it the *talking cure*. She would remember distressing memories, give vent to the emotion, and the symptom would vanish! It was just like Charcot's teaching: traumatic memories seemed to be triggering the symptoms. Breuer utilized hypnosis, just like Charcot, but with one difference. Charcot created artificial symptoms for his scientific demonstrations, and then he removed them by the same hypnotic method. Breuer was treating a young woman with *genuine* symptoms of hysteria, and he was trying to *cure* the symptoms. And he found that when the patient relived those memories and vented the emotion—she had the catharsis—the symptoms actually disappeared." He pauses and sits back in his chair. "It was such an exciting new method at the time."

"And that is what we are doing today, Professor. In a sense, we have returned to your original theory of the neuroses. The patient has memories, sometimes of a major trauma, sometimes of less dramatic but still painful events and situations. Those memories, and the associated blocked emotions, are the etiology of the problem."

Freud blows out a puff of cigar smoke and looks at me sharply, as if I have missed the point entirely. "But there were problems that arose with this work," he says, "even though it was promising at the time. Problems with the theory, as well as problems with the technique. Hypnosis did not work very reliably. That is why I developed my free association technique."

"We don't use hypnosis," I say. "And we don't use free association. We just challenge the defenses until the emotions can be expressed. It is the emotional experience that is the key. Just as Breuer said. Just as *you* once said. The patient must remember with emotion."

"Hmm. We thought so, too, at the time. Until I realized that the unconscious *ideas* are the critical element."

That is all he says. I want to say more, of course. I want to return to a discussion of modern psychotherapy, so I can convince him that we are doing the work that he and Breuer first began. I want to tell him that we are honoring his work, not detracting from it. It does not matter what I want to say, though. Freud has put a pause in the discussion again, and when he pauses in a certain way, the discussion comes to a halt.

He looks neither dismissive nor receptive at the moment. I cannot quite read his expression. He stands up and walks over to look again at a painting on his wall. In the painting, a room is filled with men who attentively study the events unfolding before them. A young woman has collapsed into the arms of a man standing behind her. To one side of the woman is a well-dressed, gray-haired man who confidently faces the audience. He is not particularly tall, but he is clearly in charge of the gathering, extending the index finger of his right hand to emphasize a point.

"That is Charcot," Freud says, pointing at the figure. "The Napolean of the Neuroses, they called him. His patient is exhibiting her hysterical crisis, la grande hysterie, at one of his morning Leçons. The man supporting her is Joseph Babinski. You know the Babinski reflex in neurology, yes? In the audience—here, the man wearing the apron—is Gilles de la Tourette. You know about Tourette's description of tics, yes? Those were wonderful days. Absolutely wonderful."

Gretchen quietly returns to pick up our teacups. The clock is ticking, and I suddenly become aware of the time passing. It is clear that we are done with our discussion. He has gone as far as he wants to go with this. I came here to talk about modern psychotherapy, but it seems hopeless. Well, it was an interesting afternoon, if not what I had hoped for. I make some excuse about needing to get back to my hotel for a dinner date, and I thank him for his time. I assume that this will be the only meeting we will ever have. He graciously thanks me for coming, and shows me to the door of the consulting room.

Gretchen silently leads me out through the waiting room and down the stairway. She deposits me on the street with a shy smile and a little curtsy, and she closes the door. The rain has stopped, and I stand for a long minute or two wondering what to do with the rest of my afternoon. Originally, I had planned to stop at a café and take some notes on our meeting, and perhaps plan the theme for the next one. Then I was hoping to take a stroll in the Innere Stadt, the old section of Vienna, one of Freud's favorite places to walk. Now all this seems quite pointless. Perhaps I should just go back to my hotel and work on a lecture I have to give when I return home. I am just about to start walking when the door opens. He is standing there in the entranceway, smiling.

"Next time we meet, perhaps we could discuss a specific case of yours," he says.

"I would like that very much, Professor."

"Then perhaps I could understand more of your modern ways. Bring a typical case from your practice. Anxiety, depression, something very common, yes?"

"Certainly. I look forward to it." The door closes again, and I start walking down the street. A man sitting on his horse-drawn cart smiles and nods at me as he passes by. I decide to look for a friendly little café, after all.

2. The Root of the Problem

*M*y office at Albany Medical Center is a small, boxy allotment of space, but it is sufficient for the necessities of psychotherapy: a desk, an old oak file cabinet (my attempt to bring a little character into the room), several chairs, and a small bookshelf. On top of the bookshelf sits a small plastic figure of Freud, holding his trademark cigar. The room easily accommodates me, Freud, and the friendly young woman sitting across from me. There is also space for a small video camera sitting on a tripod to the left of my seat. The young woman has agreed to let me videotape our sessions and use the tapes for my teaching.

Her name is Carla, and she is twenty-six years old. She has an Italian last name, which agrees quite nicely with her dark hair and dark eyes. She works at our hospital as an x-ray technician. Because this is her day off, she arrives in T-shirt and jeans rather than hospital garb. Even on a casual day off, she obviously takes some pride in her appearance; the bright, clean T-shirt is a colorful promotion for the New York Yankees, and the jeans look new. She is pretty, and she smiles the easy smile of someone who is used to having other people respond kindly to her features. She knows that she makes a good impression.

She looks directly at me, and she seems comfortable sitting here, or at least as comfortable as anyone can feel in her first psychotherapy appointment. She wastes no time in announcing her agenda for our first meeting. She reports that she is chronically nervous, and she finds it difficult to relax. (In today's terms, she has a *generalized anxiety disorder*; Freud would have called it a *neurosis*.) She has a second problem that is even more disturbing to her than the anxiety. She gets angry at her fiancé and says mean things to him, words that he does not deserve. She just cannot control what she says when she gets angry. She has no idea why she is so nasty to him, but she knows that it bothers her, and she fears that her behavior will end the relationship before the wedding date ever arrives. She knows that she needs to get help with this.

So she has anxiety and she has a relationship problem. These are not the root of her problems, of course; they are the symptoms at the surface. Still, it is a good sign that she can state these problems clearly and succinctly. Some people come to therapy and they cannot even articulate a clearly defined problem. They come to the office because a friend or a spouse urged them to make an appointment. They have "a lot of issues," but they cannot name a single one. They describe all kinds of difficult events they have experienced in life, but they cannot tell me how those past events are still affecting them now and why they are seeking therapy.

I also notice that she is describing problems about herself, rather than blaming others. She could have said that she is mean to her boyfriend because he is a terrible person who makes her feel irritable. Instead, she seems able to take responsibility for her own behavior. She has an intrapsychic focus, a focus on something about herself and her own psyche that she wants to work on. She does not externalize the problem and blame her environment. So far, so good. Now I need to get some details.

"How much of the time are you nervous and tense?" I ask.

"A lot. I'd say, half of the day."

"Half of each day, typically?"

"Yeah." Then she sighs. She takes a big breath, as if she is now feeling some anxiety that has tightened up the intercostal muscles of her chest and limited her to short, shallow breaths. She looks like she needs more air; she needs to get free of the tension and breathe more deeply.

"You sighed?"

"Yeah," she says. "It just seems like I'm always rushed. I always have a million things to do. I never sit still, you know. I mean, that's kind of my personality. I go, go, go. But last night, we just got a movie and sat on the couch, and it feels so good just to relax. I feel like I'm never relaxed."

I explore this a bit more, and I run through a mental checklist of anxiety symptoms with her. I learn that she has no panic attacks, no obsessive-compulsive behaviors, no social phobia, and so on.

"And you say that you get angry and you have trouble controlling what you say. Can you give me an example of that?"

"I sometimes hold things in, and then—with Jimmy, my boyfriend—I get irritated about something. Or when he's driving, you know. I tell him I'm going to punch him in his face because I get so mad."

"You actually say those words?" I ask.

"Yeah, I do."

I notice that she is doing something with her mouth, perhaps putting her tongue against her cheek. Maybe she is chewing on the inside of her cheek. Yes, I think that's it. She is chewing the inside of her lip and cheek. She must be getting more anxious as we talk about her anger at Jimmy. Perhaps there is something about this anger that makes her more tense and anxious. It is a perfect example of what Freud said in one of his theories of anxiety: the ego can send out a signal of anxiety because the patient is coming too close to an impulse or emotion that is dangerous or unacceptable. *Signal anxiety* is the label he gave it. This chewing might be a clue to me that she is getting anxious about troubling feelings lurking beneath the surface.

"I'm not really going to punch him in the face, but ... He'll say something to get me going. He knows how to get under my skin, and I'll say, 'Oh, shut the ... heck up. I'm gonna punch you in the face if you do that.'"

Clearly, she did not say 'heck' to him. She is cleaning up her language a bit as she tells her story. I suspect that she uses pretty rough language when she is mad at him. I would not have guessed this just by looking at her. Her whole appearance gives the impression of someone who is sweet and even-tempered.

"What might he say that would make you angry?"

"That he's going to show me how, um ..." She has been starting to smile, and now she breaks out with a small laugh. "Let's see, what happened the other day?" She laughs more openly now. We are getting closer to something. As long as she could keep the topic general, she was managing fairly well, just a little tense. Now that I ask for a specific example, the tension rises and she starts to laugh.

The nervous laugh. It is such an interesting phenomenon. She gets anxious and the chest muscles contract and she sighs, trying to get more air. When the tension increases further, Mother Nature provides an escape valve with the nervous laugh, which suddenly loosens up those chest muscles, and she automatically takes bigger breaths of air to support the next burst of laughter. At the same time, the laughing turns a difficult situation into a funny one, so it also functions as a defense mechanism against feelings that are threatening or painful. What a marvelous invention, this nervous laugh! No wonder we all make such liberal use of it. It is a very pleasant social invention, as well. I could easily join her in the laughing.

"I don't even remember what he said to me," she continues, "but it was just the whole situation."

"So you were really angry."

"Oh, yeah!"

"And how do you feel right now, talking about it?" I ask.

"Just aggravated." She's laughing again. "Because I'm thinking about it, and I just can't get him to ..." Suddenly she brings her hands up, fingers spread wide and slightly flexed, as if she would like to grab him and shake him. She presents me with such an interesting mixed message: her hands are energized with anger, but her face says it is all just a funny story.

"You laugh, I notice."

"Yeah, I can't ... it's funny, because it's like ... I think about it now and it's almost funny."

"But the laugh doesn't match the emotion of the moment, does it?"

"No." She is laughing freely now, and she looks like she is really enjoying it.

"But I wonder if the laugh covers up the anger," I say.

"It could." She is still smiling, but the laughing stops. "Yeah, it could."

Good. I made my first attempt at pointing out a defense mechanism. I told her that the laugh does not match the anger she describes.

She seems quite comfortable with my comment. Next, I suggest that it is a defense that covers up the anger. Again she is on board. She could have responded with more defenses. (*Well, I'm not really angry with him anymore.* Or: *Oh, I already let the anger out. I told him he's a jerk!* Or: *Well, there's no sense staying angry. I'm just a forgiving person.*) Instead, she seems to be comfortable with the hypothesis that she is hiding some kind of anger with the laugh. There is a certain irony to the situation: she is sitting here complaining that she gets *too* angry at him, yet there seems to be something about her anger that she avoids by laughing and making light of it. Something about her anger is beyond her conscious awareness, buried in her unconscious.

Implicit in my comments today is the idea that experiencing her emotions fully could be helpful to her. I have no idea how she will react to this notion, of course. So many people hold to the belief, prominent since the ancient Greeks, that life should be governed by reason, free of the distracting nuisance of emotion. They view emotions as unwanted intruders that need to be controlled, contained, and banished from the premises. So far, she is amenable to my implied suggestion that emotion should be considered a welcome guest at the table. But we shall see.

"So if you don't laugh, what does the anger feel like?" I ask.

"Like a stirring up inside." Her hands go up again, as if to grab him. I wonder if she even realizes what she is doing.

"And you feel it right now?"

"Um, kind of . . ."

"Your hands come up and—"

"Yeah. I can't believe he would act like that." She is smiling, but the laughing has stopped. This is a good sign, because I will have to interrupt her typical defenses if we are going to get anywhere. Otherwise, we may just have an interesting chat and stay at the edges of her emotions.

"So you get angry and aggravated and you say pretty rough things, like *I'll punch you in the face.*"

"Yeah. I call him a loser," she adds.

"Oh, you do? You get insulting like that?"

"Um-hm."

"You call him a loser?"

"Yup. Over money situations. And then I feel bad about it. I really do. It's like I can't control what I'm saying to him." She pauses for a long moment. "It's like I take that stuff out on him, and I don't want to do that."

She "takes it out on him." What might that mean? Is she implying that her anger is really meant for someone else, but she takes it out on her fiancé? If so, she is using the defense mechanism of *displacement*. She is like the person who gets angry at the boss but holds in the anger, and then comes home and yells at the kids.

"What do you mean when you say you 'take it out on him'?"

"Well, like I ... I get angry at the fact that he doesn't make enough money at his job, and I kind of throw it in his face. *You're a loser.* You know."

"So you're kind of mean," I say.

"Yeah. I get mean to him." She says this as a simple matter of fact, without flinching. I like her candid style.

"So where does that nasty anger come from?"

"I don't know."

"I wonder where you learned that way of dealing with anger. Did you grow up with that? Did you grow up with people being derogatory?"

"Yeah ... my parents ... yeah. I would say my mom did it to my dad. Because my dad was an alcoholic back then. He would go out drinking every night and not come home, and they would fight and scream at each other, and throw things at each other, and hit each other."

No one would ever guess, just by looking at her, that she comes from this kind of family history. It is a bit hard to believe. I can understand the dilemma that Freud encountered in his early years of treating patients. When so many young women who came for treatment reported a history of sexual abuse, he concluded that this abuse must be at the root of all cases of "hysteria." At some point, he changed his mind, finding it hard to believe that so many children could be victims of abuse by adults. He decided that these young women must be reporting sexual fantasies, rather than actual memories. He has since been criticized for recanting, of course, but I can easily sympathize with his about-face on this issue. Carla just does not *look* like someone who has experienced trauma in her family. Nothing about her easy smile or her well-put-together appearance would give anyone a clue, and who really wants to believe that such things happen in a child's life? But surely she is telling the truth, and this must have been traumatic for her.

"Really? They fought?"

"Yeah."

"You say that they *hit each other*?" When I repeat her words, I say it with a bit of dramatic disbelief. Because she grew up with domestic violence, she has probably come to think that it is just normal. I want to make it clear that I do not find it normal at all. In addition, because there is often no one responding to the obvious distress of children in such situations, I want to make it clear by my response that I find her story genuinely disturbing. If I show no reaction and sit with stoic indifference—the popular caricature of Freud that was never true of his actual behavior—I might leave her thinking that one more person in this world is indifferent to her suffering.

"Yup. They hit each other lots of times." She is biting her lip again.

"Really! What was that like for you?"

"It was terrible." She speaks quietly now. "I mean, a lot of it happened when I was little. They split up when I was fourteen, so it happened when I was quite young. But I remember everything before the divorce."

"What do you remember?"

"Mom would take us out in the middle of the night and go to my aunt's house because she wanted to get away from him. My dad would get in these drunken ... he would get very drunk, and he would throw chairs in the house."

"He would throw chairs?"

"Yeah, he got arrested once." She is still biting her lip and the inside of her cheek.

"How do you feel talking about this?"

"It feels like forever ago. It doesn't seem real to me. 'Cause I love my dad. I was really close to him when I was little." She can talk about this, but she speaks without any emotion. She is putting up another defense mechanism by isolating the emotion from the story. The defense mechanism of *isolation of affect*, as I learned it in residency training. *It feels like forever ago*, she says. Part of her mind wants to say that the story is so old that she no longer has any feelings about it. One can hardly blame her.

"I get nervous about my brother, Anthony." Why is she bringing her brother into the discussion? "I get nervous about … I just worry about him all the time. If I try to call him and he doesn't answer, I get nervous that he's been in a car accident or something."

"Really?"

"Yeah."

"One brother?" I ask.

"And one sister. It's me, my brother, then my sister. I'm the oldest."

"So why are you so worried about your brother Anthony's well-being? Were you worried about him when you were growing up?"

"Yeah."

"Oh, why was that?" There is a pause and then a halting reply.

"Because … my mother … my mother used to physically abuse my brother."

"She did?"

"Yeah, but not us girls."

"Just Anthony?"

"Just Anthony."

"And when you say she physically abused him, what exactly do you mean?"

"She would hit him. Sometimes she used an electrical cord." She winces as she says this.

"Really?"

"Yeah. I can't even believe it."

"She hit him with an electrical cord?" I repeat the words with some emphasis. I want her to hear them, in the hope that she will start to realize how terrible her story really is. She winced once, but otherwise she is able to maintain her composure. One would think she is telling me about someone else's life, except for that wincing.

She is detaching herself from the emotional power of her story, but perhaps I have been doing the same thing. Until this point, I have been listening to her with interest, and I have tried to show her an occasional moment of emotional reaction, but in truth I have also maintained a certain clinical detachment. Her story is not like my own life story, and I have been listening to it from the other side of town, where we nice middle-class people lived quietly (as far as I knew) without the plagues of alcoholism and domestic violence and child abuse. When she mentions her brother, though, my conveniently placed border between our neighborhoods collapses. I have brothers, too, and I have a quick flash of memory. One of my little brothers fell off his bicycle and broke his arm. I can imagine myself wincing at the time, and the connection is made: we are all the same. She worried about her brother, and I worried about mine. There is no difference between us.

I pull myself away from my own memories and I see that the biting of her lip and cheek is more obvious now. Perhaps it is time to bring it to her attention.

"As you talk about this, it almost looks like you are biting the inside of your lip."

"Yeah. Maybe."

"I noticed it before, when you were talking about your father and the throwing of chairs. It looked like you were chewing on the inside of your lip or cheek. So what does that tell us?"

"I don't know."

"Tense? Nervous?" I ask.

"Probably. Yeah, 'cause I don't talk about this stuff that often."

"But when we go back and talk about your childhood, you talk about it with no feeling, like it never happened, or like it's somebody else's life you're describing."

"Yeah," she agrees.

"But I wonder if you have feelings left over from your childhood that are exploding in your relationship with Jimmy once in a while with this derogatory talk."

"It could be."

"And your temper seems to be over the top sometimes."

"It is, yeah."

"And the physical threats to Jimmy. *I'll punch you in the face.*"

"Yeah."

"Where does *that* come from?" I ask.

"I don't know."

"But you have a history of domestic violence where people were hitting each other."

"Yes," she says.

"So I wonder if you have blocked feelings that are ... This is just a first theory ... that you have feelings about your childhood that are creating a lot of tension and ... vague stress and anxiety, and then this temper that blows up at your boyfriend."

"I know, 'cause I can't control it."

"But that would mean we might want to look back at how you felt about your family."

"I was scared. It was always scary."

"Well, that fits. You're kind of scared now. Anxious, stressed. You can't relax. You're scared that your brother will be harmed."

"Yeah."

"You are nervous now and you were nervous then."

"Yup. I know. Definitely." Now she pauses for a moment, as if lost in thought. "Oh God, it was awful!" She starts to rub her own arm, as if to comfort herself.

"What was the most awful? Is there a specific memory that comes to mind?"

She seems a bit more animated now. I suspect that the buried emotion is not far from the surface. In order to release it, we should talk about a specific memory. As long as she speaks in generalities, she might be able to distance herself from the feelings indefinitely.

"Just the way that my parents fought. One time my mother wanted to take us and leave the house late at night. It was terrible." She is back there now, back in the old house, not just telling the story but reliving it. Her parents have been arguing all evening, oblivious to the intense fear that their three young children are experiencing. Her mother gets up and announces that she is taking the kids and leaving. She has had enough. Carla's father is drunk and unsteady on his feet, and he starts bellowing curse words at his wife. He staggers to the front door, leans up against it to block his wife's exit, and he makes terrible threats about what he will do to her if she tries to leave. She pretends to acquiesce, and she goes up to their bedroom. Placated, he leaves his post to go into the kitchen looking for more beer. A few minutes later, there is a loud knock on the door. Quickly and quietly, her mother hurries downstairs and opens the door. She speaks briefly to the two police officers who enter the house and walk back to the kitchen, followed by mother and three kids. When the officers try to talk to Carla's father, he becomes bellicose again and picks up a butcher knife. In a terrifying instant, they throw him to the kitchen floor, and one of them draws his gun. Carla is back there again, as if it is happening right now.

"How do you feel right now?" I ask.

"Upset, probably."

"And what does 'upset' mean?"

"I don't know. I just think about it and I …. It's just sad." She looks close to tears.

"Very sad. *Very* sad."

"Yeah." She is starting to cry now. "I don't usually think about it."

As she cries, I can sense that she is opening up. Opening up to her feelings. But what does that mean? Up to this point in our session, she was shut down. But what does *that* mean? She was emotionally closed, and now she is emotionally open. The words sound right, but my mind searches for something more formal, more theoretical. I know I have read something like this, but I cannot remember where I read it. She is recovering and starting to speak to me.

"It's just awful that we had to see that. Me and my brother and my sister. If I had kids, I can't imagine doing that to my kids. I would *never* put them through that!"

"They put you through a lot of frightening experiences."

"Yeah! Both of them!" She cries quietly again for a minute. "I just don't understand why they had to act like that toward each other. I suppose it was the alcohol. If my dad wasn't drinking, they got along great. They did have good times, but what I remember is the fighting. I don't remember the good times. I just remember them hitting each other." She is wiping her eyes with a tissue.

"You have a lot of feelings about this, obviously. As one would."

"Uh-huh."

"You can block it out or pretend it never happened, but the feelings are just under the surface."

"Yeah."

"And maybe this would explain some of your anxiety and anger."

"Yeah. Yeah."

"It sounds like the house was full of anxiety and anger."

"Oh, all the time. We were so scared. My little brother and sister would come into my room, and we would huddle together and block our ears."

"Because the fighting was going on?"

"Yeah. 'Cause it would happen downstairs and we were upstairs. And we would just listen to the noises of them hitting each other. My mother would be screaming at him. And she would always throw bottles at him. She would throw his empty beer bottles at him."

"Really?"

"Yeah."

"That sounds terrible."

"She acted like I do with Jimmy.... She would bottle up all her emotions and then she would throw the beer bottles at him, because that's how she would react to him. And I feel like that's what I do with Jimmy, except that I don't throw bottles."

"So you're feeling like your mother felt but just leaking it out verbally."

"Yeah." Here she comes to a wonderful bit of insight into her behavior. Her verbal aggression toward her fiancé is modeled after her mother's physical aggression toward her father. It seems like a new insight, something that was never conscious before now. She has no trouble remembering the facts, unlike some of Freud's original patients who had forgotten the story itself by using the defense of repression—*dissociative amnesia*, in today's terms. But the source of her current behavior was unconscious. She did not know it was a copy of her mother's behavior, because she has never before connected the dots between the past and the present. And she has not been aware of what all this means to her and how much it hurt her. That is, her emotional reactions have been hidden and unconscious.

We are clearly working together now and making all this conscious. She is already forming a partnership with me, a *therapeutic alliance*. We talk a bit more, she cries a bit more, and then she sits quietly for a minute or two. At this point, I have the sense that we have reached the natural completion of a psychological project, and she needs a rest. This is enough work for one day. I shift gears to gather some background information. Does she ever suffer from depression? Does she have any medical problems? Is there a family history of anxiety? When I am done with my questions, I ask about her reactions to the session.

"What's it like to talk about this today?"

"It's just sad."

"And obviously you have tried to pull away from these memories of childhood as if to put them in a box and keep the box shut."

"Probably." She nods, and then strengthens her statement: "Yeah, that's what I've done."

"But that's probably why you have these symptoms."

"Yeah."

"I'm guessing that you've never had a chance to talk about this and get it out."

"No, I haven't."

"And you've blocked some feelings, and then they leak out at Jimmy."

"Uh-huh."

"Not fair to him or to you." She is starting to cry again. "You look so sad again."

"Yeah," she says.

"What is it?"

"Just that I haven't talked about it. I've never had therapy for it. And a lot of things happened that I don't talk about. My sister will bring it up once in a while, but she doesn't like talking about it either."

"It's not exactly party talk," I say.

"No. No, it isn't. It just doesn't seem like it ever happened. How could that have happened?" She cries again, settles down again, and looks more relaxed.

I glance at the clock, and I realize that we will have to bring our first discussion to a close soon. "Any last thoughts about our discussion so far?"

"It's been good," she says.

"The hardest part we talked about was the troubles in your family, of course."

"Yeah."

"What do you think of that part of our discussion?"

"It's opened up ... Like you said, I've kept it boxed up. This just opened up a lot of feelings."

Yes, I think to myself, *you are open now. You have been closed, but now you are open. Where have I read this?* We talk for a couple of minutes about her thoughts about this first session. I explain to her that there are many ways to do psychotherapy, and not all of them involve an exploration of past memories. She states very clearly that she feels she needs to look back at these painful memories and talk about them, and we agree to meet again in a week. As she leaves, she stops momentarily in the doorway and thanks me, quietly and shyly; then her face abruptly brightens into a broad smile, a very public and pretty smile, a smile that tells people: *I'm fine. I come from a wonderful, happy family just like you. I don't come from a background of alcoholism or child abuse or domestic violence. Really, I don't. I'm just fine.* And with that, she leaves.

At the end of this first session, I can already see where we are going. A few years ago, I would never have believed that I could get such a clear view of her problems in a single meeting. True, I have not resolved any of her problems, and there is no guarantee that I will, but I can see the lay of the land, and that is surely promising. But where did I read something about being emotionally open or emotionally closed?

After writing my notes on the session, I stand up and walk over to the small bookshelf in my office. The plastic figure of Freud stands on the top shelf, cigar in hand, looking quite confident, pleased with the creation of his psychoanalysis. I look at him for a moment as if he might give me a clue about the book I need. I only know that I am not looking for Freud. Even though I cannot remember where I read something about being open and closed, I know it was not in his books. In my little bookcase, I only have space for a few favorites, and I scan the shelves until my eye stops: *Reich. Wilhelm Reich.* Of course. Not Freud, but one of Freud's most brilliant young pupils, and still one of my favorite psychiatrists. I have a couple of his books on the shelf. Following my instincts, I choose one and start thumbing through the last few chapters. I seem to remember that there is something there, toward the end of the book, although I cannot say what it might be. The word *expansion* catches my eye, and I have found what I remember reading several years ago.

The essence of our biological functions, according to Reich, is the alternating process of expansion and contraction. That's it. Expansion and contraction. This is what I vaguely remembered, although I have translated his terms into the more colloquial "open and closed." Expansion, Reich wrote, is a physiological process as well as a psychological one. It involves blood flowing to the skin surface and a sense of moving toward the world. The emotional experience that accompanies it can be pleasure and joy. In Carla's case, I would say that grieving openly is also an emotional expansion.

Wait, wait, wait. I think I am reading the answer to a question that I never really asked: *What is emotion?* It occurs to me that nothing in my psychiatry training could help me to answer this. Somehow, it was never discussed in four long years of residency. But how can I treat emotional problems if I have no definition for the word *emotion?* Maybe this is why my mind made a mental note of these few pages in Reich's book when I first read them: he was giving the answer that I have always needed, even though I have never consciously articulated the question. *What is emotion?*

I go back over the same lines. Pleasure and joy, blood moving outward to the skin surface. Reich made the case that all living organisms experience two poles of pulsation: expansion and contraction. Expansion is associated with elongation and dilatation. I picture someone stretched out in a hammock, arms and legs extended, feeling relaxed and happy. Contraction, in contrast, involves blood being withdrawn from the skin surface, making the skin cold and pale. The organism tries to shrink into a smaller volume. It is a movement away from the world and back into the self. The emotional component can be anxiety. I picture a photo I recently saw of a child in Iraq crouched down behind a wall during a gun battle in his neighborhood. His knees and elbows were flexed, as if he were trying to curl up in a ball to make himself small and less likely to get hit by a stray bullet. There was obvious fear in his eyes. Expansion versus contraction. Open versus closed. So emotion is more than a "feeling"; it is a physiological process of expansion and contraction in response to our surroundings. We stretch out and relax when the environment is friendly; we curl up in a tense ball when the environment is threatening. Our awareness of this process is the "feeling."

I put the book down and mull the idea over. Some emotions are the result of a process of expanding, opening up. I pick up a pen and make a short list of emotions that might be consistent with expansion: love, longing, compassion, joy, anger—a healthy, assertive anger, not the destructive rage of people shooting at their neighbors in Iraq. Surely, Carla's overdue grieving is an emotional expansion as well.

Other emotions are the result of contraction and shutting down. My list: fear and anxiety, shame, guilt, depression. For me, this simple dichotomy makes sense out of the chaos of human emotion. Here is the basic function of all emotion: expanding and contracting. I wonder why Reich's ideas on emotion, published back in 1942, have not been widely accepted by others in the field. But why would I be puzzled over this? Not a speck of Reich's work has been accepted. He was the pariah of psychoanalysis, rejected by his peers, expelled from their professional association, dismissed as eccentric or insane. For some reason, his banishment has always made him more attractive to me.

Thinking of Carla, it occurs to me that there is more to reap from Reich's model of emotion. Expansion and contraction are opposite states, physiologically and psychologically, so she can only be in one state or the other. She cannot be expanding and contracting at the same time. In plain language: *she cannot be open and closed at the same time.* If she is tense and anxious, she is not experiencing emotions of expansion like joy, grief, or compassion. If she is experiencing these emotions of expansion, then she cannot be tense and anxious. A turtle can either stick its head and limbs out to explore the environment or withdraw into its shell. An amoeba can either extend a pseudopodium to take in nourishment or round up into a tense little ball. In all of nature, it is one way or the other.

I suppose I am overstating the case, though. Suppose a person stands up to receive an award. She is happy and excited to receive it, but nervous about making an acceptance speech. So she cannot fully expand and just be happy, but she is not completely shut down with anxiety either. So perhaps a modification is in order: *The more you are open, the less you are closed.* Yes, that will do nicely. But I prefer the absolute clarity of the first version: *you cannot be open and closed at the same time.*

Oh well, no sense in ruminating over the words. Carla walked in feeling anxious and contracted; when she allowed the grief over the traumatic memory, she felt relaxed and expansive. This dichotomy supplies a theoretical basis for generations of therapists who have urged their patients to "get in touch" with their feelings. What they are saying is actually shorthand for this: "Get in touch with emotions of expansion and you'll stop feeling emotions of contraction."

I have a sense of satisfaction, sitting at my desk and contemplating Reich's work. I feel pleased with myself for finding the passage I was looking for, and pleased that it helps me to make sense of things. I also feel gratified by this first session with a young woman named Carla. I was able to identify her defense mechanisms and show her what they are. We were able to move past her defenses so she could get in touch with some of the buried emotions—emotions of expansion—about her traumatic past. I was able to offer a first interpretation linking her current behavior toward her fiancé to her troubled childhood: "You have blocked your feelings, and they leak out at Jimmy." And she joined the work by elaborating on the past-present connections between herself and her mother: "She acted like I do with Jimmy ... except that I don't throw bottles." We have already begun to see the root of the problem. The problem, of course, is not a "disorder" called *generalized anxiety disorder.* The problem is that she has blocked her emotions. All else follows from that.

My plastic figure of Freud looks down from atop my bookshelf and he, too, looks pleased.

3. Inspired

"This is not psychoanalysis!" That is his entire response, a merciless verdict delivered by a stern judge in a terse four-word sentence. I have just spent the better part of an hour describing the case of Carla in some detail. He has listened, but as I proceeded, I could see his expression growing more distant, more cautious. At first, he looked interested and asked a few questions, but he gradually became silent and aloof. Now he stands up and walks over to get one of his cigars. Is this a sign that the discussion is over? Should I just get up and leave? Outside on the streets of Vienna, it is a beautiful sunny day in May. Perhaps I should abandon my hopes for a dialogue with Freud and go sightseeing.

He stands by the bookcase near a photo I noticed during my first visit, a photo of a woman with very intense eyes. As he examines his choice of cigars, I find myself attracted to the photo. I see intelligence in her eyes, or at least I imagine that I do, and perhaps a tendency to be passionate about things that interest her. What I cannot discern is the nature of the emotion in those eyes. One could read a heavy sadness in them, but maybe she just looks serious. I can imagine her eyes becoming angry, but she is not passionately angry at the moment of the photo shoot. Maybe it is not anger at all. Is she trying to contain some kind of distress, some inner turmoil, her eyes warning the photographer not to come too close? She looks at me with a direct, engaging look, but she will not let me know what lies within. But why am I so absorbed by a photograph on a bookshelf? I suppose I would like to enlist her help in getting him to listen to me. Would she help? Who is she, anyway? And why does her photograph deserve a special place on Sigmund Freud's bookshelf?

He has yet to light the cigar, after some fiddling with matches and an ashtray; he comes back to his chair and sits down with his pleasure still unlit. I still have a chance to make my case, although I can see that the odds of success are diminishing with each passing minute.

"But Professor, this is a direct offshoot of your psychoanalysis. It's just a newer version of your original ideas."

"You have no couch, correct?"

"That's correct. The patient and I sit facing each other in chairs."

"You do not ask her to tell you her associations as they occur to her. Correct?"

"That's true. I don't tell her to just say whatever comes to mind. This is a more directive approach to treatment."

"No couch. No free association. This is not psychoanalysis!" He stands up again, and now he paces back and forth. He not only disagrees with what I have presented; he is clearly angry. In fact, he looks insulted, as if I have personally attacked him. I am stunned that a man of his stature can be so easily offended. I have read about this aspect of his character, to be sure. No matter how much positive attention he received in the world, he was prone to misinterpreting even the most balanced critique as a vicious attempt to destroy him and his theories. Friendships fell apart because someone dared to disagree with him. I must have been dreaming to think that I could interest him in a reasonable discussion about modern changes to his original technique. Still, I feel that I might as well try to finish my argument, as long as I have come all this way.

"But if you look at my case, perhaps you might agree that this is a variant of psychoanalysis. Just look at my use of defense mechanisms in the session. At first, Carla laughs when she talks about her anger at her fiancé. A nervous laugh, of course, but the laugh also functions as a defense against facing her rage at him. I point it out to her, and she agrees that the laugh might be masking other emotions."

Freud stops pacing and nods, almost reluctantly. His concept of defense mechanisms was one of the most original ideas in his voluminous work. He must be stopping to consider whether I am honoring his concept by using it wisely or defaming it by blatant misuse. I decide to continue.

"Later in the interview, I ask her how she feels and she again employs defenses. She says, 'It seems like forever ago.' She separates her emotions from the story. 'It doesn't seem real to me.'" Freud is listening now, and I can hear myself becoming more hopeful as I try to sell my argument to him. "By pointing out these defenses, I am educating her about the workings of her psyche. At the same time, I am trying to turn her against the defenses, so she will face the unacceptable ideas and emotions that she has refused to face until now." At this point, I reach for the book that I brought with me, as a lawyer reaches for the critical piece of evidence that will prove his client is innocent. "May I read something to you?" I ask.

"Certainly," he says, still looking quite skeptical.

"*These patients whom I analyzed had enjoyed good mental health up to the moment at which an occurrence of incompatibility took place in their ideational life—that is to say, until their ego was faced with an experience, an idea or a feeling which aroused such a distressing affect that the subject decided to forget about it.*" I look up from the book to make sure he is listening. "From your paper, 'The Neuro-Psychoses of Defense,' written in 1894. One of your earliest papers. As a child, Carla was faced with terrible, frightening events, events that she would rather forget about. We are now using your concepts and challenging the defenses to get to the disturbing 'experience, idea or feeling.' For this patient, she has never really faced the painful reality of what happened in her childhood home. And you can see what happens by the end of the session. She experiences a breakthrough of emotion and begins to realize the magnitude of the situation she endured as a child. She *remembers with emotion*, just as you and Breuer prescribed in your book *Studies on Hysteria*."

Freud is standing in one spot now. He no longer looks agitated, and he seems to be considering my line of thought. He takes his chair again, much to my surprise. He is thinking, and he takes his time before offering a thought.

"So you are using my concept of defenses as a direct technical intervention with the patient. You actually tell her about her defenses as they arise."

"Exactly," I say.

"And by pointing them out to her, you are trying to weaken their hold on her, so that the repressed contents of the mind can emerge."

"Exactly! The thoughts and memories can emerge, and she can open up with her feelings. She can emotionally expand again." Freud looks puzzled by my last comment. I want so much to talk with him about Reich's concept of expansion and contraction. I want to tell him: *You cannot be open and closed at the same time. Carla started the session in a state of emotional contraction, and later she was able to re-expand emotionally.* But this might be too much to lay on the table so soon. And who knows how he might react to the topic of Reich and his revolutionary ideas? I need to stay focused and talk about short-term dynamic psychotherapy. "Yes, the contents of her mind can come forth. That's exactly what I am trying to accomplish. If I can loosen the grip of her defenses, then we can dig down beneath the surface and find out what lies buried. Like an archeological dig." I know that Freud loved to compare psychoanalysis to archeology. He would sometimes point to his vast collection of miniature antiquities to make the metaphor to his patients. I worry for a moment that I am trying too hard to ingratiate myself to him, but he nods his approval at the comment. At this moment, Gretchen opens the door to his office holding a tray with tea. Freud waves her off, apparently not wanting to be distracted now.

He sits pondering what I have said. Here, in the last couple of minutes, I have seen the two sides of Sigmund Freud as I have read about him. On the one hand, he could be remarkably thin-skinned. He was always determined to make a name for himself, and his ambition could sometimes lead him to be competitive, distrustful, and vindictive. To use the psychoanalytic term, his *narcissism* got in his way. True, he had his detractors, and he endured some unwarranted hostility from colleagues, but he sometimes took an honest disagreement as a narcissistic injury, a blow to his basic self-esteem. On the other hand, he had a quick mind and an intense love of ideas. When he was immersed in the world of ideas and theories, without feeling threatened, he could be a kindly mentor, a committed analyst, and a devoted friend. One could easily see how two people could come away from him with two diametrically opposed impressions of the man.

At the moment, his intense curiosity has overtaken his bellicose instinct to protect his intellectual territory. He asks more questions about how I use defense mechanisms in therapy. Which defenses do I see most often? Are certain defenses associated with particular symptoms? How do I proceed if the defenses do not yield to this approach? As he talks, he sits back and lights his cigar. Now that he is engaged, I make my next move.

"Here is another point I would like to make, with your permission. Just look at your concept of anxiety and how I used it in the session, and you will see why I say that this is still psychoanalytic work. You remember that I noticed how she was biting her lip and the inside of her cheek? This happened early in the session, and it became more obvious as she began to tell the story of her violent, chaotic family life."

Freud nods, puffing on the cigar.

"And you recall that I pointed this out to her as a possible physical manifestation of anxiety. The anxiety was triggered by the difficult topic at hand. It was your *signal anxiety*: anxiety that gets triggered by some unacceptable thought or emotion within the person. In your terms, the ego sends out a signal of anxiety because there are uncomfortable feelings lurking beneath the surface. In plain English, she is afraid of her own emotions."

Freud nods again.

"In Carla's case," I continue, "the anxiety was prompted by the stirring of hidden grief over her childhood. Her anxiety, which caused her to chew her lip, alerted me to the presence of unacceptable thoughts, feelings, and memories. When I asked her about the significance of the chewing, she realized that she was anxious, and she was anxious because she was starting to talk about the trauma. Soon after that point, her sadness began to emerge."

"So you are using my signal anxiety as a marker in the therapy," he says. "Once you see it, this biting of the lip, you know that the emotions are not far behind."

"Yes. Exactly! And it can be any sign of anxiety: fidgeting of the hands, gripping the chair, tapping the feet. Any of this might mean signal anxiety, and then I start to suspect that buried feelings are closer to the surface."

Again, he asks questions. How do I know when the anxiety is *not* due to buried thoughts or feelings within, but due to a real threat—financial problems, illness, and so on—in the immediate environment? Not all anxiety is signal anxiety, he cautions me. What do I do if the patient's anxiety gets too overwhelming? How soon do I address the anxiety in a session? He calls for Gretchen, and we drink tea and talk for quite a while about defense mechanisms and anxiety, until he has satisfied himself that he understands the approach I am describing. For the moment, at least, the struggle to get him to listen is over, and the battle is mine.

"So this new technical innovation, this is your own construction?" he asks.

"No, not mine. I learned it from Davanloo."

"Davanloo? And who is this Davanloo?"

"Habib Davanloo. A psychiatrist in Montreal. He was after your time."

"What kind of name is this? Davanloo."

"He was originally from Iran. Persia." I have no idea when Persia changed its name to Iran, so I offer both names. "He studied psychiatry in the United States and then settled in Montreal, in Canada. It was his idea to employ your theories like this. He was one of the people who developed short-term dynamic psychotherapy."

"Well, that is interesting. I still cannot call this psychoanalysis, but it is very interesting." He asks more questions about Davanloo, and I tell him a bit more of his background and training. "How did you meet him?"

"Oh, I had heard about him, and I attended one of his conferences in Montreal. I was younger then. I was a psychiatry resident when I first heard him."

"Was it well attended?" He seems interested in getting a sense of Davanloo's notoriety, as well as his ideas.

"The auditorium was packed. He drew quite an audience in his day. I think he has retired now."

"It was a good conference?" he asks.

"Oh, it was amazing. It was so different from anything I had ever seen." I can still remember my first sight of Davanloo walking out onto the stage at the front of the auditorium. He was a short, bald man who was clearly past midlife, but something about his energetic presence made it feel as though he had leaped rather than walked onto the stage. He might as well have landed by parachute as part of a military operation to liberate Montreal from the enemy forces of psychotherapeutic ineptitude. He spoke in a loud, authoritative voice with a thick Persian accent, and he spoke with great confidence and certainty about his method of therapy. He assured us that he could get to the core of the patient's difficulties in a relatively short time. He could overcome the patient's resistance (a word he pronounced with a French Canadian accent: *résistance*), penetrate to the core of the neurotic conflict, and accomplish a breakthrough into the realm of the unconscious. He kept talking about the *unlocking* of the unconscious.

This was strange talk to anyone whose primary orientation was traditional Freudian "dynamic" psychotherapy. The model of therapy that I was learning in my residency at the time was heavy on general theory and light on specific techniques. We were taught to practice "long-term psychodynamic psychotherapy," and part of the training was to learn the art of patience. We were instructed to follow a person's thoughts and listen for hidden, unconscious meanings in his utterances. When I grew restless with this method, when I wanted to take action and *do* something, I was repeatedly coached to "sit with the patient" and curb my wish to see rapid changes. I had to learn to "tolerate ambiguity" and avoid premature interpretations. There was some wisdom in all of this, of course, when applied at the right time. However, when this approach to therapy was carried too far by a couple of our instructors, it became a paralyzing message. If the trainee actually wanted to move ahead quickly and efficiently, and alleviate the person's suffering, he was chastised for being naïve and exhibiting a beginner's impatience. With this as my educational background, Davanloo's introductory claims sounded immodest, preposterous, and immensely intriguing.

He did not spend too much time on this first description of his method, though. He probably spoke for a half an hour or so, and then announced that he would show a videotape of a session to illustrate his technique. We were told that taking photographs was not allowed during the video, to protect the patient's privacy. Behind me, I heard someone say that Davanloo was reluctant to have any photos taken of him under any circumstance. This struck me as odd, as he hardly seemed like a man who would shy away from a camera.

"Videotape?" Freud asks. I have to explain video cameras to him, of course. We talk for a moment about motion picture technology in his day, but he quickly returns to the subject. "Your man Davanloo sounds like Charcot," he remarks. "First there is the lecture, and then he brings out the patient."

"Right," I say. "Charcot brought out the live patient. Davanloo brought out the videotape of the patient. But Charcot showed you the symptoms, not a treatment for the symptoms. Davanloo showed us a complete method of psychotherapy on his videotapes. It was really unbelievable." In the first few minutes of the tape, a young woman described her problems with anxiety and depression. Davanloo asked a few questions. So far, it looked like any other therapy. Then he told the patient very bluntly that she was being passive with him. She agreed, and I began to feel confused and uncomfortable as I sat watching the videotape. How could he make such an outlandish pronouncement after spending two or three minutes with her? Then I realized that she did seem a bit passive. He asked a question, and she answered. Otherwise, she offered very little on her own, so perhaps he was right. She not only agreed with him but also told him she was *always* passive in her relationships. I felt anxious. How could he identify one of her most problematic personality traits in a few minutes? And what was I doing in my own therapy cases? Was I accomplishing *anything*? Was I not also being too passive by following the advice of my instructors?

Davanloo questioned her further about her symptoms and her relationships with other people. At one point, she started a sentence with the word "maybe" and he stopped her in midsentence. *Maybe? You say maybe? Are you always vague like this?* His confrontational stance made her feel uncomfortable, of course, and I got the feeling that many of the therapists around me in the audience were likewise uncomfortable. A minute later, the woman answered: *I guess so.* Again, Davanloo pounced. *You guess so? Why do you say you guess so? Either you think so or you do not. Why do you keep everything so vague?*

A narrator's voice had been added to the video at this point. Davanloo, according to the scripted commentary, was challenging the patient's defenses, not the patient. Her vagueness was a defense against her unconscious thoughts and feelings, and it must be addressed directly. Likewise, her passivity was a *character defense*, a personality trait that functioned as a defense mechanism against the unacceptable contents of her unconscious. This passivity might be hiding some assertiveness or anger. All this must be challenged, and the therapist must *turn the ego against the defenses*. This challenge was going to trigger a set of complex, ambivalent feelings: the patient would feel gratitude for Dr. Davanloo's persistence as well as anger and irritation about the confrontation. If the patient was ambivalent, I was too. One minute I thought he was being rude and obnoxious; the next I could see how this might be a brilliant and productive approach.

Davanloo confronted her yet again, this time about her passivity. *What are we going to do about this passivity?* The patient was flustered, as I was. She did not know what she was going to do, of course. She did not like being passive, she told him, and that was one of the reasons she came to therapy. He would not be appeased. *But what are we going to do about this passivity of yours? If you continue being so passive, I will be of no use to you.* She became quiet. He continued his relentless confrontation of her defenses. *You come here to get help, but if you keep up your passivity, you make me useless to you and I cannot help you.* This confrontation went on for another minute or two, and then he asked her what she was feeling. She was clearly starting to look sad. And then came the most startling part of the interview. She began to talk about how awful it felt to be so passive with everyone, and soon she was talking about her authoritarian father. She had to become passive with him, or run the risk of asserting herself and facing the consequences of crossing him. She was openly crying. Davanloo now changed his tone dramatically, as he gently explored with her the psychological roots of her problems.

All of this was both exciting and disturbing to me. I remember looking at my watch, and I was astonished to see that I had been sitting in the auditorium for only about an hour, and part of that time had been Davanloo's introductory speech. The video segment I had just watched could not have been more than twenty minutes. *Twenty minutes!* I could not have accomplished all that in twenty sessions!

At this point in my story, I realize that I have stood up from my chair in Freud's consulting room and moved to the window. I have been doing a bit of dramatization as I told the story. There is no way to convey Davanloo's style of psychotherapy unless one speaks in a loud confrontational tone, and I have tried to mimic that tone. I have also tried to imitate his accent (Persian with hints of the Quebecois French spoken in Montreal), and then I have spoken softly to give the impression of the passive woman on the tape. Freud is looking at me and smiling broadly.

"Obviously, you met your Charcot at that conference." He is clearly delighted. "And everyone should have a Charcot in his life. This calls for a celebration!" He stands up and goes for a cigar, his second for the afternoon. Like all addicts, Freud uses every possible justification to indulge. "One should have some passion to be in this business. One should feel inspired. Obviously, you were inspired by this Davanloo, as I was inspired by Charcot."

"Well, I guess so," I say.

"You guess so? Listen to your own story. You were inspired! That is wonderful."

"Yes, of course." I cannot bring myself to say what I am thinking: *No, that is not right. Interested, yes. Amazed, astonished, yes. But not inspired. That is not the right word.* "But Davanloo was not Charcot," I say. "As you said, Charcot played a pioneering role in clarifying the nature of several serious neurological diseases like multiple sclerosis. His work with hysteria was in addition to his prominent contributions to neurology. Davanloo was a talented therapist, but just one of many therapists who contributed to modern dynamic psychotherapy." *Impressed, yes, but not inspired.*

"But obviously you saw him as I saw Charcot: bright, articulate, fascinating. And you learned something from him, yes?" How odd that Freud is now defending Davanloo, despite Davanloo's bold changes to the technique of psychoanalysis. And he is right, of course; I learned a great deal from Davanloo's conferences. He had breathed life into classical Freudian concepts, and he gave us a practical means to implement them in the therapy session. Until I heard him speak, I really had no way to integrate what I was reading with my actual work in the office. In all of Freud's voluminous publications, he had precious little to say about technique, so generations of dynamic psychotherapists had felt a bit lost when they actually sat down with their patients. In my own training, decades after Freud's time, there was still so much theory and so little technique. Davanloo changed all that. *But it is not the same. Not the same as Charcot. Inspired is the wrong word.*

"Well, his conferences were fascinating," I say, "so I suppose you could compare them to the weekly lectures of Charcot." In between spoken sentences, I wrestle with Davanloo's importance. I have a problem with him: his method was too harsh, too confrontational. Many of us studied his methods, but then we had to struggle to make his approach gentler and less threatening to the patient. Not every "maybe" or "I guess so" is a defense mechanism. Am I still doing work that is consistent with his teaching? Yes, I answer myself. Yes, definitely. Even though many of us have modified his approach and rejected some of his techniques, I still learned a great deal from him, and his contribution was enormously important. *But he was not my Charcot.*

"Very good. Very good." Freud is pleased. It seems that my description of a Davanloo conference has curiously done a great deal to further the alliance between us, and I should leave it at that. "Obviously the experience of attending his conference has changed your life. How do you spell this name: Davanloo?" I spell it out for him. "Ah, two *o*'s at the end. I was thinking of it as a French name, with *i–e–u* at the end. But you did say he is Persian." He holds up his cigar, as if it were a pen, and draws two circles in the air.

I imagine him with an actual pen in hand, sitting at a desk, writing one of his books. The scene in my mind is late at night, after his wife and children have all gone to bed. He sits alone at his desk, an ashtray on the desk holding a cigar that has been lit but forgotten as he wrestles with a question. He struggles with an idea that will not quite yield to a clear solution. Maybe he is trying to understand why one particular patient resists getting well. Maybe he is trying to understand some larger question about civilization in light of his psychoanalytic theories. He sits alone at his desk, unable to move forward, unwilling to give up, incapable of admitting defeat. Then, in one triumphant instant, the confusion clears, the fog lifts, and he sees the answer right before him. He puts pen to paper and begins writing as quickly as it comes to him, and it comes very quickly indeed. I imagine that he no longer senses himself as a man writing an idea, but as an idea being written through a man. He is a conduit for the knowledge of the human condition that has been known by poets and sages for thousands of years, knowledge that he will now put into systematic formulations for generations to come. The book seems to write itself as the Muse of psychology shines upon him.

"Oh, yes," he says, pulling me out of my fantasy scene, "You have found your Charcot. We need to find inspiration, you know, especially early in our careers. We need to find someone who inspires us by his excitement for the field. Whatever else that person does, whatever his mistakes or excesses or faults, he has done an important job if he has inspired the next generation."

"Yes, I totally agree with you, Professor." *But it's not him, it's not Davanloo. It's you. You are my Charcot. You are the one who inspired me. How is it even possible that you don't see this? Do you really not know this? Why do you think I come here?*

"Good, good," he says. "I must hear more about this Davanloo and his techniques. More about your Charcot."

4. The Sight of Blood

*O*ne never knows how a patient will react after the first visit. I have my predictions about Carla, and they are positive ones, but sometimes there are unexpected negative reactions to the first session. Maybe she went home and felt that the first emergence of hidden emotions was just too frightening. She could walk into the office today with a rationale for stopping the therapy process. She might offer a genetic theory and ask for medications. *Everybody in my family is anxious. It's in our genes.* She might say that looking back is a waste of time. *I just want to move forward.* If she cannot face another session, even though the first one seemed quite successful from my point of view, she might not appear at all. I have my predictions, but one never knows.

She does arrive. When she walks into the office, she seems comfortable being here again. She greets me and makes direct eye contact. She asks me how I am this morning. Again, nothing in her appearance or her bearing would suggest a traumatic background. In fact, she seems naturally cheerful and animated, despite the dark history of her childhood. She has *resilience*, as they say in the research on child development. She somehow has the capacity to bounce back from terrible adversity and construct a successful life for herself. She even shows a bit of goodwill toward others.

She talks first today about her boyfriend, Jimmy. She still blows up at him, and she still feels bad about it. She belittles him for not making more money, and she calls him a "loser." Ironically, he is the first man she has dated who does not have trouble earning and saving money. Carla tells me that all her other boyfriends really were losers, as they wasted all their money on alcohol. Obviously, it has never occurred to her that her choice of those men was influenced by growing up with her father, who drank too much and failed to support the family. She has clearly been in the grip of Freud's *repetition compulsion*; she has unconsciously been compelled to repeat a pattern of getting involved in a relationship that recreates the early trauma of living with her father. And I suppose that Freud was right in thinking that the unconscious goal of such a reenactment is to gain mastery over the trauma. *This time,* says the unconscious mind, *it will be different. This time I will make my father* (whose role is played by a hard-drinking, irresponsible boyfriend) *change for the better. He will apologize and change his ways.* Sadly, this cleverly designed strategy of the unconscious mind never, never, *never* works, and only leads to more suffering.

I would conjecture that part of Carla's anxiety is triggered by the fact that Jimmy is not like the others. He works hard, saves his money, and promises to be a very reliable mate. But this must present her with a terrible dilemma: when she rants at Jimmy for not being a good provider, she knows that the attack is misplaced, and she is faced with the disturbing idea that the anger is meant for someone else. We are not yet ready to deal with that idea, but it must be lurking somewhere in her thoughts.

She tells me that she talked to Jimmy about our first session. I consider this to be a good sign. If she spoke with him about it, she was obviously willing to look again at the subject matter of that session. I feel less optimistic when a patient never talks about the therapy to anyone, and worse yet if she never thinks about the sessions after leaving the office.

"Jimmy didn't even know some of this stuff," she says, settling into her chair. "He asked me how my first session went with you and I was telling him, and I was talking about my past more freely after I left here. And he said, 'What did she do? Your mother did *that?*' And I said, 'Yeah.' And he said, 'Why would she do that?' And I said, 'I don't know.' And he thought it was terrible."

"Of course," I say.

"He was laughing because he couldn't believe it."

I suspect that this may be the first time she has told anyone outside the family about what happened in that home. It must be good for her to hear him express his surprise and disbelief. Perhaps it will help her to gain a new perspective on the traumatic home life that was the norm for her.

"It's kind of embarrassing though," she adds.

"Well, it's not something you'd want to tell everybody at a social gathering."

"Yeah, that's for sure."

"Were you embarrassed telling *me*?" I ask.

"No, not at all. I was more embarrassed to tell Jimmy about it. If that makes sense. He knows my mom. And I don't want him to hate her because of what happened."

"Are you worried that Jimmy might hate your mother, or that *you* might hate your mother?"

"I don't have angry feelings toward my mom."

"No?"

"I mean, some, probably. Like how she …"

I challenge her contradictory statements. "You don't have anger, but you do."

"I do, I do probably have a little bit, 'cause she's weak. I can't stand it when women are not strong in their relationships. When a woman is not even her own person."

"Your mother was weak?"

"Yes. She still is!" Carla talks about how her mother tolerated her father's behavior year after year and failed to stand up to him effectively. When she finally left the marriage, she went through a series of boyfriends, and she was equally submissive with all of them. Carla sounds critical thus far, but then she abruptly shifts into a more idealized version of Mom, perhaps the version of a young child. Mom always protected the kids from dad's drunken rages, she says. Mom would scoop them up and take them to her aunt's house as soon as dad started raising his voice. Dad is the villain of this fairy tale, and Mom is the fairy godmother who rescues her children again and again.

Carla is contradicting herself, of course, but I am not surprised. The behavior of her parents was often so erratic and unpredictable that her experiences could never become fully integrated into a single, consistent narrative. Her parents would show up at her soccer game to cheer for her, and three hours later the same parents were drunk and beating each other while the kids cowered in a corner of the room. How can one construct a logical, coherent childhood story from such chaos?

As the story continues, it changes again. My narrator matures into a teenaged girl who begins to move beyond seeing Mom as a helpless victim. Now she begins to contradict the fairy tale version. She recounts the prolonged fights between her parents, and she highlights Mom's contribution to the troubles. Finally, she returns to her original indictment: Mom was weak. Mom should have left Dad after his first drunken explosion so the kids could be extricated from the constant turmoil.

"So, you see your mother as weak."

"Yeah." She gazes off to the side for a moment, as if to glance at a memory waiting in the shadows. "One time she cut herself on a glass. She had a gaping wound on her hand. And the blood was just coming out, and I was just crying and scared for her. I was so young."

"That was during a fight with your dad?"

"Yeah. I think he had thrown a glass and she bent down to pick up the pieces, the shards of glass. He might have pushed her at the moment she had glass in her hand. Or maybe she just cut herself. I don't know if she ever got a black eye. I can't remember a black eye ever." Again, she talks casually, as if we are discussing someone else.

"Do you have any feelings now?" I ask.

"No. Just sadness that it happened to her."

"You feel sadness? Or you say the word *sadness*?"

"I say the word. I'm not really feeling sad." There is no real experience of emotion here. This is the kind of therapy session that sounds good but arrives nowhere. She is obviously talking about important events that took place in her life; she is "working on her issues." Nonetheless, she is experiencing nothing, and the benefits of the session will be limited unless we get past her defenses again.

"So where's the feeling?" I ask. In Reich's terms, she is experiencing neither expansion nor contraction; there is neither an expansive release of anger or grief, nor shrinking away in anxiety or guilt. No emotion at all. Nothing. Her defenses block it all.

"I don't know," she says. "I don't feel anything about it." She pauses for a moment. "Sometimes that happens with traumatic incidents in my life. I just feel numb." As she says this, she uses one hand to start picking at the other. She seems to be digging with her fingernails. It takes me a minute to notice it, but then I am struck by the possibility that this is a nonverbal enactment of the story: *Is she picking at the cut?* She is trying to distance herself from the emotional impact of the memory, but perhaps at the same time she begins to act it out with her hands.

"Well, that's a common defense. Just to shut the feelings down. But I think this has left you with residual emotional problems like the anger at Jimmy and the anxiety. Maybe there is some sadness under the surface that you don't let yourself feel anymore. You saw your mother bleeding, and you saw what she went through."

"Yeah, Mom bleeding. My father always drunk. Just never had a functional family. You know, they just didn't do the normal things to take care of us kids."

"You didn't get the care you needed."

"Yeah. Didn't get the care. And then there was Anthony. My mother was so cruel to Anthony. She took everything out on him"

"In what way?" As soon as I ask the question, I regret it. She was talking about the cut on her mother's hand, and then she mentions her brother Anthony. It could easily be a diversion; she may be using an unconscious ploy to move away from the memory of Mom's cut. And here I am going along with it, colluding with the defense. I sit quietly listening for a minute, as she goes into the memories of Mom mistreating Anthony.

"Mom would say mean, humiliating things to Anthony. She would slap him and hit him."

I am about to interrupt and go back to Mom's cut when she yawns widely. The yawn makes me think that perhaps this is not a diversion, after all. The common theme is about family members getting hurt, and the yawn might suggest that talking about Anthony is threatening to stir up painful emotions. Instead of experiencing the feelings, she gets tense. She is breathing too shallowly and needs air, so the yawn functions as the nervous laugh of our first session; it delivers an emergency supply of fresh air.

"You're yawning, I notice."

"I know. I think it's because this chair is so comfortable."

"But you're talking about your brother being abused."

"Yeah."

"It seems to me that you block your feelings so much that you could talk about this and drift off to a nap."

She bursts into a big laugh. "I know it's not funny!" she says, still laughing.

"But that's how cut off your feelings are right now." I didn't use the word *cut* intentionally, but now I hear the reference to her mother's cut. In a sense, my unconscious is talking to hers: *You are cutting off your feelings about your mother's cut.* Should I go back to that subject or stay with the story about her brother? "And I'm sure you have feelings about what happened to your brother."

"Yeah, I feel bad for him. 'Cause I imagine that's why he has so many problems with women now." She starts to describe one of Anthony's relationships with women, but this certainly will be a diversion away from the emotion if I allow it.

"So I don't know what you're feeling. Underneath the yawning."

"I don't know either."

"You sound like you could be describing a movie you saw last night. It doesn't sound like it's your family and your life."

"That's how I talk when I talk about my grandmother passing away last summer." She begins to describe the scene of finding her grandmother dead at home. She tells me she was very close to her. "That was such a traumatic thing, but it just doesn't feel like it happened to me. It just seems like so long ago."

"You really cut these feelings off," I say.

"Um-hm. I don't know why. Like you say, it's a defense." She sits quietly for a long moment, and all the vitality is gone. All the energy has disappeared. "I feel like I should have feelings about it, but—"

"I presume that you do. Somewhere."

"I do. Somewhere. I don't feel them right now, though."

"We talk of these important topics, your mom's cut and your grandmother dying and Anthony, but there's no emotion."

"At first, when I was young and my mother was beating my brother up, I was upset and cried then. But now I've made it so I don't really feel anything about it."

"It's all sealed off."

"Yes," she agrees.

"But I wonder if this too contributes to the outbursts of anger."

"It could, yeah. Why do I get that angry at Jimmy? But he knows how to get under my skin, you know."

"Well, he may be good at irritating you, but that doesn't explain the type of anger that comes out of you."

"Exactly. The mean words that I say and the names that I call him."

"And the threats to punch him in the face," I add.

"Oh, yeah. I just have to zip my mouth. The other day, I was with some friends and—"

"But before we jump to your friends ..." I have interrupted her in midsentence, as I saw Davanloo do when I attended his conference in Montreal. It is not the most polite manner of interacting, but it is time to block her defenses before she can use them to escape.

"You do have a tendency to jump around a bit."

"That's how my mind works. But it makes me feel scrambled, too. Even in our first session, I felt like I jumped around too much."

"Oh, I see. But then we don't solve any particular problem if we jump around all over."

"Right," she says.

I know I need to interfere with her tendency to change topics, but old voices haunt me from my residency days. I can hear my supervisors telling me to let the patient say whatever comes to mind. I should just follow Freud's technique of free association, they say. After all, this is the fundamental rule of his psychoanalysis. I argue back in my head against Freud: If I just adhere to the fundamental rule and follow her line of thought, I will be led on a defensive ramble that takes us farther and farther from the emotional center of the problem. But I am not being fair to Freud here; certainly, many Freudian analysts would also point out the rapid shifting of subject matter and recognize it as a defense. I suppose some of my supervisors just took the fundamental rule to an extreme, so my argument is with them, not Freud.

Carla stifles another yawn.

"We were talking about your mom ... Are you starting to yawn?"

She smiles. "I'm trying not to. I don't even know what causes yawning. Calmness or something? Maybe I'm not breathing enough?" I am surprised that she seems to understand the physiology behind the yawn.

"I was just going to say that. I wonder if you are breathing shallowly and then you have to take a big yawn ..."

Now she surrenders to an enormous yawn, her mouth becoming cavernous. "Yeah, 'cause ..."

"You need to get air. Maybe it's not just the mind shutting down. Maybe it's your body that shuts down and slows down a little bit when you talk about these things, so that you're not getting enough air."

"Maybe. 'Cause it's only happening when I'm talking to you about these things."

"Only when we talk about your mother and Anthony. You are physiologically slowing down so you don't have to experience your emotions."

"Um-hm."

"What do you think you're blocking in there? We were talking about your mother's cut and then your mother and Anthony. Someplace in the middle of these stories, stories about people getting hurt, you started yawning and slowing down."

"Yeah, I'm probably just avoiding the feelings that I felt at the time. Being so scared."

"Scared? When?"

"Probably when I saw my mom bleeding. And, you know, she's crying 'cause she sees the blood too." How interesting that she mixes present and past tenses. One minute, she is describing an event from long ago; the next minute, she is reliving it in the present moment. "And I was so scared and ... I don't ever remember hating my dad, though. I never got so upset at him. I was more worried about him all the time. I was worried he was going to kill himself."

"Worried he was going to kill himself?"

"Yeah. He threatened to do it all the time."

"He did?"

She nods.

"But we were talking about your mother bleeding. And there must be a lot of feelings about your mom. Before we go to your dad and your grandmother and ten other things..." She is actually a bit more challenging than I realized after our first visit. Not only does she jump from topic to topic, but they are all serious topics worthy of exploration: the cut hand, the abuse of her brother, her grandmother's death, and now her father's suicide threats. What better way to get a psychiatrist's attention than to mention suicide? The challenge for me is to decide when a topic is being used as a convenient escape route, and when it represents the natural direction of her thoughts. When is it a defense? When is it the thread that will lead to some healing?

From all these stories on the table, I will pick the one about her mother. After all, when she first talked about it, she started picking at her hand. The body does not lie.

"My mom. Yeah." She looks to one side, gazing again into her memory bank. "I remember we were in her bedroom ... and I'm not sure but I think she had a bandage on her hand, actually. And I said, 'Oh my God, Mom! What happened?' And I think that's when she showed it to me, or maybe she just put a bandage on it and I didn't actually see it.

I didn't remember that bandage until just now. It wasn't just like it was open and bleeding. She had it covered. I remember it bleeding and I remember it covered. Maybe I saw it both ways." Now she yawns again, her mouth opening wide and searching for air.

"Do you notice the yawn?"

"Um-hm." She laughs. She moves so quickly between a dull stillness and an animated laugh. "Yeah."

"What are you feeling physically?"

"Nothing. Just tired. And I wasn't tired when I came here today."

"But that's so interesting."

"I know," she says.

"We see that the defense is physiological."

She laughs again. "I know. That's so weird!"

"You're not tired. But somehow you're yawning and you look like you could just tip the chair back and take a nap, talking about your mother bleeding profusely from a cut." She is laughing now and she looks like she cannot stop. "We are talking about your mother engaged in a fight with your father."

"I know!"

"But you know, if you're physically slowing down, it suggests to me that there is a world of emotion in there, and you are trying—without realizing it—to block it."

"Yeah, you're right."

"I don't think you were yawning in the early part of the session at all."

"No, I wasn't." She laughs one more time. "Maybe I should stand up and walk around." She actually stands for a second and then sits down again.

"What makes you laugh?"

"I can't help myself from yawning today. How weird! When I'm at work, I don't sit around and yawn. Even when I'm tired, I don't yawn. Maybe I have to sit up straighter." Another yawn. "I don't know. Maybe it's because of the way I'm sitting?"

"Maybe it's the way you're not feeling."

"Yeah, maybe."

"So you saw your mother with the cut or the bandage and you were worried about her."

She nods. "And I was upset because she was crying, and upset because my father did that to her. Or at least I blamed him at the time." She sits quietly now, neither yawning nor laughing.

"What would you say to her? What would you say if you could go back into that memory?"

"*Mom, oh my God, what happened to your hand?* I don't remember if she lied to me, or if she said, 'This is what your father did to me.' She would sometimes blame him. She would hide some things, but not—"

"And what do you suppose is underneath the yawning?" I hear myself shifting from defense to emotion. Instead of focusing on her defenses, I have shifted to an inquiry about the emotion itself.

"I don't know. It's the feeling underneath, but I'm numb from it. I feel calm."

"Right now you're calm?"

"Yeah."

"Do you have any idea about what's beneath the surface if we conduct a little archeological expedition here?"

"Probably a lot of sadness."

"Sadness for whom? Your mom, your dad, or yourself?"

She looks quiet and very serious now. "I don't know. I don't feel angry about it."

"That's okay, but then who are you sad for?" I notice myself leaning forward slightly, as I do sometimes when I sense that I might be getting closer to the emotions and I am trying to coax the patient to relinquish her defenses and have a genuine emotional experience.

"Uh, probably sad for my mom. That she had to deal with that for so long."

"And she was injured," I add.

"Yes, and she had three kids that she had to protect and ..."

"I suspect there is something about the cut—that scene—that stirs up a lot of feeling and makes you go numb and yawn. Because you keep jumping away from that scene, and I'm thinking to myself how terrifying that moment would be for a little girl."

"Yeah."

"Because you wouldn't know how much she is going to bleed or if she's going to be okay."

"Yeah. I think she needed stitches, and she wouldn't go to the doctor. The cut was open."

"How old were you?"

"Oh, about nine probably."

"Pretty scary for a nine-year-old."

"Yeah."

We are not getting anywhere. She still seems detached from it all, and her face displays a pleasant, blank expression. I am trying to bring out the emotion by offering a bit of empathy for that nine-year-old girl, but to no avail. Perhaps I should go back to the defenses. Maybe if I keep moving back and forth between emotion and defense, we can still succeed.

"But you look pretty calm and bored."

She laughs again. "I know. I don't know why. I'm not bored. I just—"

"What else would you want to say to your mother if you could go back in time to that scene?"

She looks more serious again. "I would say, *Mom you don't have to put up with this anymore. Just leave him. It's better if you leave him. Don't stay with him. We'll make it without him.*" Still nothing. She is unmoved by all of this. Maybe it would help to shift from the memory of Mom to the memory of herself as a child.

"And then what would you say to that nine-year-old little girl?"

"I would say, *It's alright. Your mom is not hurt that bad. She's going to be okay. She fights with your dad because he makes her angry. And he does bad things and she gets mad at him.*"

"How does that little girl look in your memory?"

"Just … I don't know … scared. Crying. Just always feeling anxious, probably."

"Just like you describe yourself now."

"Yeah." Then something happens. It happens for only an instant, certainly less than a second. She presses her lips together and she shuts her eyes tight. The expression is vanishingly brief; her face returns immediately to its former still posture, like a pretty mannequin in a store window. But it was there for a moment: the face of a little girl about to burst into tears.

"Do you have any feelings coming up?"

"Starting to, a little bit."

"Really? What is it?" Now, for the first time today, she starts that motion of chewing the inside of her cheek and lip. Something is brewing and it makes her anxious. We must be very close.

"You chew your lip or something."

"Yeah, like I'm trying to hold back tears, probably."

"Why are you holding it back? Saving it for another day?"

"No." She smiles, and then the tears form. "I don't know." Her brow furrows in a clearly pained look. "That's probably where all my anxiety stems from. Because I was always scared." And she *looks* scared now. Scared and sad.

"Of course."

"I've never pictured myself in the past like this. I've never looked back and felt the anxiety feelings. So it has never gone away."

"Right," I say. Right, indeed. Her comment is a perfect summary of the early position taken by the kindly Dr. Breuer and his young colleague, Sigmund Freud. She has never looked back and felt the emotions of that time, so they never went away. They were frozen in time, and she has carried that anxiety with her ever since. She has carried the grief too, although she has not been aware of it.

Now that we have moved past the wall of defenses, she goes back to the story. First, there is the fighting and screaming between her parents. The scene is in the kitchen, where her father throws a glass—probably several glasses—against the wall. Her mother bends down to pick up the pieces. Perhaps she is cursing at her husband, but Carla is not sure about this. Maybe she is cursing at him, maybe not.

"I suppose it doesn't really matter," she says.

No, it does not matter, I think to myself. We reconstruct our memories as best we can from the available bits and pieces we have at our disposal. The goal in dynamic psychotherapy is not perfect accuracy in retrieving the details; the goal is to remember troubling events in our lives and to overcome their harmful effects on us.

So her mother is bending down to pick up broken glass, and she is cursing at her husband. The children are right there, as usual, right in the middle of the unbridled rage of two adults whose job it is to protect them and make them feel safe. *Bastard!* yells their mother, crying and scooping up shards of glass. And then he comes up from behind and pushes her. The kids are yelling, *Daddy, stop!* Or maybe they are standing there frozen in fear saying nothing; she cannot be sure about this part of the memory. It does not matter. Her mother puts out her hands to brace herself as she tips forward onto the floor, but her hands are full of glass. When she stands up, she is dripping blood from one hand. The kids are crying, *Mommy! Mommy!* Or maybe they are quiet, saying nothing, silently witnessing a scene that instantly and permanently destroys their belief in a safe, predictable world.

Mother runs upstairs to her room with Carla close behind. What happens to father, brother, and sister at this point is lost in the remembrance. Mother is sitting on the bed crying, holding a bandage on her hand. Carla is in the room with her, frightened and trying to talk to her, trying to give comfort and receive comfort at the same time, and failing at both.

"I don't get it," she says to me now. "I just don't get it."

"What don't you get?"

"Why did it have to be this way? Why did they have to act this way?" She is crying hard now, struggling to fit the words in between the sobs and the deep breaths. "It didn't have to be this way. They could have gotten help for themselves. They could have made life better for all of us." And so she cries for a while, and I sit quietly saying nothing because there is nothing more to say. She has crying to do; she must cry as the nine-year-old girl who is afraid that her mother is bleeding to death, and she must cry as the twenty-six-year-old woman who is sad about how her childhood has affected her entire life.

When she is done, she looks a bit tired but very calm. "Well, that was pretty intense," she says with a little laugh.

"It sure was." We talk for a few more minutes about her family. She remembers the poverty that they endured after the marriage finally ended and her father refused to pay child support. Remarkably, she transcends her own emotional needs as a child and expresses empathy for her mother's anxieties. She addresses her mother as if she were in the room with us, and she uses the present tense. It is all happening here and now.

"Mom, I'm sorry that you have to deal with this. I'm sorry that Dad's an alcoholic. I'm sorry that you don't make enough money, Mom. That's probably why you're scared." As she finishes with these thoughts, I decide to check on her reactions to the session so far.

"What's it like to let out some of this feeling?"

"It feels good."

"Yeah?"

"Yeah. It makes me feel like I'm *alive*." She certainly looks alive, too, more vibrant and animated.

"Yes, you are very much alive now," I say.

She lets out a deep breath and composes herself. She reaches over for another tissue to wipe her eyes. "I think I need to talk to my mom. We just argue a lot when we're together, and I would really like to talk to her."

"Well, that's entirely up to you, of course."

"I do want to talk with her. We've never talked about any of this. And maybe I need to forgive her. Maybe I need to forgive her for not protecting us. Maybe then we could be closer."

You cannot be open and closed at the same time. She certainly does not look anxious now. She is more open emotionally, and she is open to a greater understanding of what happened to her. Freud once said there are two ways of knowing. A person can know what happened to her, including traumatic events of her past, yet she may not know the significance of those events in her life. Carla lets out another big breath, like someone stepping away from a serious automobile accident, shaken up but uninjured, and very grateful to have survived. Now she knows.

5. Making the Connection

"A marvelous little invention, the sugar cube," Freud says. Gretchen has brought us our tea, and he now holds a single cube of sugar between his thumb and index finger. "When my parents were growing up, there was no such thing. Sugar came in a big sugar loaf that might weigh a kilogram, and one had to cut off pieces for use in the kitchen. One had to smash it with a hammer or chop it with a knife, and then the result was odd-sized pieces, often too large to fit into the teacup." He drops his cube into his cup. I have just finished describing my recent therapy session with Carla, and I am eager to hear his opinion.

"So what do you think about my session?" I ask.

Freud stirs his tea and continues, as if I have not spoken.

"That was the state of sugar until the 1840s. At that time, there was a man named Rad—Jakub Krystof Rad—who was the head of a sugar refinery in Moravia. That is where I was born, you know. Moravia."

"How interesting." I smile too broadly in an awkward attempt to mask my impatience. I did not come here to talk about the history of sugar cubes. I came here to talk about psychotherapy.

"So Jakub Rad was producing the usual type of big, heavy sugar loaf, until one day his wife, Julianna, cut her hand while trying to hack off pieces from the loaf." Smiling, he pauses to make sure I am taking in this last sentence. He holds up one hand with fingers extended straight and slices it across the palm of the other. "She complained to her husband and asked him why he could not make sugar in more reasonable sizes. He wanted to please his wife, of course, so he patented a sugar press that made perfect little cubes of sugar." Freud takes a sip of his tea, and then drops a second cube into his cup. "This was certainly not the only time in history when an unhappy wife stirred her husband to new inventiveness, nor was it the only time when a cut hand led to some very productive thinking. You had a very interesting session, I see."

"Well, thank you, Professor. I thought you might not think very highly of it. After all, I am not instructing the patient to say whatever comes to mind; that is, I am not using your free association technique. Instead, I am being very directive with her. So I thought you might not see this as consistent with your work."

Freud has been smiling, obviously pleased with his sugar cube story. Now his gaze turns a bit stern. "I said that your session was interesting. I did not say it was without problems. It is true that you are not using the fundamental rule of free association, which I view as an unfortunate mistake on your part. However, you are focusing intensively on the defenses, and the concept of defense mechanisms is central to the entire edifice of psychoanalysis. The patient is in conflict between the defenses and the forbidden contents of the mind: memories, ideas, wishes, emotions. This is the 'dynamic' element that exists in both psychoanalysis and your modern dynamic psychotherapy. There is a struggle within." Freud nods at me for emphasis. He gets up and walks over to the only window in his consulting room. The sun is streaming in today, brightening the dark objects of the room: dark-stained wooden bookcases, dark bindings of thick hardcover books, and somber stone figures unearthed from their dark little tombs in antiquity. He opens the window a bit to let in fresh air and light on a spring day.

I am pleased, of course, to hear his comments about my defense work. I am also apprehensive about what he might say next. As I sit drinking my tea, I catch a quiet whisper in my thoughts: *I do not really need his approval.* But obviously I do.

He is very interested in the story of Carla's mother and the cut hand. He asks many questions about Carla's symptoms, and whether she had any symptoms related to her hands. Did she ever have a paralysis of a hand or arm? Did she ever experience numbness in her hand? Were there any involuntary movements of the upper extremities? He is obviously looking for *conversion* symptoms, in which a psychological problem is converted to a physical one. He is exploring the possibility that the sight of blood on the mother's hand might create in Carla some symptom involving the functions of her own hand. Perhaps he thinks that Carla might be like the dramatic "hysterics" who were the stars of Charcot's brilliant lectures in Paris. He also mentions the early case that his mentor Breuer treated, the case of Anna O. In Breuer's case, he explains, each dramatic symptom could be traced back to a specific traumatic event or troubling idea. I explain to him that nowadays we still see these conversion symptoms, but there is not usually such a neat correspondence between a specific symptom and a single memory.

He asks about my approach to Carla's defense mechanisms. "I notice again that you tell your young lady about her defense mechanisms."

"Yes, I do. I tell her that she is numbing herself to avoid her feelings, or changing the subject, laughing, yawning, and so on. That is the first thing that struck me about Dr. Davanloo's lectures in Montreal. As a psychiatry resident, I used to write down the patient's defenses in my therapy notes after a session, but Davanloo was telling the *patient* about her defenses. It had never occurred to me to do this." Of course, Davanloo did more than discuss the defenses. He mounted a full-scale assault on the defenses, relentlessly determined to bring them down with a torrent of vigorous confrontation. Davanloo the Warrior.

"Well, surely you need to educate the patient. I did this from the earliest days of my career, and I discussed it in my book with Breuer, our *Studies on Hysteria*. In the last chapter of the book, I specifically addressed the importance of educating the patient about his attempts to resist the treatment." He looks irritated and offended, clearly unhappy that I give credit to Davanloo for something he initiated.

"Oh, I guess I forgot that part of the book. Besides, when I studied psychotherapy, my supervisors never told me to take such an approach. I will certainly go back and read that chapter in your book. I know it was so helpful to me when I saw Davanloo going in that direction."

"I see. Davanloo."

The cordial reception and the amusing sugar cube story are ancient history now. I must try to make amends. "This idea—*your* idea about educating patients—seems to work very well in this case. This patient seems to understand right away when I explain things to her."

Freud is not to be mollified. "But this is only your second session. You seem to put great trust in the psychological abilities of your patient, despite the fact that she has no training in this field. I fail to see how such a trust can be justified." Now it seems that he is just being argumentative. I do not see how the number of sessions has any bearing on our discussion. Either you tell the patient about her defenses or you do not. Besides, was he not just congratulating me on my work with the defenses? This is maddening.

"Well, she is not an analyst," I say. "But she needs to understand the workings of her own psyche. And she must join with me in working to block the defenses when they arise."

"In the second session?" He looks skeptical and shakes his head. I suspect that there is nothing I can say at this point that will please him, but I am determined to persist.

"Yes, in the second session, Professor. After I pointed out Carla's lack of emotion, she told me that she has a way of numbing her feelings when she thinks about traumatic memories. She told me specifically that she used to get upset and cry when her mother hit her brother, but then she learned to stop feeling anything about it. In other words, she has some awareness of her defenses, and now we are working together so she can understand them better. She is beginning to know herself better."

Freud sits for a minute or two, pondering this. He still looks impatient and a little irritated, but most of all, he looks puzzled. I imagine that my view of the patient is difficult for him to accept. After all, in his day the analyst was the all-knowing expert who listened to the patient talk and then delivered a brilliant interpretation that would make everything clear. He may have educated his patients about the process, but he was still the doctor, the revered healer with all the answers. It must be hard for him to view the patient as a capable partner from the very beginning of the process. It also occurs to me, though, that my patients might be quite different from his patients, precisely because of his contributions to our understanding of the psyche.

"You should know, Professor, that your work became so widely known that our patients today are much more psychologically sophisticated than they were in your time."

"Psychologically sophisticated? In what way?"

"Well, it's not uncommon for a patient to start joking about a serious topic and then say, 'Oh, but that's just my defense mechanism.'"

"Really?" he asks. "Your patients come in with an understanding of defense mechanisms?"

"Oh, yes. They often have at least some rudimentary idea about the defenses, and more. I recently asked a patient if he was angry at his wife, and he replied, 'No, at least not consciously.' In other words, he acknowledged the existence of the unconscious mind."

"Your patients have that level of understanding?"

"Yes, they do."

"These are not patients who are studying to become psychoanalysts?"

"No, no. This is true for many patients, no matter what their interests or careers might be. Your ideas have permeated Western culture to such a degree that the average person walks into my office with some basic ideas about psychology, and many of these ideas are yours. Here's another example: Often the patient assumes from the start that his childhood experiences might have some bearing on his current problems. Just as you said in your writings and teaching." As I talk, it occurs to me that perhaps I have never really comprehended the magnitude of his work. I have thought a lot about Freud's influence in the world of psychotherapists, of course, and I have recognized his impact upon the intellectual world, the world of thinkers and writers and university professors; but I have never fully appreciated the fact that he created a certain level of psychological literacy in the general public that did not exist before him.

"So my ideas have stood the test of time?" He sounds almost a bit surprised.

"Yes, yes. Many of your ideas have endured for well over a century." I expect him to look delighted, but his reaction is surprisingly somber. It seems to take him a long moment to digest what I am telling him. "Sometimes I wondered if any of my ideas would last. I wondered if future generations would discard my work entirely." He sits up a bit straighter; he holds his head a bit higher and turns slightly to one side, departing from me for a moment of solitary reflection. He looks like a general who has just received the news that the war is finally over. He looks stunned, as if he cannot take in the information. After sleepless nights filled with maps and military campaigns, after countless bloody battles and terrible casualties, after humiliating retreats, after crippling desertions by his own troops, the general learns that the seemingly endless war is suddenly and finally over. We sit in silence for several minutes while he ponders this news.

I have urges to say something, but he obviously needs time to mull this over. Besides, I am not sure what to say. Should I congratulate him? Should I tell him about all the books that have been written about him since his passing? Should I tell him about the modern research on the ideas that he developed? I would love to tell him about the brain scan studies that are shedding light on how psychotherapy works. But not now, not now. I could also tell him, of course, that many of his theories have actually been rejected. In fact, there are certainly people in my field who think very little of his work and love to belittle anything Freudian. I have had my own disagreements with many of the things that he claimed to be true. Did he overemphasize the Oedipal conflict as the origin of neurotic problems? Absolutely. Was his free association technique as useful as he claimed? Certainly not. But he also developed a system of brilliant and useful concepts for understanding the mind, and he succeeded in spreading these ideas beyond the confines of this little consulting room in Vienna. I want him to know this, and I am happy to be the messenger of such good news.

Athena

Finally, he gets up and disappears for a minute into the adjoining room, returning with one of his little antiquities. "This is Athena," he says. "She is one of my favorites. Goddess of reason and intellect. Goddess of literature and the arts. Also a goddess of war; she was quite fierce in battle." She is smaller than many of his antiques, only a few inches from helmet to toe. He turns the tiny statue in his hand, studying the figure. I suppose she had been his Muse during all the years of thinking and reading and writing. Perhaps she was also his inspiration in battling against others whom he perceived, correctly or not, as his adversaries. "She sprang fully formed from Zeus's head, and she was clad in armor, ready for battle." He hands his Athena over to me so I can have a better look at her. The bronze figurine is a well-preserved female form. In her right hand, she is holding a bowl. Her left arm is raised in the air, as if she were holding something in that hand too. "I believe she was originally holding a spear, but that has been lost. Well, perhaps she will not need it anymore." I hand her back, and he gingerly sets her on the shelf of a bookcase. "So my work has survived."

"Survived and flourished, Professor."

"When you arrived for your first visit here, I quickly got the impression that you were one of a small group of individuals who still use my concepts in practice. I did not get the sense that my theories had spread so widely. I had hoped for such acceptance during my lifetime, naturally, but when you first spoke about the changes in my methods, I began to assume that most of my work had been … well … rejected."

"Not at all. Most therapists do not identify themselves as psychoanalysts any more, but some of your ideas have become part of our intellectual heritage. They are passed from one generation to the next as part of our common knowledge, part of our psychological vocabulary."

"Indeed." His face is beginning to brighten now. He nods his head slowly, considering the outcome of his long struggle. "So the technical approach to treatment has changed, but the basic ideas remain."

"Some of them. Yes. Definitely."

"And the term 'psychoanalyst' is used less, but my ideas—some of my ideas—have survived. They have been widely accepted."

"Exactly."

He begins to smile slightly. "Well then, all right. So we will not worry about the name 'psychoanalyst.' As Shakespeare said:

'What's in a name? That which we call a rose

By any other name would smell as sweet.'"

He fetches one of his cigars and stands by the open window while he lights a match. A pleasant spring breeze makes the flame flicker, almost blowing it out, but he is able to light the cigar with it. Oddly enough, I pity him. I feel sorry for the most famous psychiatrist who ever lived. The man who shook the thinking of Western civilization had his doubts. I am looking at the man who integrated the best psychological thinking of his day, expanded upon it, added to it with his own innovative theories, and started an international movement; the man who translated Charcot from French to German, read Shakespeare in English, and studied archeology and Greek mythology when he was not writing his own extensive corpus of work; the man who convinced his own and future generations to consider not only *what* they do but also *why* they do it. Freud, the man who accomplished all this, still struggled with his own loneliness, doubt, insecurity, and—I cannot escape the word—*anxiety*.

"So let us get back to your case," he says. Just like that, in an instant, he emerges abruptly from his contemplation and returns to his seat. Remarkably, he is done with his reflections on how history has judged his work, and he is ready to apply his intellect to the next task, which happens to be my case. No doubt, this is one of the marks of the great innovators of any time: they would rather engage in the next challenge than dwell on what they have accomplished in the past. What drives them is not ambition, although they may be relentlessly ambitious, but the creative work itself, the act of applying their talents and energies to the raw materials that the world lays before them.

"As you describe the session," he says, "it sounds like you alternate between the emotion and the defenses."

It takes me a minute to catch up with his rapid transition back to our case discussion. "Well, yes, I suppose I do. Yes, that is exactly what I try to do. This is what I have learned from Dr. Davanloo's technique." I wonder if it is a mistake to mention Davanloo again, but Freud seems comfortable now. His mind is back at work. "First, I ask her what she is feeling. When there is no emotion, I address her defenses against her feelings. Then I go back to speaking directly to those trapped feelings."

"In a sense, then, you are doing the work of the archeologist who digs up a buried artifact of past history." He gestures to the bookcase where Athena sits. "First you dig around the object to remove the dirt that prevents you from bringing it into the light of day. Then you gently pull to see if it comes free yet. If not, you dig a bit more. Back and forth until you can free your little treasure. Just so, you go back and forth between emotion and defense."

"Yes. I like your archeological metaphors, Professor."

"There is a difference, though, between your work and the work that I did. I was pressing the patient to recover a mental construct: a memory, a thought, or an idea; specifically, I looked for an idea that is unacceptable to the ego. It is an idea with strong emotional import, of course, but an idea nonetheless. You, however, are pressing your patient to have an emotion. This seems backward to me."

"Well, sometimes I do press the patient to recover a thought, but it is more often fruitful to pursue the emotion first."

"That is a serious mistake you are making. You should be focusing on the memory and her thoughts about it, her associations to it. The emotion will take care of itself."

"I suppose so, Professor." But why do I always try to agree with him? *No, that is not right at all. The emotion will not just take care of itself. That is the problem with classical psychoanalysis. Always the thoughts, always the intellect, but where is the actual experience of emotion?* "I did focus on the memory, of course. But she also has an emotional problem: she is very anxious." Anxiety: a state of emotional contraction, as Freud's student Wilhelm Reich said. But I dare not mention Reich. Freud will undoubtedly see him as a rebel, a traitor to the cause of psychoanalysis, and that will be the end of our meeting. If he sometimes finds it difficult to talk about the good Dr. Breuer, his old friend and mentor, he will never tolerate an open discussion of the revolutionary Reich.

"Yes," he says, "she suffers from anxiety, but you should explore the traumatic memory and the associated thoughts—the ideas— that give rise to the anxiety."

"Granted," I say, "but she must also open up emotionally and reconnect with her mother. She wants to forgive her mother."

He looks at me with an uncharacteristic look of incomprehension. "Reconnect? Forgive?" He repeats the words as if he does not understand their meaning.

"Yes, she needs to reestablish an emotional bond with her mother." He still looks perplexed.

"All the chaos and violence in the house made it impossible for her to feel close to her mother, and she wants to repair this gap in their relationship," I add.

"Are you suggesting that the patient should visit with her mother? Is that your approach to psychotherapy?"

"No, I didn't tell her to do that. That would be her choice. What I'm saying is that she has to repair the internal mother-daughter relationship in her mind. If she thinks she can also repair the actual relationship by talking with her mother, that's her choice. Near the end of our session, Carla spontaneously spoke to her mother, as if her mother were in the room with us. She expressed some compassion for the hardships her mother had to endure. She obviously needs to feel reconnected with this woman. She said she wants to forgive her. She wants to reestablish a healthy attachment."

Freud looks impatient, as if he is getting frustrated listening to a foreigner who cannot quite speak his language and should just stop trying. "What she needs to do," he says with authoritative emphasis, "is to explore her memories, follow the associations, get beyond her defenses, and find the contents of the unconscious mind. She needs to discover the unacceptable *ideas* lurking in the unconscious. In her case, I would strongly suspect that she may harbor some unconscious hostile wishes toward both mother and father."

"Well yes, I am sure that is true," I say. "But at the end of all this psychological exploration of her individual mind, including hostile wishes, she will need to open up emotionally and recover a sense of attachment to others, including her mother. She must learn to relate more openly to other people. Didn't you once say that mental health consists of the ability to work and to love? I think it would be a big step toward mental health if she could forgive her mother and feel closer to her."

Freud's expression clearly signals that my comments are either totally senseless or wildly irrelevant, and therefore do not merit a reply. I am surprised by his response. After all, he certainly recognized the importance of deep, lasting human connections, and he helped us all see their origins in early family life. I remember reading passages of his in which he clearly spoke of a child's love for his mother, and the fear of losing her love.

Then I reflect a moment on his own way of dealing with relationships. According to what I have read about him, forgiveness was not a major component of his emotional repertoire. If you offended him, or threatened (in his opinion) the future of his psychoanalytic organization, he might cut off the relationship and never look back. If that left him isolated at times, so be it. That was his approach to conflict. So why would he expect Carla to want to resolve the conflict with her mother?

It occurs to me, not for the first time, that theories of the mind are not created in a vacuum, independent of the theorist's personality. If there is one dominant motif running through Freud's prodigious outpouring of creative thinking, it is conflict. In his Oedipus complex, the boy is in conflict with his father for the love of the mother. The sexual and aggressive "drives" are in conflict with the demands of civilization. Most important, as he was just saying a few minutes ago, the mind is in conflict with itself: upsetting thoughts and emotions are blocked by defenses; the ego battles against a tyrannical superego; the wish to get well is countered by the resistance to the therapist's efforts. Everywhere there is conflict.

But what about resolving conflicts and sustaining a healthy relationship? What are the elements of such a relationship? How does the mother–child relationship create a healthy capacity for resolving discord with others? These questions were left for later generations of psychotherapists to answer. He would not know the names of the people who influenced me in this line of thought. He does not know that some of my contemporaries who still call themselves psychoanalysts identify their work as *relational* psychoanalysis. For them, and for me, we are not motivated by innate drives of sex and aggression; we are primarily motivated by a need for a relationship with others.

I look at him sitting across from me, very formal and proper, his suit immaculate and his beard perfectly trimmed. Even in his most gracious moments, when he exudes that Old World charm and hospitality, there is a certain reserve about him. I think it fair to say that he is a bit distant. Maybe this whole business of maintaining emotional attachments is difficult for him personally, even if he can think about it intellectually. And yet he did nurture some of his friendships for years. He is, in so many ways, an enigma.

I try again to explain my position. I tell him that Carla could not get her attachment needs met from her mother. Mother was unable to keep her safe, unable to comfort her after the violence. Mom could be violent toward Carla's brother, just as her father could be violent toward her mother. All this trouble kept mother and daughter at an emotional distance, and now Carla keeps her boyfriend at a distance. She needs to forgive and end the conflicts, with her mother and her boyfriend alike.

Freud says nothing. He is not angry with me now, just quietly disengaged. We are clearly at an impasse here, and I begin to suspect that eventually I will simply have to admit defeat and move ahead to another subject. But not just yet. We sit quietly for a couple of minutes as I search for another strategy. My attention wanders to the photograph of the woman on his bookshelf. I still wonder who she is. Apparently, Freud notices the direction of my gaze.

Lou von Salomé

"Lou," he says, in answer to my unspoken question. "That is Lou Salomé. Born Louise von Salomé, actually. But she called herself Lou."

So *that is* who she is.

"She was originally from Russia," he continues, "but she came west to study."

That would explain the thick fur around her neck, suitable for a Russian winter.

"Oh, yes," I say. "I read about her in a book on the history of psychoanalysis. I found her so interesting that I also read a biography of her."

Freud ignores my comment, apparently assuming that I could not really know anything about her from books. He seems all too eager to tell me about her, and probably just eager to change the subject and get away from this annoying business of forgiveness and attachment.

"She was a very distinguished person among writers and thinkers throughout Europe," he says. "A very competent psychoanalyst, and a dear friend of mine." I decide to accept his digression without trying to avert it; we probably both need a brief change of topics. "She was a brilliant thinker, quite well versed in philosophy, and she befriended the philosopher Nietzsche."

"Oh, yes, Nietzsche," I say. "But that was a very complicated relationship, as I recall from my reading."

Freud stands up and gets the framed photo, handing it to me as if he is introducing me to an old friend who just walked into the room. When he sits down, there is a long silence. At first, I assume that he is going to respond to my comment once he collects his thoughts, but then I realize that no such reply is forthcoming. When he glances at me, though, I can see that he knows what I am talking about; he just refuses to discuss it. I can see in his eyes that he knows the whole story. He knows that his friend Lou was very close with Nietzsche for a time, but simultaneously interested in Nietzsche and a fellow philosopher, both of whom were fond of her, and both of whom she ultimately rejected. *Apparently, your friend Lou did not allow herself to get attached to either one of them. So is this not the same problem I am trying to discuss in Carla's* case? Carla keeps pushing her fiancé away with her nasty comments, and Lou von Salomé pushed away her two philosophers. In both cases, one could argue that there is a problem in establishing and maintaining an intimate relationship.

"She was also an important influence on the great poet Rilke," he adds.

Influence? He is being rather selective with his facts.

"Wasn't she married when she knew Rilke?" I ask. I am pretending to be unsure about this; as always, I tend to monitor my words with him and censor anything that might be too confrontational. But there is no doubt in my mind; I remember perfectly well what I have read about her. She had a long love affair with the poet Rainer Maria Rilke, despite being fourteen years his senior and married to another man. So she was never fully committed to either Rilke or her husband. Or Nietzsche. Freud offers no answer to my question. Apparently, his strategy is one of total avoidance.

"Lou von Salomé," he says. "Actually, I should call her Lou Andreas-Salomé. She married a very fine scholar named Friedrich Andreas."

Married in name only, Professor, but never faithful to him, I think to myself.

He continues, unaware of my secret commentary. "After establishing herself as a successful novelist and essayist, she became a very competent psychoanalyst." Freud talks about admitting her into his Wednesday evening discussions, which made her the only woman in the group. Clearly, he is very fond of her, and he is bent on protecting her from anything but praise.

He puts the photo back on the shelf and continues to reminisce about his friend Lou for a while. I make no further attempts to challenge his highly edited version of her life. I am doing my best to look interested and attentive, but I am scanning his words for an entry point so I can get back to my case—and back to the subject of emotional attachments. When he finally pauses for a moment, I make my move.

"Professor, I think we may have different views of this subject because we have different views of relationships, starting with the early mother-child relationship. Since your seminal work, many researchers and theorists have written about the importance of the mother-child relationship and its effect on all future relationships."

"An important relationship, of course. The child looks to the mother to meet his basic needs for food and warmth. The mother provides relief of instinctual tensions. I wrote about that."

"Yes, but generations of later therapists have recognized the child's need for a more complex, psychological relationship with the mother."

"More complex?" he asks.

"Yes. The mother—if I may use 'mother' as short-hand for mother, father, grandparent, or whoever is raising the child—helps regulate the child's emotions, calming the child's fears and helping her talk about her feelings of anger, sadness, happiness, and so on. Carla's mother didn't do this very well. The mother is supposed to keep a child feeling safe, but Carla's mother was not able to do this in the midst of all the domestic violence in the home. Mother teaches the child how to repair the inevitable ruptures that occur in close relationships, but nothing was ever repaired in their relationship. So that first critical relationship was a troubled one, and it affects Carla's relationship with her fiancé today." I reach into my book bag and pull out a volume I brought with me today. "'*An infant becomes attached to figures who interact socially with him rather than with figures who do little more than attend to his bodily requirements.*' From a British analyst named John Bowlby, who studied young children and their parents. His work is known as attachment theory, and it deals with the young child's emotional attachment to the mother, which sets a pattern for future relationships."

Freud is listening now, and I give him credit for trying. He asks questions about the theories I describe. He wants to know about Bowlby and others, and he is curious about how these theories were received in their day. But does he understand what I am saying? Does he understand why Carla would feel the need to repair the relationship with her mother? I still doubt it. Maybe he thinks that Carla should be like his Athena, born from the head of Zeus the father, having no mother at all. I suppose I need to let this argument go. I think he misses something about the essential importance of the mother-child attachment and its consequences. Well, maybe I should not be so hard on him. After all, he got so much right, even when he was partly wrong. It was Freud who taught us to look at the earliest childhood relationships in order to understand the psychological problems of adults. True, he focused too much on the idea of an Oedipal conflict, but he wisely emphasized the intense feelings of children toward their parents. He was inconsistent in his position about the frequency and importance of childhood trauma, but he certainly brought it to our attention. He tended to view a child's mother from a limited biological perspective, as a source of basic gratification of physical needs, but he also wrote that a young child experiences a mother's anger as a loss of love, a psychologically threatening experience.

So what does he *not* understand about Carla and her mother? Does he not see that our needs for close emotional attachments begin in infancy and persist into adulthood? Perhaps his notion of a healthy adult is a person who maintains a stoic independence from others. Does he not believe that conflicts in intimate relationships can be resolved? Does he view forgiveness as a fairy tale?

Whatever the problem is, I am not going to get him to accept my viewpoint. I must abandon my efforts in this argument. I glance back at the photo. *What about you, Lou von Salomé? You were Nietzsche's confidante, Rilke's lover, and Freud's colleague. But who did you belong to? Who were you attached to? Certainly not to your husband, Andreas, whom you left at home as you traveled around Europe with other men.* How funny that I can hear myself sounding angry at her, as if she betrayed me, too. Louise von Salomé. A perfect companion for the slightly reserved Professor sitting across from me. A brilliant woman (a genius, according to her peers) who worked hard to analyze the emotional lives of her patients. But did she ever fully understand herself? She belonged to no man and she had no children of her own, yet I imagine her as the mother—and Freud as the father—to the intelligentsia of Europe. An emotionally distant mother, I would think. She looks at me from the immutable boundaries of her picture frame while Freud sits in his reserved silence and my mind wanders a bit. An image of my own mother comes to mind: a young mother bustling about in the kitchen, preparing dinner for the family. In my memory, I envision a sweet woman, one of the gentle souls of the earth, but always a bit reserved, always a bit distant.

"Well," he says. "it sounds like your case is progressing nicely enough, in spite of these rather drastic changes you introduce with your modern theories and techniques. You are still focusing on the traumatic memories she carries in her mind. The memory of the mother's cut hand."

Obviously, he wants to bring the conversation back to familiar territory. I am a bit disappointed, but not entirely reluctant to get back to a less controversial area.

"Yes, I think things are moving along well," I say. "And she seems to understand the process well. Near the end of the session, she commented that she has never looked back and felt the anxiety about her parents' fights, so the anxiety has never gone away. She makes me think of the quote from the philosopher Santayana: 'Those who cannot remember the past are condemned to repeat it.'"

"Yes, absolutely," Freud says. "Your Carla understands what Breuer and I said: *Hysterics suffer mainly from reminiscences.* She is living with disturbing memories that have never been resolved. And her symptoms can be understood as the manifestations of the buried past."

"Yes, that is how I understand her case. Even her critical comments to her fiancé are really just a reproduction of her mother's anger at her father. Carla uses the defense of *identification with the aggressor*, as your daughter Anna wrote about in her book on defense mechanisms. Carla takes on the aggressive qualities of her mother, becoming an aggressor rather than a victim." I immediately regret my effort to ingratiate myself to him by mentioning his daughter, and I only feel worse when I see how well I have succeeded.

"You have read my Anna's book?" He is obviously delighted.

Anna Freud

"Yes, we all read it in residency." I cannot stop myself from pandering to his paternal pride. "I remember that she devoted an entire chapter to this defense."

Freud beams with pleasure. "Anna wrote that book in 1936. You and your colleagues read it?" Anna was the only one of his children to follow him in becoming an analyst, and he takes a long minute to savor the news about her book's enduring success. He talks at length about Anna and her career as a psychoanalyst. I manage to overcome the shame I feel at my ploy, and gradually I am able to sit back and enjoy the fact that we seem to be on a more collegial note.

The time is passing, though, and eventually he makes a comment about some reading he wants to do, and I take it as my cue that we are ending today's meeting. At the door, he has one final thought on my case.

"Your patient has revisited a traumatic memory, and she has vented the emotion, the grief. She has had a catharsis. But you are not done, my friend."

"Certainly not. We still have a lot of work to do."

"And some of this work will inevitably involve feelings of anger and aggression."

"Yes, no doubt," I say. "She came in with the complaint that she gets too angry at her fiancé."

"And all this anger is certainly not deserved by this young man of hers. You say she identifies with the mother's nasty behavior by expressing anger toward her fiancé, and that is a wise insight. But you must help her face the real object of her rage. Who is she so angry at? Mother? Father? Both? Or is it possible that you are more comfortable dealing with grief than with anger?" He pauses, but only for a brief moment. Clearly, he is not expecting an answer to his question. Perhaps he thinks that I have no answer, at least not a conscious answer. "A catharsis of grief will not be enough to cure this woman."

"I totally agree. Thank you for your advice, Professor. And thank you for another interesting chat." But once outside, I realize how irritated I am. Walking back to my room at the Hotel Regina, I feel annoyed that he never seems quite satisfied with anything I do. As I cross the street, I have to step around a man coming toward me with a push-cart and I feel like shouting at him. *Look where you're going, you idiot! Don't you see me walking here?* And I have a memory flash of my father sitting in the audience at my medical school graduation, saying nothing at all about my accomplishment after I walk across the stage to receive my diploma. *Don't you see me walking here?* Now Freud becomes the father in the audience, sitting in silence, looking unimpressed. Sigmund Freud is the father and Lou von Salomé is the mother. A terrible thought crosses my mind: Am I transferring old feelings about my father onto Freud and then expecting him to act like my father? Am I developing a father-transference to Freud?

6. An Incompatible Idea

We are at session number five, and Carla begins directly with the subject of anger. She has been angry at her fiancé again, and she has also been angry at a co-worker. In fact, she has been "angry at everybody." As she often does, she manages to jump from one topic to the next, all the while seeming to be on a single focus. The subject is anger, of course, but she quickly scurries from one angry episode to another, from one person to the next. She continually shifts her psychological location, like someone who is running from the police, spending each night in a different place to avoid being questioned about having been at a crime scene. Chasing her will never work; following her from topic to topic with the hope of getting the facts from her will be exhausting and fruitless. The only sensible strategy is to convince her to stop running, take the witness stand, and tell the truth.

"I notice that you are jumping around again. First you're angry at this person, then that person."

"Yes, but I just feel angry at everybody!"

"But we'll never get anywhere if we talk for ten seconds about each of a dozen people. We'll never really understand your anger unless we slow down and deal with one episode involving one person."

"Yeah, I know. I do tend to jump around. But I have been pretty angry. Monday I was *so* angry!"

Good, maybe we can focus on a specific event. That will give us a better chance to get to the root of this anger.

"Really. Why were you angry?" I ask.

"I have no idea. I was just really aggravated. Do I even know what happened on Monday? Oh, yeah. This one radiology technician just makes me crazy. He never does his work. You know, he's supposed to do a certain number of x-rays, but he's lazy and the other techs always pick up the slack for him. And then he has the nerve to complain that he works so hard! And I have to listen to it all the time. 'Oh, poor me, I did this and I did that. I work so hard.' I've never seen a person so lazy and irresponsible."

"So you're mad at him."

"Yeah, 'cause I have to listen to it."

"What is his name?"

"Peter. But we call him Drama Queen." She laughs a bit, but I decide to ignore it for now. Not every laugh is a defense mechanism.

"Do you feel mad when you think about him?"

"Oh yeah."

"Right now?"

"Oh yeah! He decided he had to leave early the other day, for some flimsy reason, so I was told that I would have to do his x-rays for him. Once again, he slips away and other people have to do his work. See, I'm all agitated. 'Cause he takes no responsibility. None!"

"Let me ask you this: How would you imagine things if your anger just came out at Peter? In a fantasy, not reality." In my mind, I can imagine Davanloo the Warrior on a videotape I saw at one of his conferences in Montreal. I can hear his voice, loud, authoritative, and unrelenting: *Can we look at this anger?* I can hear him urge the patient—perhaps a stronger word is needed: he *pushes* or *challenges* or *commands* the patient—to express a fantasy of letting out the anger. I am trying to do the same, albeit in a gentler, less confrontational approach than he takes. "What would you say or do in a fantasy if your anger just burst loose?" I do not expect her to respond with a full expression of her anger, though. I expect a defense. She might start to describe an angry image, but I will be surprised if she gets very far before she blocks her emotions with a defense mechanism.

"I would yell at him," she says.

"You would yell."

"Oh, yeah."

"And what would you yell?"

She starts to laugh, and there is the defense. Something about this anger is intolerable, and it probably has nothing to do with this fellow Peter. In Freud's words, the idea of getting fully angry at someone is an *incompatible idea* for Carla; it stands in direct conflict with other elements of her psychological composition. Perhaps the anger generates wishes or impulses that could be dangerous or destructive, hurtful impulses that transgress her ethical or religious beliefs. I suspect that the anger at Peter activates a more complicated, unconscious anger whose emergence might threaten an important relationship with someone dear to her. Is she angry at her father for his drunken rages? How could she *not* be angry at him? Is she angry at her mother for failing to protect her? Or for mistreating her brother, Anthony? Undoubtedly. But which of these relationships is being activated by her lazy co-worker? Whatever the answer may be, it is neatly concealed with a laugh.

"I would tell him to grow up and do his work!"

"But you laugh, as you tend to laugh things off."

"Yeah." There is a pause.

Before I go any further with Davanloo's approach, I need to assure myself that it is safe to proceed. I run a mental checklist: Does the patient have good control of her impulses? Yes. She is not physically aggressive toward others, and she does not respond to angry feelings by drinking or cutting herself or acting in some other destructive manner. Do we have a decent working alliance in place? Yes. She obviously understands my approach to therapy, and she seems to accept the idea that exploring buried emotion has a central role in helping her get well. Has she been able to tolerate some strong emotion so far? Absolutely. We have explored grief and guilt, and she had no negative reactions to the process so far. It looks safe to proceed.

"So you laugh again," I say.

"Yeah. I know I shouldn't. I suppose I just laugh to hide the anger in some way."

Great. She has learned that her laughing functions as a defense mechanism, and she does not forget this from one session to the next.

"So if you didn't laugh to hide the anger, what would you say?"

"Well, I'd probably start yelling. I do that with my fiancé too, you know. And last night I was talking with a girlfriend—"

"But now you change the subject."

"Yeah, I know."

"But this jumping around doesn't sound like anger."

"But when I get really, really angry, I just say such mean things."

"Yes, I know, but I wonder if this jumping around hides something about the anger. Something that the mean words don't release completely."

"Well, yeah, maybe the jumping around is a way to avoid all my mean words."

"But then you don't get to the root of your anger today. And you came here for the first session complaining about your nasty anger. So if you're carrying a lot of anger inside, maybe we could get it out here today. Maybe we could free you of something."

"That's what I'm hoping."

"You are hopeful, perhaps?"

"I am! It gets tiring holding onto all this anger," she says.

"Ah hah. I do believe that."

So far, so good. She understands that there is something about her anger that remains hidden. She knows she is using defenses, and she puts up no resistance to looking at it. Still, our path could be a difficult one. She has been exposed to one role model of drunken rage and one of an abusive parent; she may harbor a fear—an unconscious fear—that if she really gets in touch with her anger, she will be just as bad as her parents. We will soon find out.

"So, if you don't laugh it off, and you don't jump around, can you imagine just letting all your anger out at Peter? In a fantasy. Nothing to do with reality. If all of your anger just burst loose, what would happen then?"

"What his response would be? Or what I would do?"

"What would you do?"

"I'd be yelling. A lot! And I'd probably break something."

"What would you break?"

"Well ... I can envision ... there's a coffee pot we keep in the radiology office. I can imagine just smashing that, because I'm so aggravated." She employs the defense of *displacement*; she will take out her anger on an inanimate object and spare Peter.

"Just to do something physical," I say.

"Physical. Yeah."

"But you laugh again. We start to get close to the anger and you laugh again."

"Yeah, I guess I do. I mean, obviously I do. I can't figure out why."

"Well, we both need to think about this and figure it out."

"Right."

The nervous laugh is fine; she could do worse in terms of defenses. She could turn the anger against herself and start criticizing herself. She could sink into a depression. She could dissociate, feel confused, and forget what we are talking about. All things considered, the nervous laugh is fine. In fact, all of these defenses—laughing, changing the subject, using displacement—are pretty benign defenses, none of which would indicate that I should avoid a thorough exploration of her anger.

"So it seems like you start to get angry, and there's a physical urge to do something with your hands."

"Right," she says.

"But obviously you're not mad at the coffee pot."

"Right."

"You're mad at Peter."

"Right. I mean, if I could, I'd wring his neck, but then I'd be in prison." She laughs more loudly, as if her own words have triggered a jolt of nervous excitation. "And that certainly wouldn't do me any good."

She would wring his neck. I can feel my mind being pulled in different directions. There are the approaches that I learned in my psychiatry training. I could ignore the vivid wording of her sentence and let her continue to say whatever comes to mind, or I could embark upon a general discussion of anger and how to deal with it. Those methods would come naturally, and they are easy enough to follow. But then there is Davanloo, the Warrior of Words, who has also taken up residence in some of the synapses of my brain. Ever since I first heard him lecture in Montreal, he has changed the way I view the challenge of dealing with anger. Right now, he is telling me to ignore the urge to turn right or left onto old, well-paved roads, but to barrel straight ahead and look the monster in the eye. She says she would wring his neck. Maybe, Davanloo whispers, I should take those words as a message from the unconscious about the depths of her rage. She has an urge to wring his neck? By all means, let us wring his neck!

But then I have the voices of other colleagues joining the Great Anger Debate in my head. They argue that anger is a secondary phenomenon, a reaction to pain and hurt. They are right, undoubtedly, but their solution is to bypass the anger completely and steer the conversation toward a search for other feelings that lie beneath the anger. (Is Carla hurt by Peter's lack of consideration for her? Is she sad that people treat her with such disrespect? Is she humiliated that she did not stand up for herself?) Davanloo speaks up again in a booming, authoritative voice: The anger itself demands a full exploration! I agree with him, but why? Why can we not bypass the monster?

I am drawn back into the room by Carla's body language. She puts her hands down by her sides, and it appears that she is starting to slide them under her thighs, almost sitting on her hands. She laughs one more time.

"And now you laugh and the anger gets short-circuited," I say.

"Yeah. It feels like it has no place to go."

"So you said, if you could, you would wring his neck."

"Yeah, he's so frustrating."

"So what do you mean by 'wring his neck'?"

"I would just shake some sense into him."

I am about to comment on the position of her hands, but she spontaneously raises both hands and gestures vigorously, pantomiming the act of shaking him. A very positive sign, indeed. So many people talk about their anger but experience nothing, sitting with limp arms hanging at their sides and making up a tepid fantasy to please the therapist.

"It looks like you just did it."

"Yeah. I guess I did."

"I'm inviting you to imagine this, because this is one way that might help you to free up some of this anger. What does this look like in your imagination, this shaking? How do you grab him?"

"By his neck and shoulders." She motions again with her hands. Is she side-stepping the most troubling part of the fantasy by moving from his neck to his shoulders? We shall see.

"And so you shake him. Your hands actually move."

"Yeah."

"So I want to invite you just to imagine that for a second."

Another laugh. "He'd be surprised," she says, "because he doesn't expect it."

"I see. And you're shaking him."

"Yes, I'm shaking him."

"And then what?" I ask.

She shakes her head. "I go nowhere after that. I just ..." She makes the motions again, this time with more force. We are on the right track. "I just ..."

"Oh, your hands look strong, though. Like you're really feeling it, which is good."

"Yeah."

"And you say you go nowhere?"

"Right," she says. "It just ... I can't envision anything else."

Small wonder that this was the most difficult part of Davanloo's method to learn, at least for me. It can be technically quite challenging. When should I push her to imagine the anger? And when should I pause in that process in order to deal with the inevitable obstacles that get in our way? After all, if I fail to acknowledge her defenses, we will never get to the core of the feelings. If I fail to appreciate her fear of expressing anger, I may come across as lacking compassion. If I miss some negative reaction to my interventions, she may just feel harassed rather than helped. This method demands far more art than I thought after hearing my first Davanloo conference.

"Maybe you avoid the anger again."

"That could be, because I want to laugh again. I can feel it. I just want to laugh like hell again."

She is working with me, helping to identify the defenses as they arise. And interestingly, they keep trying to sneak back into position and block her emotions, even after she has started to experience the anger and move her arms in the pantomime of an angry attack. It still surprises me sometimes to see how persistent the defenses can be. Obviously, there is a significant force in her mind that fights against looking at the anger. I suppose there is part of me that does not want to look at it, either. After all, these fantasies of anger can be so difficult to hear. What if she comes out with a fantasy of real violence? Who would want to hear this lovely young woman give a voice to fantasies of violent aggression? No one, absolutely no one. We therapists do not want to hear what is lurking in the mind of such a normal, civilized creature, lest we have to face the alarming possibility that we might also harbor some of Freud's "incompatible ideas." I am sure that many of Freud's contemporaries did not appreciate his efforts to tell them that we have such aggressive thoughts. We would rather persist in the comforting belief that such heinous impulses belong only to the violent psychopath, not to the rest of us.

"So there it is. You keep dodging the anger."

"But I don't know why. It ... it does it by itself."

"It's automatic," I say.

"Yeah."

"Yes, and I'm trying to help you break an automatic mechanism here." Yes, I need to reassure her that I am trying to help her, not just badger her. "It's an automatic defense mechanism that blocks the anger. And I can see that you have the urge to laugh again."

"Yeah, I can feel it."

"So then you can't just say what you would do after shaking him."

"No, I don't know what I would do after that. I do it and then I'm done. But I'm not really done, 'cause it still hasn't solved anything."

"Is all the anger out?" I ask.

"No. No."

She makes my work easier. She knows that she is not done, and makes no effort to convince me of the contrary.

"So let's take one more look at shaking him," I suggest.

She immediately brings up her hands for another round of shaking. "I *do* just want to shake him."

"Right. Go ahead and pantomime it. It seems like when you put your hands up, you do feel the power of the anger."

"It's just … it's just … talking to him is just so frustrating…. Oh, there is something! I wanted to just slap him around." She makes the slap in the air with her right hand. "You see, I'm very violent. Is this normal?"

As I suspected, she has a fear of becoming violent like her parents. "You're not violent. You may have some violent images come to mind, but who cares? You're not acting like that."

"It's true. It's not like I'm actually going there and slapping him." She laughs, but then swings her hand again, this time with a bit more force. The smile vanishes from her face. Perhaps this is the right time to reach for an unconscious connection, if only she can face it. Surely, all this anger is not only about an x-ray tech named Peter.

"Does anybody else come to mind as you slap him and shake him?"

"My father."

The answer is immediate, and I speak just as quickly, before she can change her mind and pull away from the challenge that lies before her. "Your father. Why your father?"

"Because he left us! He just walked out on my mom and us. He never paid child support, not a dime! But somehow he always found money for his alcohol."

"So he didn't do his job, either."

"Exactly!"

"Just like Peter."

"Right! And we had nothing. Sometimes the electricity got shut off because my mom couldn't pay the bill, and he never helped a bit." Her voice is a bit breathy now, and her hands are actively gesturing, palms intermittently extended toward me as if to show me something she is holding in her hands. *See, look at this,* she seems to be saying. *Look at what I've been holding all these years!*

"So you're agitated about your father."

"Yeah. Very agitated!"

"So how would you imagine the anger coming out at your *father?*"

"I just ..." She struggles to speak, stumbling over her words, her hands closing into fists, her face struggling to declare itself in a definitive emotion, unable to decide between rage, grief, or fear.

"What are your hands doing?"

"I want to hit him!" She has tears forming in her eyes, but I do not challenge this as a defense mechanism. She is not covering her anger with tears now; she is experiencing a sudden flood of feelings about her father, one emotion spilling into the next as the breach in the dam widens.

"So picture hitting him," I say.

She laughs briefly, but only briefly; she still seems engaged in the process.

"It's your fantasy," I say. "He'll never know."

"Well, that's true," she says.

"Where do you hit him?"

"I hit him in the stomach, partly because I can reach there. He's tall." She tries to smile, but only for a moment.

"You punch him in the stomach?"

"Yeah. So he comes down to my level."

"You mean he doubles over?"

"Yeah!" She holds up two fists, like a professional boxer ready to go in for the next round. I mimic her pose as a way to ask my next question.

"What are you doing now with these fists?" I ask.

"I just want to hit him—again and again!"

"Okay. So picture it. It's fine. Picture it. Where do you hit him?"

"In the head at this point, because now I can reach his head." She is choking back tears and feeling enraged all at once. "And I just want to shake him!"

"So you're shaking him."

"Yeah."

"What does he look like with all this punching and shaking?"

"He's a little bloody, I mean ..."

"He's bloody," I repeat.

"His nose is bloody and ..."

"Of course. He's all bloodied up."

"And he's *hurt*. Really *hurt*," she says.

"As you were hurt when he left and refused to pay child support."

"You're damned right!"

So here we are at the root of her anger. It is not about a lazy co-worker named Peter, nor is it about her boyfriend, Jimmy. The root of the problem is her buried rage at her father, a rage that was hiding in the unconscious mind until now. Its release creates a palpable energy in the room. Still, I have the sense that she is not quite done with this.

"So is all your anger out?"

"No! 'Cause now that I picture him on the ground and he's hurt and he's bleeding, now I want to kick him!"

I wonder for a moment if she is going to stay with the anger indefinitely as a way to avoid some other feeling, using one emotion as a defense against another. But this still feels like the genuine article, and I decide to follow her lead. "What does it look like?"

"What do you mean?"

"Where do you kick him? I can't see into your imagination."

"In the stomach. Anywhere I can get him."

"So you're kicking him repeatedly."

"Yeah."

"So you're going wild with rage."

"Yeah, rage. Just plain rage." But there is a shift taking place now, a rapid shift in the level of her emotional arousal and a shift in the energy palpable in the room. She is looking down and slightly to her right, staring at one specific place on the rug in my office. She gazes at that spot, as if she is looking at her father lying on the floor between us. "Just plain rage." The words are like an echo now, softer than the original words and coming from a distance. Her face is calmer, her hands rest in her lap now.

"So is he still breathing?" I ask.

She looks at that area of the rug again for a long moment, and then shakes her head. "No. He's not breathing," she says, without looking up.

"So?"

"So now he's dead."

"He's dead," I repeat.

"Right." She says nothing for a moment. She has to adjust her mind to letting go of the anger and moving on the next step of the drama. "Then it's over. Then I can't ..." She starts to cry, but catches herself long enough to finish her sentence. "Then I can't talk to him."

"And what would you want to say to him as he lies there?" I gesture to the rug in the direction of her gaze.

"Why did you do that?" she says to the imaginary dead man sprawled out on the floor in front of us.

"Do what?" I ask.

"Why did you leave us? It wasn't supposed to be like that! Why couldn't you just—?"

"Just ...?"

"Why couldn't you just *be my dad*?"

And with that, she cannot speak any more. It seems that she cries for a long time, even though it probably lasts for only a minute or two. I find myself feeling close to tears, too. Mother Nature accomplished an amazing task when she programmed our brains to feel what another person is feeling. Thanks to the complex interrelated systems of emotional expression (Carla's) and emotional mirroring (mine), I can go beyond an intellectual understand of the ideas she is verbalizing; I can actually experience a moment of her inner world, or at least something close to it. I wonder why Freud counseled his students to maintain an emotional detachment from their patients. It seems to me that I would not really understand her as well if I did not allow myself to resonate a bit with her feelings.

She wipes her eyes with a tissue and blows her nose loudly without any awareness of me. She takes one slow deep breath, and finally looks up at me. "Well, at least I don't have to worry about him anymore."

"You worried about him?"

"Yeah. They divorced when I was fifteen. We kids stayed with Mom, but I spent a lot of weekends with Dad. My brother and sister basically would have nothing to do with him, so it was just me and him. He lived alone in a little apartment, and he would get pretty depressed. Sometimes he would threaten to kill himself."

"Yes, you mentioned that once before. He threatened suicide."

"Oh, yeah. Many times. Always when he was drinking, though. And he never actually tried to hurt himself."

"But what effect did this have on you?"

"Oh, I was worried sick. Sometimes I would go into his room at night just to make sure he was all right."

"You were checking to see that he was alive."

"Right." She pauses and glances at the spot on the rug. "How weird. I was always worried about him dying and here I've done it."

"You worried he would kill himself, and here you have killed him."

"Yeah, right," she says. "And you know what? It's a relief. The stress and the worry is gone. I don't have to worry that he'll kill himself or kill Mom."

"So you don't have to worry about being responsible for Dad."

"Right. *Right!* I felt responsible for him for a long time!" She pauses and sits quietly for a moment.

I suspect that she is just realizing this for the first time. For the past decade, she has been living with a secret mission statement filed away in her unconscious mind. *I am responsible for Dad. If I do not watch him, he will surely die.* Small wonder that she has been anxious! But this was not a meaningless free-floating anxiety or an inherited anxiety "disorder." This was an anxious vigil with a noble purpose, designed to protect the father she loved.

"What a complicated mix of feelings," I say. "You loved him, you felt responsible for him, you worried about him, and you were afraid of him. And terribly angry at him."

"I guess so." Again, it looks like this is a new realization. "Obviously I was really angry at him. But I'm less angry now."

"Right now?"

"Yeah."

"I actually feel better."

"Well, that's good."

"Yeah, it's funny, but I feel better."

"Well that's the point of all this, right? To get you some relief. And it seems that part of your anxiety has its roots in the relationship with your father. Worrying about him, whether he would kill himself or kill your mom. And now that you allow yourself this fantasy of anger and death, you feel better."

"Yeah," she says. "Because now it's over."

"He's dead—in fantasy—and it's over."

"Right."

She looks so calm, so relaxed, and so different from the tense, angry woman who came into this office at the beginning of the session. Now she has faced the hidden truth of her anger, and she has re-expanded emotionally with the experience of the anger. The scope of our discussion widens now to include her whole family. We talk about her parents' marriage again, as well as her siblings, a couple of aunts, and a grandmother. But now she views them all through the lens of a new knowledge: she loved her Dad, but she also felt responsible for keeping him alive, and none of her relatives ever helped her with her worries about him. This unbearable burden created a relentless anxiety for her. Worse, she harbored a murderous rage against the father she was protecting. Could there be a more classic Freudian conflict? She feared that he would die, but she wanted to kill him.

As our discussion comes to a close and she pulls herself together in preparation for leaving, I cannot help but think about our session as an example of true psychoanalysis, even though we call it short-term dynamic psychotherapy. We have been analyzing her thoughts and feelings toward the family; the difference is that we are doing the analysis *after* the emergence of the unconscious emotion. If we had talked about all these relationships before the emotional catharsis, we would have had a very limited access to the contents of her mind. We would have been talking about the conscious thoughts, not the unconscious ones. It might well have been an interesting intellectual discussion, but I am not sure that it would have led to clear benefits. Now that she is emotionally open again, the analyzing is not censored by defenses that were built to avoid the painful emotions and the unacceptable ideas. *Incompatible ideas*, as Freud called them. The murderous rage at her father is incompatible with other thoughts (*I love my dad*), and incompatible with her image of herself (*I am not a violent person*). In Freud's words, we have made the unconscious conscious.

Carla thanks me and leaves the office. The session was a successful one. Still, the question lingers in my mind: Why do we have to explore fantasies of anger? True, not all patients will give such a graphic account, but why should we explore the anger at all? Why can we not just go straight to the pain and sorrow beneath the anger and circumvent all this unseemly aggression? Davanloo never really explained it to my satisfaction. How can I explain this to myself?

Carla felt better after the imagined murder. Let us start there. Why did she feel better? First, I suppose it was a relief to imagine the crime—a crime already planned in the unconscious—and realize that it was only a fantasy. No one really got hurt. Second, some of her anxiety was probably due to the unconscious fear that she might act on her anger toward her father. Now that the deed is done, but done only in fantasy, there is nothing left to feel anxious about. Also, there must be terrible guilt, albeit unconscious guilt, accompanying the hostile impulses. It probably helped that there was another person in the room bearing witness to her fantasy without judging her.

I think that she might now see the price she pays for avoiding her anger at her father: she redirects it at her fiancé and threatens the future of the relationship. Perhaps now she will be able to experience a rational anger when the need arises, without getting anxious and without complicating the interaction by unleashing a backlog of unresolved anger meant for her father.

I have to agree with Davanloo: there is no shortcut around this. The unconscious anger carries with it a tangled web of troubles, and the best solution is to look the monster in the eye.

7. Beyond Words

*A*pparently, I have crossed a line, stepped over some invisible boundary delineated in Freud's mind, committed some transgression the penance for which is beyond negotiation. He sits in stony silence and says nothing. I could see this coming halfway through my description of the pivotal session with Carla. I could feel the atmosphere cooling, and with it my excitement and pride over the case. Of course, I know that what I did in that session, inspired by Davanloo the Warrior, is dramatically at odds with Freud's psychoanalysis; however, somehow I had convinced myself this morning that he would nonetheless see the value in my work. How could he possibly disagree? I chide myself for my naïveté. This is not my first meeting with him, and I should know better.

He did look interested in the beginning. When I described my early conversation with Carla about her anger, he seemed quite engaged. True, he had his criticisms, and he was characteristically direct in expressing them. ("You talk too much!" he said, forever carrying the banner for his free association technique.) But overall, I thought I was winning him over. I was so certain that he would be swayed by the logic of my presentation.

"Well, clearly you have your own point of view on these matters." He is not even looking at me, and his tone suggests that he does not find my position worth arguing about.

"Yes I do, and my point of view is psychoanalytic, Professor. You taught us that we often hold back anger at those we love, and the anger is often unconscious. Here I have helped Carla to find the unconscious anger, feel that anger, and give a voice to it. And this process has helped her a great deal. This is psychoanalysis."

"It is no such thing! In psychoanalysis, we allow the patient to explore all the complex associations with her anger. There are likely many other thoughts, associations, and memories connected to this discussion, but you interrupt her and steer her into this contrived, dramatic scene of violence."

I do not even understand why this particular session makes him so angry. I suppose I am treading on one of the most valued parcels of his vast intellectual acreage: his theory of an unconscious aggressive "drive." And I am not doing it his way.

"Yes," I say. "I am challenging her to describe an angry fantasy." As often happens to me in his presence, I cannot bring myself to say what I really think. *Contrived? Dramatic? How can you be so pigheaded? This is what you wrote about! Exploring the patient's forbidden, unconscious fantasies.*

"You need to learn some patience, sir. You need to learn to sit with her and *listen.*" With that, he is done. He reaches over to the small table near us to pour some tea for himself, without offering me any. I am so angry that I could start smashing his precious little collection of antique statues. I am angry at his stubborn refusal to see my point of view. I feel not only frustrated but also humiliated that I cannot really speak my mind, and this makes me even angrier at him, as if he was physically preventing me from speaking. Why is it so difficult for me to get angry at him? How can I help Carla, or anyone else, if I still have such defenses against my own anger?

Sit with her and listen. This is the same advice I had from a couple of my supervisors back in my residency training days. The long-term psychoanalytical model that I was taught was not classical psychoanalysis, but not far from it. I had two chairs instead of the Freudian couch, but I was supposed to let the patient "say whatever comes to mind," and occasionally—only occasionally—offer some kind of brilliant interpretation that would help the patient understand his life. When I reported the contents of my sessions to these supervisors, I would be chastised for being too active in the therapy. "You are talking too much! You have to learn just to sit with the patient." I felt paralyzed by their injunctions.

"Well, I understand your point, Professor, but ..." My voice ends midsentence. *But when should I do something to help the patient?*

My grandmother could sit and listen. When will you acknowledge that I now have the skills I need to help people?

Freud says nothing, and my thoughts turn to the work of his protégé, Wilhelm Reich. Early in my psychiatry residency, I found myself wanting a more active approach. I found just that in Reich's books, which documented his work in the first half of the twentieth century, long before Davanloo began his innovative approach to psychotherapy in Montreal. If only there had been video cameras in his day, so we could see what Reich really did in session back in the 1930s. I wonder if his approach was similar to Davanloo's. No one in my program taught Reich's work, of course, because he had been declared *persona non grata* in psychiatry even before his death in 1957, decades before I entered the field. But I read his books and found in them a kindred spirit. A rebellious spirit, to be sure. He was the one who refused to emulate the older analysts; he complained that they were having serious conversations about trying to stay awake during the analytic hours. He was the firebrand who counseled action, rather than sitting in silence while the patient lies on the couch and says whatever comes to mind, in accordance with the "fundamental rule" of free association. Reich, for me, was the real pioneer of short-term dynamic psychotherapy, even though he never used that label. He was the one who took Freud's theories and put them into action. Davanloo added significantly to our techniques, but Davanloo the Warrior could not have existed without Reich the Revolutionary. How sad that Reich gets no credit.

Freud returns to his chair with his tea, but does not look at me or speak to me. I am stunned to realize that he is done with business for the day, and he is only waiting for me to leave. I have an urge again to spew sarcasm, but nothing comes out of my mouth. *Is that all you can do, sit in silence? Wilhelm Reich did not just sit and listen. He actually helped people!* Freud's meticulously trimmed beard, which I have admired until this moment, suddenly becomes despicable to me, the sign of the well-groomed bourgeoisie, those self-satisfied champions of the status quo. *Reich talked to his patients. He directed the sessions, rather*

Wilhelm Reich

than sitting and listening to an endless chain of associations that lead deeper and deeper into a labyrinth of self-indulgence. Freud's black bow tie, neatly tucked beneath his shirt collar and modestly revealing only part of itself, is now just the emblem of turn-of-the-century Victorian-era inhibition. In contrast, I remember a photo of Reich with open-collared neck, no tie at all, looking friendly and happy. He was probably just relaxing on vacation at the time, but to me it is the lively image of a modern revolutionary. I am ready to join his ragtag band of rebel forces and head for the woods. *Vive Reich!*

Question: Why do I always find myself turning to military terms? Davanloo the Warrior. Reich the Revolutionary. The answer comes to me quickly: Freud loved military metaphors. He wrote of defenses, resistance, opposing forces, and conflict; a civil war in which the weakened ego must defend itself against both the primitive id with its bestial impulses and the hostile superego. It seems that even when I am arguing with Freud, I am inescapably influenced by him. Fine, then, I will use military metaphors: I will pull out my best ammunition. I reach into my briefcase to pull out one of Reich's books that I have brought with me. Although I never expected this level of conflict today, I thought that I might need some reinforcements to defend the more active approach to dealing with anger in psychotherapy. Perhaps if I quote a certain passage, I will have a better chance of convincing him.

However, when I bring out the book I packed, it is not Reich at all. I have mistakenly packed one of Freud's books. What a foolish mistake! Or perhaps it was not a mistake at all. Perhaps it was an unconscious choice not to pack it, a Freudian mistake. Unconsciously, I did not want to bring it. I suppose I am avoiding conflict; maybe I am sabotaging myself and not letting myself win. I look at the book for a frustrated moment and shove it back into my briefcase.

"It would appear that our conversation for today is coming to a close," Freud says, looking only at his teacup and stirring his tea more than necessary. "You seem rather quiet, and I can only assume that you are perhaps tired and done with our chat. I would not want to keep you longer than you wish to stay."

"Yes, of course." *I seem quiet? You give me the cold shoulder like some petty autocrat who is miffed because I refuse to be an obsequious sycophant, but I seem quiet?* I stand up to leave. "Thank you for the interesting conversation, Professor." I say this without enough conviction to fool either one of us, and I start toward the door of his consulting room. At the door, I turn to look over my shoulder and deliver a cold farewell. As I am trying to choose my words—I search for an artful construction of brevity, wit, and righteous indignation—a soft knocking at the door distracts me, but I do not realize that Gretchen is opening it from the other side until I turn to the sound and the door hits me hard in the face.

"Entschuldigung! Entschuldigung!" Gretchen looks horrified as she repeats her apology. I am reflexively holding one hand over my nose, as if to ward off a second blow, while the other hand is raised in a clenched fist. I want nothing more than to punch the door. Freud says something to her, and she disappears, closing the door behind her, channeling her distress into frantic flight, leaving me alone with him again. He dutifully asks if I am all right, and I nod. I am taking deep, involuntary breaths, my entire body on the alert in response to the surprise attack upon my nose. When the throbbing pain starts to subside just a bit, the remaining arousal of my sympathetic nervous system pushes me past the barriers of my inhibitions.

"Good day to you, Dr. Freud. Next time, perhaps I will visit with Wilhelm Reich. He was a man who was open to new ideas!" My hand is on the doorknob.

"Willie? You are familiar with the work of Willie Reich?"

"Yes, indeed I am! And he would have listened to me without trying to discredit everything I do and make me feel like my work is nothing!" I feel invigorated by the surge of anger coming out of me. Freud, however, simply sounds curious now.

"Are you saying that Reich's work has stood the test of time? People in your generation still read what he had to say?"

"No, for the most part, they don't," I say with open defiance, "but *I do*. I choose to read him because he was open-minded and excited by new ideas. He didn't reject them out of hand. He would have been quite receptive to Davanloo's active approach to anger." I am ready to leave, but now Freud is engaged again, at least with the subject of Reich.

"He was a fine young man, Reich. A brilliant student, you know. He came to me as a young medical student and studied psychoanalysis. And he moved up very quickly in the field. Practicing, teaching, writing. But later it became impossible to continue with him. I had to distance myself from him."

"I'm sure you had no trouble doing that," I say bitterly.

He doesn't seem to hear me. "His ideas drifted so far from the basis of psychoanalysis. And then he became involved with the communists, you know. He wanted to change society through an integration of psychoanalysis and Marxism. Impossible. He wanted a sexual revolution. Absolutely impossible. So our paths had to split apart. We had to go our separate ways. A fine young man, though." Freud looks a bit wistful. He looks at me curiously, as if he is suddenly noticing me standing in front of him, and then looks off into his memories again. "Perhaps I was a bit too harsh in my judgment of him, too quick to cast him aside. He had such potential. Such intelligence." We both stand in place, I with one hand on the doorknob, Freud immersed in his reverie about the young Wilhelm Reich. A long minute or two pass by. It feels awkward to leave, but pointless to keep standing here.

"Good day, Professor."

"But wait," he says, emerging from his thoughts. "Let me get you some ice for your nose. That was quite a blow."

"No, thank you. I'm fine."

"Well, at least sit for a minute and make sure that you do not develop a nosebleed."

"No, really, that won't be necessary."

"Please," he says, gesturing toward a chair with a sudden outpouring of Old World charm that I find difficult to refuse. "At least sit for a few minutes to make sure you have recovered sufficiently to negotiate our busy streets here in Vienna." He pours a second cup of tea and hands it to me as I take my seat. I accept it without thanking him. "I had such great hopes for young Willie Reich. He joined our Vienna Psychoanalytic Association when he was still in his early twenties. A gifted analyst, an outstanding teacher. But you know, there has to be some common ground if one is to continue a working association with a colleague, some basic agreement on principles." Again, he looks pensive, wistful, and he takes a deep sigh. "Well, we cannot turn the clock back, you know. But perhaps we could take a fresh look at the session you were describing."

I still say nothing. The pain in my face is subsiding, but not completely gone. The anger that came to me at the door is likewise diminishing, but still a lingering presence. All the biological and chemical soldiers deployed in response to pain and anger must complete their assigned maneuvers, and this requires some time. Stress hormones must be deactivated in the liver or scooped up by nerve cells in the brain for storage until the next crisis. My heart rate and blood pressure must drift back down to a peaceful level of homeostatic tranquility. Endorphins released from brain cells must finish the job of easing my pain. I cannot rush these physiological processes, so I sit and wait quietly. I reach over to the table and put a lump of sugar in my tea, then a second, and even a third. I suppose I am trying to comfort myself.

"You were talking about the unconscious anger that your patient felt," Freud says.

"Yes, I was." The defiance is gone from my voice now. I take a sip of the sweet tea, enjoying the return to normalcy.

"And your position, if I understand it correctly, is that a vivid imaginary scene of anger is therapeutic. You think it can be helpful to the patient."

"I don't think so. I know so." I am surprised by the assertiveness in my words now. Maybe I should have smashed my face into a door sooner.

"And why is this imaginary scene an improvement over my psychoanalysis, in which the analyst helps the patient become aware of her unconscious wishes, without all this drama?"

"Because this is what lurks in the patient's unconscious," I say. "She not only has the thought: *I am angry at my father*, she also has urges, impulses—wishes, as you would say—to hurt her father. In the language of modern emotion theory, we would say that her anger brings with it an *action tendency*, a tendency or readiness to act in a certain way."

Freud mulls this over, apparently trying to give me a fair hearing now. "But how do we know that she really harbors such a specific wish to hurt him in this way?" he asks. "How do we know that she is not simply creating this imaginary drama to please a zealous analyst?" The pain in my face is basically gone now, and I cannot help but respond positively to his curiosity.

"That's a fair question, Professor. I'm sure that can happen, if this technique is not done properly. But when done correctly, the patient is simply allowing herself to imagine the disavowed action that has been in her mind all along. This drama, as you call it, has already been set up in the theater of the unconscious."

"This is theory, of course. One can hardly prove it to be so."

"Granted, but the proof of the pudding is in the eating. We see patients get well using this theory. We see good outcomes."

"All right, then," he says. "We shall have to wait to see how your Carla progresses, and whether this helps her."

"No, we don't have to wait. I have had two other sessions since the one I just described."

"Two more sessions," he says skeptically.

"Yes, and they were good ones. She now reports a sharp decrease in anxiety, and she has stopped being so critical of her fiancé."

Freud raises his eyebrows, obviously surprised to hear this.

I forge ahead. "She no longer has to displace the anger toward her father onto her fiancé, because she has faced the original anger. She has gone from emotional contraction to emotional expansion, using Dr. Reich's terms. The way I think of it, I would say that she has re-expanded, opening up emotionally after years of being contracted and shut down. And she is even feeling closer to her mother."

"Well, this is very impressive news," he says. Skeptical still, he is at least listening now, at least thinking about what I am saying. He gets up and chooses a cigar for himself, so I know that he is settling in for a continuing conversation. As we continue to talk, we seem to be renegotiating our positions. It seems that he now takes the stance of a judge who has declared certain evidence admissible in the courtroom, despite his initial objections. I can still see him struggle at moments to contain a negative reaction—a brief pursing of the lips, a shifting of his posture in the chair—but he recovers quickly and continues to remain engaged with our discussion. Maybe he is determined not to reject me like he rejected Reich and others. I find myself wondering if this has anything to do with me, or if he is simply trying to atone for past sins. Does he really respect my work? Or am I just a representative of his past victims, a symbolic recipient of the reparation that should have been offered to them? I suppose it does not matter, as long as we are still talking.

For my part, I seem to be a bit more assertive. I am no longer angry, but my outburst seems to have opened the door a bit so that I can hold my ground now. The change is not complete, but I am somewhat less hesitant about advocating for my viewpoint. The visual imagery that Davanloo employed in Montreal to reveal the unconscious anger has been allowed into our discussion now, and I have the impression that I have established a new status, and with it the right to bring up any topic I deem worthy of conversation.

We even talk about Reich, and I find myself telling Freud what I liked about him. "Reich went beyond the patient's words to observe the manner in which they were spoken. He looked at body posture, tone of voice, facial expression, manner of speaking—all the nonverbal aspects of communication. In other words, he looked at the physical, biological language." Freud ponders, without objecting, so I continue. "When Carla bites her lip, or starts to yawn, or sits on her hands, she is giving me clues to her state of mind, just as surely as her words give me clues. And it was Reich who taught this." I spare him the rest of my thought: *While you and your colleagues were waiting for the next verbal utterance, the next bit of ver-*

bal "material," Reich was beginning to mine a wealth of material that had nothing to do with words.

"The unconscious will reveal itself quite nicely in words," Freud counters. "By free association, by slips of the tongue, and by the patient's reporting of dreams. These are the roads to the unconscious."

"Those are all fine," I say, "but Reich added so much by noticing the nonverbal messages. And he saw more than just the patient's state of mind at a given moment. He also used these clues to understand the patient's unhealthy personality traits—the *character traits* or *character pathology*. Did the patient look haughty and contemptuous?" I strike an arrogant pose to illustrate my point. "Did he seem too eager to please the analyst? Did he act distant and aloof? Passive and submissive?"

Freud almost smiles at my attempts to act out these character attitudes. He relaxes his guard a bit.

"All this," I say, "Reich gleaned from the nonverbal communication." I remember Davanloo in Montreal on videotape: *You are so passive with me. If I don't question you, there is silence. And you agree with everything I say. Are you passive like this with everyone?* Surely, he must have been influenced by Reich.

"Reich did some good thinking about character traits, this is true," Freud says. I am surprised at the admission.

"He did," I say, "and his work is enormously helpful in the office. Carla did not have a great deal of serious character pathology, but there were certainly times when she adopted the pose of the "good girl," the perfect, well-behaved child who tries to please and covers all her troubles with a smile."

Freud reflects for a minute. Is he thinking of his own cases?

"Reich wrote a book called *Character Analysis*," he says. "My daughter Anna made reference to his work in her book on defenses." This is a lucky break. If his daughter Anna was willing to acknowledge Reich, then he will be more open to discussing Reich's work. And he seems to maintain some respect for Reich, even though he is obviously not in agreement with his approach. Of course, I wonder if Freud saw what

Reich saw. Freud sat in a chair at one end of the couch while the patient reclined. The patient could not see him, and Freud was not facing the patient. I wonder how well he could observe his patient without being face to face. How much of the nonverbal communication did he miss from his vantage point?

"I also like the way he explains that these character traits become permanent," I say. "*Character armoring.*" It occurs to me that Reich also used a military metaphor here. I wonder if he too was influenced by Freud in his choice of language. "The patient is armored against his feelings and armored against the world."

Freud nods an agreeable nod. "Yes, yes. I spoke with Willie Reich about this on many occasions. I wrote about the development of character traits in an early paper of mine, and he certainly added to this important topic." Again, he looks pensive. "I suppose I was perhaps too quick in turning him away. Such a bright young man. But still, he went too far . . . too far."

"But Professor, he was just trying to follow your lead and develop some of your ideas more fully." But Reich went much farther indeed. I am not sure how to discuss this tactfully without offending Freud, but I am determined take full advantage of our new armistice and press ahead. If he is offended, so be it. "And I like what Reich said about the physical expression of the neuroses." Does Freud know about this part of his protégé's work? Did he break away before Reich went in this direction? I cannot tell by looking at his expression, so I continue to talk. "Reich said that we hold negative memories in our minds, but also in our bodies. Traumatic experience leads to chronic muscular tension, as well as protective character traits."

"Yes, yes, I heard about this too. We discussed it." His response is quick and dismissive in tone, as if he would like to curtail this part of the discussion. I try to present not only my admiration for Reich, but also my concerns.

"To be fair, Professor, I do think that Reich and his followers became so engrossed in the somatic work that they sometimes neglected the psychological." But Freud is clearly not comfortable with this topic. Well fine, let him feel uncomfortable for a few minutes. "I am sure that you did not approve when Reich started to work with the *muscular armor* and laid hands on the patient." Did Freud know that Reich instructed the patient to lie on the couch and breathe deeply, and encouraged the patient to overcome his habit of shallow breathing? Did he know that Reich gently pressed on the patient's chest to help him fully exhale? That he examined the patient for muscular tensions? I do my best to explain all this to him. Reich actually touched the patient, I tell him. I assure him that I do not follow that approach, but what is so wrong about it?

"Well, that is not part of psychoanalysis, nor is that necessary to help a patient with neurotic symptoms." Freud, the medical man and former neuropathologist, ultimately came to identify himself as a psychologist, while Reich was moving psychoanalysis in the direction of the physical realm. Obviously, Freud could not approve of that direction, nor could many others.

I stand my ground. "But Reich was only offering a simple message to his colleagues in psychoanalysis: We have bodies! When we contract with fear and anxiety, we do so physically, not just psychologically. We breathe more shallowly due to the contraction of chest muscles. I can see this happening in the office with my patients. I saw it plainly with Carla. Other patients develop symptoms like neck and back pain from holding in the emotions. When we release the anger and grief, there is a physical expansion that occurs. I can easily see that Carla's body posture is more relaxed after she opens up emotionally. Reich taught us that emotion is a physiological—not just a psychological—phenomenon, a process of expansion and contraction." Why would anyone have trouble seeing the wisdom in this?

"So you are pushing on your patient's chest?" he asks with obvious disdain.

"No, I don't use his somatic techniques. I am only arguing for the soundness of his theories."

"Pushing on the patient's chest is no substitute for exploring the mind!"

"Well, as I said, I think that Reich and his followers put too much emphasis on the somatic work, but that is no reason to dismiss him entirely." I feel like I am arguing for a brother or a cousin who has been unfairly banished by the patriarch of the family. And I have not even mentioned Reich's theory of an atmospheric energy; that would surely meet with more resistance.

"I admit that I was too hasty to turn away from Reich. But you must realize that I was not the only one. The International Psychoanalytical Association voted to expel him from the organization in 1934. That was not my choice; it was their vote. He just went too far astray. A very bright young man, but he went too far." With that, Freud is done. A long silence follows, and I have the sense that we are done talking about Wilhelm Reich, if not quite done for the day.

We seem to have arrived at a new place in our relationship this afternoon, though. We cannot agree on everything, but it is now permissible to disagree. We talk a bit more about psychoanalysis, and Freud mentions a couple other people who trained with him. It is not easy for him, but he is trying to open the door and let other ideas enter the room. Eventually, he shifts the topic to his time in Paris listening to the lectures of the great Charcot, the Napoleon of the Neuroses. I suppose it is comforting for him to close with a pleasant memory of an easier time, a time before his battles with colleagues over his new ideas.

When we part for the day, there is still a slightly stiff feeling to our good-bye; we are a bit too polite, too forced and formal. But we agree to continue our meetings, so the storm has passed. I suppose I owe this new shift in our interactions to Reich, as Freud changed his tone when I first mentioned him today. Another debt to Wilhelm Reich. Vive la révolution!

8. A Hopeless Case

I might as well be sitting alone in my office, even though there is another human being in the chair opposite mine, just a few feet away. There is no real connection between us, despite the fact that we have sat together—or at least in the same space—three times before. I know a few things about him, of course. I know that his name is Tom, he is in his late thirties, and he works in the nanotech industry that is blossoming in the Albany area these days. I also know some of the facts about his depressive symptoms, but I do not feel that I really know him at all.

On this, our fourth session, I am still not even sure that he wants to be here. In fact, it would be a considerable stretch of the imagination to say that he is *in therapy* yet. He comes to my office and sits here looking rather miserable for the allotted amount of time, and then he leaves, untouched by the experience. It was his wife who called to set up the first appointment for him, so I suspected from the beginning that he did not really want therapy. She called on his behalf, he explains, because he does not like to ask for help. He would rather deal with things himself. Now he looks like the hapless husband whose wife has dragged him to yet another place that he had no wish to go: a shopping mall, a church service, dinner with the in-laws, and now the therapist's office. This is one more thing he must suffer through in the course of his melancholy life.

And suffer he does. He tells me that he has been depressed for years, for decades, for as long as he can remember. He is relentlessly critical of himself, and never misses an opportunity to indict himself for an endless list of perceived shortcomings. He is less than forty, but he sounds like a despairing old man of eighty, bitterly unhappy with what he has done in the past, totally unable to enjoy the present, looking forward to nothing in the future except getting old and dying. No, he would never kill himself, he assures me, but he takes no pleasure in the continuation of this dreary existence. As one would expect, he is not very hopeful that this therapy will help him. He has tried several therapists in the past, as well as several rounds of antidepressant medications, all to no avail. All of these experiences just confirm his deep-seated belief that he should deal with things on his own.

I have been wondering whether I should try to treat him at all, since he seems so uninterested in what I have to offer. If I do continue to try, it certainly will not be *short-term* dynamic psychotherapy, but that would not matter as long as I could help him. Perhaps I should refer him to a colleague who offers another type of therapy. However, there is one small bit of information that he offers today that keeps me from quitting: there is a "background story" to his depression, he says. When he was twelve years old, his father died suddenly of a heart attack. He does not add anything to this one sentence. After delivering it, he falls silent, unsure where to go with the conversation. He is lost in the woods without compass or map, and his previous efforts to retrace his steps have only gotten him farther and farther from home. His sidelong glance announces that he has little faith in me to guide him out of the wilderness, but seeing the storm clouds gathering overhead, he has reluctantly offered me the only clue he has about the original trail he was walking: he remembers passing a gravestone with his father's name on it. He seems to know nothing about how he got from that sad monument to this particular patch of ground where we encounter each other today.

I speculate that he is offering me a psychological theory, sparse though it is. His father died, and *therefore* he is depressed. At least, that is the implication. Having said that, he is done talking. Worse, he is quite convinced that looking back at his past is both painful and unproductive. He assures me that he has looked back many a time and seen only foolish mistakes, missed opportunities, and irritable behaviors on his part, memories that only lessen his already bleak estimation of himself.

A few minutes later, though, I get a fleeting glimpse of his emotional life. He mentions his father again, and speaks briefly about how depressed and withdrawn his mother became after she lost her husband. He talks about her last years—she died only a few years ago—and he suddenly becomes quite visibly sad. "I miss her." But this lasts only a few seconds, and then he recovers his equilibrium and sits stoically in his chair, waiting for the session to end. The energy in the room is stale, and I wonder what he thinks of this dull state of affairs.

"What do you think about our session so far?" I ask.

"So-so," he says, with an expression that would be useful for telling a waiter that the food on the table is quite tasteless and not worth the price listed on the menu.

"It does seem a little slow now," I say.

"Yeah, we aren't doing anything."

"What do you make of that?"

"I don't know. My mood goes up and down."

"At the beginning of the session, you mentioned the death of your father. You talked about how withdrawn your mother became after his death. You even felt a bit of sadness about her. Since then, it seems that you closed the door again. Is this what you do? You open up a little and then close the door again?"

"Yeah. If I open the door, it's never good."

"Why is that?"

"I don't handle emotions well. I don't feel like that's a good place to go. It's not going to solve anything, so I don't see the point. It's never worked for me in the past."

"What's never worked?" I ask.

"Bringing anything up."

"You mean bringing up your feelings and experiencing them?"

"Right," he says. "Experiencing my feelings has never worked for me."

Why is this man even sitting here? He certainly does not want therapy. Not dynamic psychotherapy, anyway.

"So you've taken the opposite strategy and locked your feelings away and isolated yourself, which leaves you feeling very unhappy with life."

He nods agreement, but seems not the least bit disturbed by what I am saying.

"It's so bad," I add, "that you look forward to getting old and dying. It seems to me that your strategy is not particularly productive."

"No, it's not." He shakes his head, again agreeing with me, but obviously with no intention to change course. There is an air of stubborn resignation, even a hint of contempt for anyone so naïve as to think that this problem could be resolved. "It's a lose–lose scenario here for me. If I dwell on things, I get upset. And the alternative is not to dwell on them but also to be unhappy. That's just the way it is." Earlier in the session, I could see a small opening, a breach in the wall. Now that opening has been sealed and buttressed, and the fortress is once again totally impenetrable. This is resistance with a capital *R*.

Our biggest obstacle is his negative view of emotions. He starts to experience an emotion (his grief over his mother), and then quickly stifles the feeling before he can get any relief from letting it out. Afterward, he concludes from this quickly aborted experiment in the emotional life that emotion is a useless phenomenon, a needless bit of discomfort that leads to nothing good. Worse, he makes no distinction between emotions of contraction and emotions of expansion. For him, it is all muddled together as the dreadful experience of feeling "upset." He endures feelings of painful depression, he dwells on negative memories in a vortex of depressive rumination, and he feels shame and guilt; from this he extrapolates to a general condemnation of all emotions. I will never succeed by just pointing out his defenses and clearing the way for the emotions, unless I can convince him that there might be some utility to this exercise. Without using Wilhelm Reich's terms, without saying *expansion versus contraction*, I begin a discussion about the difference between emotions. I explain to him that some of the emotions that people avoid, like anger and grief, can actually lead to a sense of relief if we let ourselves experience them fully. He seems willing to have the discussion.

"I close off emotions," he says. "Not just bad ones. All of them."

"Right. And you seem to think that if you open up your emotions, you'll just dwell on something for a few minutes and then you'll feel worse."

"I've never felt better by doing so."

"To me that says you've never really let it all out."

"Probably not," he says.

I take a moment to examine his answer. He offers only these two words, but the words feel like the genuine article. I think he actually sees my point. Perhaps there is hope for us yet.

"You've never opened up and remained open to the world. Instead you're isolated and miserable."

"I don't like the world," he says. The door slams shut again. He looks angry and defiant. "And I don't trust people." A message for me, no doubt.

"You don't trust people?"

He shakes his head definitively.

"Well, I'm people," I say. "That statement would include me, then."

"Right." He nods unapologetically.

"You don't trust me?"

"Not yet." He shrugs his shoulders and holds his palms upward as if to ask, *Why should I?*

I really doubt that I can help this man. He has a moment here and there, a moment of bona fide emotion, a moment of understanding in which he seems to be willing to join me in exploring his emotional life, but then he always pulls away and retreats to his stubborn isolation. Still, I am reluctant to send him away, and I find myself wondering why. There is something about him that I find almost likable, despite his sarcasm. But liking him will not cure him.

"So where does this leave us in therapy?" I ask. "Earlier in this session, you had the experience of starting to open up here, but rather than taking the ball and running with it, you went back to being shut down and very unhappy. And it sounds like you've decided that's the path for you."

He sits in silence for a long minute or two. He moves a leg back and forth, left and right, so I suspect that something is brewing. Is he feeling a bit of anxiety about staying on his current path and remaining unhappy? I certainly hope so.

"It's not a choice," he says.

"Oh I'm suggesting that there *is* a choice. Maybe you're not making a *conscious* choice, but—"

"Well, right," he says. There it is again: the tiny crack in the wall. He seems willing to listen. Maybe he understands what I am implying about his unconscious choice to continue feeling miserable.

"We all make choices," I say. "You can choose to explore what you mentioned earlier this morning and push it further to see if that helps, or you can choose to stay shut down and unhappy. But it *is* a choice." I must help him see this. He cannot continue to see himself as the hapless patient with a disease called depression, the unfortunate victim of his genetic fate. He must see himself as an active agent who can either prolong his own suffering or fight to overcome it. To convince him of this, I will be battling not only against his resistance, but also against the general misunderstanding that has permeated my profession these days. Everything is attributed to genes and biochemistry; every problem is blamed on a spontaneously occurring chemical imbalance, as if what happens in our lives has no effect on brain chemistry or emotional well-being. "You still have a choice."

He is nodding in agreement. "Right," he says.

"But it's not a choice that I can make for you."

"Right."

"I can sit here and tell you that I think that the better path is to open up, but it doesn't matter what *I* say. It all depends on you."

He continues to look amenable to my comments, but I do not expect our fragile alliance to last for very long. There is something maddening about talking with him. We seem to be on the same page occasionally, but then he returns to his isolated, adversarial stance. Now that I have another small window of opportunity, I talk a bit further with him about trying to work together and solve his problems. Not surprisingly, he seizes upon selected comments of mine to arrive at a very unproductive conclusion. Yes, he realizes that he has to participate, he tells me. In fact, he knows that I cannot fix him, and he must fix himself. In other words, he still takes an isolated stance, rather than an active stance as a partner with me in this process.

"It sounds like you're here trying to do it all by yourself," I say. "Trying to fix it yourself."

"Well, no, I don't know what to do. This is why I'm here. Because I don't know how to do it."

"So maybe you're implying that you need my help to do this."

"I don't think it's implied," he says. "I am here, after all. It's pretty blatant. It's *obvious.*" He goes from ally to adversary in seconds. He is quickly becoming annoyed. "If it was implied, I might drive by your car and wave at it hoping that you would understand that I need to come in. I think it's pretty obvious that I'm here."

"And why are you here?"

"Well, that's obvious. I'm here to ask for help."

"That's an interesting thing you just said. You're here to ask for help. But most of the time, you don't seem to be asking for help. Your wife called to make the first appointment and—"

"Well, I guess if I'm supposed to walk in the door and say, 'Hello I'm asking for help'—if that's the system, you know, it seems kind of dumb to me."

I am surprised that he can be so abrasive. "You sound annoyed with me."

"Yeah. You could say that."

"So why are you annoyed with me now?"

"Because we're doing the same thing we did last time." For a split second, he almost looks close to tears, but I am not sure. He covers his tracks so quickly.

"You look a little upset," I say.

"I don't have time …" He pauses, but I cannot read him. "I'm making the time to be here."

"But why are you annoyed with me?"

"Because I don't understand the process of … *your* process of therapy. I've been to other therapists who have specific goals in mind …" He shrugs thinking of them. "And they didn't work. I didn't like their approach. But this … I don't get this."

"But you got annoyed with me around the issue of asking for help. I said it's not that obvious that you're asking for help, and you became irritable."

"Well, I think it is obvious that I'm asking for help. Just by coming here and being in your office. I mean, we're not sitting here in preparation to go somewhere else, right? It's not a gate at the airport to get onto a plane."

"It's not so obvious to me that you're asking for help. It's not obvious that you want to be here."

"Well, you see, I think the implication of being in your office is that I'm asking for help. If I have to say the words, I can say the words, but that's—"

"But this seems to annoy you."

"No, I can say it." He slaps his leg for punctuation. "Doctor, I need some help. Please help me. Would you like me to write that down for you?" This should be called the porcupine defense: the tendency to bristle with anger and irritability in order to keep everyone from getting too close.

"More annoyance, I see."

"Sure!"

"And some sarcasm."

"You bet! Because I'm here— "

"There's something annoying to you about this whole discussion right now."

"I should just stop talking, which is what I usually do in arguments with my wife." He looks ready to give up and walk out of the office. It is interesting that some patients can get under the therapist's skin and provoke a lot of anger, while others can be rude and insulting without arousing a strong reaction at all. I become aware of myself for a moment and I realize that I do not feel the least bit threatened or offended by his comments. It is so obvious that he is feeling rattled by the discussion, and he is just trying to protect himself in some way. I need to move quickly, though, before he actually walks out. Somehow, I need to let him know that this conversation is an acceptable one.

"But I think this is a very important topic," I say. "It's a rough conversation that we're having, but I think we should pursue it because I think it might lead to something useful. I think you need help. You're not happy. And we all need help at times in life. But it's very difficult for you to ask for it. So when I bring this up, and you say that you need help, you get irritated as Hell with me. I think it makes you annoyed that you need help, and I wonder if you're also annoyed that I haven't given enough help yet."

"I'm not sure that I expect help."

"But what is so annoying about this discussion? Help me understand that."

"Look," he says, "if I pull my car into the car wash, the guy should say, 'I think this customer wants his car washed.' What if he asked, 'Are you here because you need a new suit? Tell me why you're here, sir.' I'd say, 'Don't be a moron!'"

We are skating on thin ice. I still do not feel rattled by his comments, even though they are getting pretty nasty, but I wonder if he can ever move past this protective layer of vitriol and do some meaningful work.

"So you're implying that I should understand you and stop acting like a moron."

He is mute, looking like a man who just blurted out something quite rude at a party and then realized that the host heard what he said. When he does speak again, he tries to repair the faux pas by claiming that he is not calling *me* a moron, but just making a point. After a brief pause in the conversation, he shrugs his shoulders, as if to acknowledge that I am obviously not convinced, and to let me know that it matters little to him what I think.

"You're very conflicted about this idea of help," I say. "Your strategy is to fix it yourself. You're not going to rely on anybody. But that doesn't work. And on the other side of the coin, you sit there thinking, 'Why doesn't this moron see that I came here because I need help?! When is he going to help me?'"

"I don't think I can fix it myself. I know I need help. What you said just now was accurate." Again we are momentarily back in synchrony with each other.

"Yes, you sound conflicted about it. You want help, but you don't want to rely on me."

"I ... I don't want to be disappointed."

And with these few words, I see him put down his shield and change his demeanor entirely. Suddenly, he looks vulnerable, sad, and too weary to keep struggling against my attempts to gain entry to the hidden world of his psyche.

"Well, that makes sense," I say.

"I would rather not be disappointed in other people. If I don't engage them, I can't be disappointed by them."

"Oh, I see."

"If I don't ask a friend to help me with something, then I can't be disappointed in my friend." His voice becomes faint by the end of his sentence; it almost breaks. He looks away and struggles against the emotion.

So there it is. There is the impetus for his ferociously self-reliant character style. He cannot take the risk of leaning on another human being, because he is nearly certain that he will just be disappointed once again, as he was disappointed by both of his parents. Instead, he is the self-made man, the rugged individualist, the man who needs no one. At the moment, he looks sad and vulnerable, but usually he sits across from me looking distant, aloof, and uninterested in any meaningful connection. Wilhelm Reich would have spotted his ferocious self-reliance in a minute, and he would have recognized it as character pathology—character *armor*. It functions both as a defense against his internal emotional life and as a resistance against letting me get close enough to help. He just cannot risk another disappointment.

The theme of disappointment now takes center stage. He was disappointed in his parents, and now he is disappointed in himself and how he has lived his life. I am suspicious here. *He is disappointed in himself.* Is this statement a genuine attempt to reflect on his life? Or is he starting to use this topic to criticize himself for being such a disappointing person? He shifts back to talking about his father, and I relax my vigilance, but just a bit. He can take any topic and turn it into a weapon against himself.

"I remember when he died," he says. "He died when I was twelve. And I remember for a time feeling like it was—and I knew it was silly—but for a short time, I remember blaming myself. Because I didn't really like him very much."

"I see."

"So, somehow my twelve-year-old brain was thinking that it was my fault, because I didn't like him, so ..."

"So he died," I say.

"Yes, he died," he repeats.

"Well, that's how kids think, of course. They blame themselves."

"I learned later that this obviously wasn't the case."

"But you had this thought, that it was your fault."

"Yeah." He sits looking down at the floor and says nothing else. I decide to venture a hunch. "Did you ever wish him dead?"

He looks up directly at me. "Yeah."

"You did?"

"I did. I hate him. I hate him!" I notice the use of the present tense, but there is no time to comment on it. "He was an ass. He was always so angry. And I think he was hardest on me, since I was the oldest kid in the family. I still remember him hitting me with his belt when he was mad, and I was little then. I just couldn't relate to him as a kid at all. He was a very tough person." Another long pause. "In fact, I remember going to school one day and telling my friend that I hate my father and I wish he would just drop dead."

"Really?"

"Oh yeah. Absolutely. And then he died."

"How much later?" I ask.

"I don't know. I think a few weeks later, but it could have been longer. But I remember that: I wished him dead, and then he died. Afterward, I remember thinking: *I wish I had never said that.*"

"But I wonder how this affected you. You wished him dead, and then he died."

"Yeah, I felt like it was entirely my fault, because ..."

"So you've carried some guilt."

"Yeah."

"I wonder if this is related to the fact that you don't let yourself enjoy things. Maybe you think that you don't deserve to enjoy things."

He looks down again, and he seems close to tears.

"You have some feelings coming up?" I ask.

"I *do* want to enjoy things. I want to be a happy person."

"Do you think you deserve to enjoy life?"

"I don't know. I don't think I make enough effort to enjoy life." Again he blames himself, and I must interrupt this process.

"You don't make enough effort to enjoy life. So it's your fault that you're not enjoying it."

"Well, yeah, isn't it?"

"More self-blame, I notice."

"I guess so."

"But I want to go back to your dad. I wonder how his death affected you. You hated him, for obvious reasons, because he was so difficult. You wished him dead, and then he died. And then you spent the next twenty-five years or so not enjoying life, and maybe unconsciously punishing yourself. As if you're saying, *I don't deserve to enjoy anything. I killed my father.*"

"Could be."

"Maybe you've lived a life of suffering and penance for that. Unconsciously."

"That sounds right," he says.

"It's just an idea."

He sits for a bit with this idea, and at moments he seems to be nodding just slightly, as if he agrees with me. Or perhaps he is just agreeing with whatever is running through his own mind at the moment. Then he looks up at me to speak.

"But how can his interactions with me, which only lasted for the first twelve years of my life, have screwed me up for the rest of my life?"

"You look sad," I say, ignoring his question for the moment.

"Yeah." This monosyllable comes out in a strained, painful whisper.

"What makes you sad?"

"Because I wish *I* were dead!" he blurts out more loudly. "I've felt this way my whole life, and I've hidden it for the most part. I have survived by focusing on whatever would keep me going. Like work."

"Work kept you going."

"Work and whatever else distracted me. But there was so much time in my life that I just hated being me. Just the other day, I was trying to fix a leaky faucet and I couldn't get it right. I'm not that handy. So I struggled along for a while, and then I just lost it."

"Lost it?"

"Yeah, I just lost my temper. I was literally walking around the house yelling at myself. *Stupid! You idiot!*"

"Attacking yourself."

"Yeah, and that was mild."

It is hard to tell at this moment whether he is opening up and experiencing sadness about how poorly he treats himself, or whether he is sinking into another depressive swamp of self-criticism. How confusing it is that tears can represent either situation. One would think that Mother Nature would have designed a better system, with one physiological marker for the emotional expansion of active sadness and grief, and another for the emotional contraction that we call depression. My guess is that each time he starts to open up with grief, he unwittingly blocks it by mentally attacking himself and turning it into another round of depression. So the tears of grief, which could be healing, are replaced with tears of depressive self-hatred.

"But I get the sense that you go into a tailspin of despair here. We are talking about the enormous effect your father had on you, but you shift gears into a monologue of self-hatred."

"This is what I do. And I'm very good at it."

He certainly is. Here we can agree on something. "But I suspect that it gets in the way of exploring your feelings about your father. You flip into a negative evaluation of yourself, rather than facing your feelings about the negative effect he had on you."

"Well, for a while he did have a negative effect. And then he just wasn't there anymore. No effect. No father."

"So you had no father to rely on."

"And I had no mother to rely on either." Is this a ploy to avoid talking about Dad? I am not sure. I wait to see what he will say next, and how it feels to me. "After he died, she just seemed to fall apart. You know, she spent lots of time in her bedroom with the shades drawn." This sounds important, and it does not feel like a defensive maneuver.

"So she withdrew," I say.

"Oh, yeah. She completely withdrew for long periods of time."

"So you couldn't lean on her either."

"Oh, no. She wasn't really involved. My mother never pushed me to do my homework, or anything like that. Doing well in school just wasn't a priority for her."

"Could you rely on her at all?"

"Not for that. I don't ever remember relying on her ... I did the laundry. I cooked."

"You cooked? At what age?"

"Twelve or so."

"I see." I can imagine a very lonely twelve-year-old boy trying to put together a meal by himself.

"Not like I was making every meal, but I would cook. Breakfast, things like that."

"Would you cook for her?"

"Yeah, sure, if I was making breakfast, I would make it for her. I got up every morning and made her coffee." His says this in a very matter-of-fact way, as if all kids make coffee in the morning for their mothers.

"Was this before he died? Or after?"

"After. When he died, that changed everything. That changed the whole dynamic of the family.

"In what way?"

"Well, he wasn't that old when he died. It was a devastating loss to my mother. It really affected her forever."

"It sounds like the roles got reversed at times, and you were taking care of Mom instead of vice versa."

"To a point. Sure."

"So you must have learned at the age of twelve that you can't really rely on Mom in the normal ways."

"Right."

"In fact, she was relying on you. For coffee …"

"Right."

"So the roles were switched."

"Yeah." His answers are monosyllabic, but he is clearly engaged in the discussion now. His eye contact is better and his posture is more erect. He is here in the room with me.

"I assume this is where you learned that you can never be in a dependent role, because there's no Dad, and Mom's not up to the job."

"There was no net," he says.

"Right. Well said. There was no safety net for you. So you were just on your own."

"Right."

"And I think you've constructed, from age twelve onward, a way of being. You developed a character—a personality that says, *I'm going to get through this on my own.* Because that's the only way it can be. Total self-reliance."

"Right. I mean, what choice did I have?"

We are on the same page again now, and my hope for him is on the rise, at least for the moment. He will not be an easy case, of course, but maybe we can do this. It will not be a quick case, but Short-Term Dynamic Psychotherapy is not always short. I wish Davanloo and the other pioneers of this method had given it another name. Well, short or long, maybe we can get through the hard parts and get to the bottom of this. Or maybe next time he will just come in with his resistance in place like a concrete wall and we will fail. Time will tell.

We spend another few minutes elaborating on his relentless insistence on being self-reliant. He sees it in various examples from his life. We are actually working together after a rough start. There is a change taking place in his expression at the moment, though, and I am not sure what it means. He just looks less animated; in fact, he looks troubled again.

"I feel bad for her, too," he says.

"For your mother?"

"Yeah, for her. I mean, losing her husband really devastated her. She faced financial hardships. She obviously got depressed and withdrawn. It just ruined her life." He has been looking down at the floor, but now he looks up at me. His eyes are wide and plaintive, the eyes of a twelve-year-old boy who has a terrible secret to tell: "I ruined her life."

9. Prophet and Disciple

I am dreaming a dream and it is only a dream, but it feels as real as anything in my waking life. I have been given a new job to do, and it involves mapping out a path to a house in the woods. I know that I must find the house and mark the route to get there, but the instructions from my boss are not very clear beyond that. Should I just make the map and return to the main office? Am I supposed to do something when I arrive at the house? Do I enter it or just pass it by? Nothing in the instructions from the boss addresses these questions, and I feel quite anxious as I get near the house.

It is a small brick home, but it has a solid iron banister leading up the stairs to the second floor. In the dream, I am surprised that I know this because I have never been in the house, but I am sure about that banister inside. I approach the door, and I feel increasingly anxious about what to do. I could knock, or I could just enter without knocking, but I am too apprehensive to do either. I content myself with looking at the front of the house, and I realize that it needs some gardening. There is nothing growing in front of the house, so I pull out a notebook and start making notes for a garden. *Dig the soil six inches under,* I write. I make some further notes, and then I decide to report to the boss.

Back at the office, the boss is not happy with me. He sits opposite me and scowls at my notebook. "Well, I guess we are just different, you and I," he says. He does not explain his comment, nor does he need to explain. I know exactly what he means. He is implying that he would have done the job the right way; he and I are different because he is a better worker.

"No, it's not that we are different," I say. "It's just that I am new at this. I don't really know what I'm doing yet." I immediately regret my words. I sound so self-effacing. Why should I accept his criticism? After all, he never told me what to do. I wish I could speak up for myself.

And then I wake up in my room at the Hotel Regina in Vienna. Half awake, I am still engrossed in the dream, and I actually think of what I would like to say to the boss in the dream: "Yes, we *are* different. I would never be so mean and critical to an employee. I would never send someone off to work with such pitifully inadequate instructions and then chastise him for not doing the job right!"

Then I am up, out of bed and hurrying. I have slept later than I planned, and I have a meeting with Professor Freud this morning, rather than our usual afternoon time. As I dress, the dream wanders in and out of my thoughts. I realize that I cannot recall the boss's face in the dream. And why was I so anxious about that little brick home? Never mind. I need to collect myself and leave a little time for breakfast before I am due at Berggasse 19. *Dig the soil six inches under.* None of this makes any sense. What does any of it mean? Or does it mean anything? Of course, Freud would say that every dream has meaning, and every dream is a disguised wish fulfillment. Modern science does not support such a sweeping generalization, but this dream was so intense that I think it must mean something.

I am dressed and ready to go. Before I leave my room, I check on a couple of books I am bringing with me, in case I get a chance to quote from them to support my position on psychotherapy. This time, I make sure that Reich's book *Character Analysis* is packed. As I am hurrying, I just barely notice the colorful fall leaves changing on the trees around me outside. Over a light breakfast at a café, I pour over a few notes I have made for the meeting today. I am no longer actively thinking about the dream, but it still lingers around my little breakfast table, just at the periphery of conscious thought.

At Freud's building, Gretchen greets me stiffly at the front door. This is the first time she has seen me since our unfortunate collision last time, and she is obviously quite nervous. I wish I could speak enough German to put her at ease. I offer her what little I have: an overstated smile and my best *Guten Tag!*—Good Day! I follow her up the steps, holding onto the wrought iron banister, and the dream comes back.

There was a wrought iron banister in the house. In some way, the house in the dream represents Freud's house, yet the little brick house in the dream looked nothing like this Renaissance-style apartment building in Vienna. Was the boss in the dream supposed to be Freud? I have not been able to remember his face since I woke up, and I think there was no clear vision of his face even during the dream. Why are things so disguised in dreams? Why do we not simply dream things as they are? Freud wrote that we have a dream censor that acts much like a defense mechanism in waking life, to ward off unacceptable thoughts and feelings. I do not see what I would need to avoid about my visits with him, though.

Gretchen and I arrive at Freud's quarters on the second floor, and we enter the apartment. She leads me to the door of his consulting room, but this time she does not knock and wait as she usually does. She is eager to part ways with me, so she quickly and quietly walks away. I raise a hand to knock and I feel a wave of anxiety, as I did in the dream. *I stand at the door to the little brick house, and I am afraid to knock.* I pause at the door, my hand raised to knock, and I take a moment to analyze my dream. Obviously, I have been afraid to confront Freud ever since we first began meeting. But why? What do I care if he disapproves of my work? I knew before our first meeting that he would have trouble accepting the modern changes to his original approach. I know I am getting good results in the office with my patients. Why do I care if he disapproves?

The boss in the dream gave me scant instructions for the job I was assigned to do. Another connection: Freud wrote very few papers on the actual technique of psychoanalysis. Most of his writing was about theory, not technique, so generations of psychoanalysts—and their heirs, we dynamic psychotherapists—have struggled with ambiguity. What should we actually do in the office? How can we translate Freud's rich body of theory into action? Yes, the boss in my dream is Freud.

"Good morning," he says with a welcoming smile. I realize that I have knocked while I was lost in my dream analysis. I greet him and move toward my customary chair. *Six inches under.* What could that mean? The phrase *six feet under* pops into my mind, and I see now that the concepts of death and burial are hidden in the dream. As I manage to talk about my session with Tom, I am simultaneously putting together the last pieces of the mystery. I wanted the boss dead in the dream. I wanted him *six feet under.* Translation: I wanted Freud dead. So my dream actually is a wish fulfillment dream, straight out of his book *The Interpretation of Dreams.* But why would I have this dream now, after I was able to assert myself during our last session and discuss Reich? I suppose it happened as a direct result of that confrontation; now I am free to let my angry feelings emerge in my dreams.

I suppose it was also influenced in part by my patient Tom, who wished his father dead. The thought reverberates in my mind: he wished his father dead. Only then does the rest of the dream yield to my analysis: the little brick house is clearly the house where I grew up in Detroit. And the wish is not only against Freud but also against my own father. I remember going out to his vegetable garden to help him pull weeds when I was a little boy. *Not that!* he would bark at me. *That's not a weed!* How was I to know? He never gave me very good instructions on how to distinguish between a weed and a young cucumber plant. Crystallizing in my mind, there is a case formulation about my first patient, myself: I have had trouble getting angry and asserting myself with Freud because it awakens the forbidden and dangerous anger toward my father.

"I see that you have a highly resistant patient here." Freud is standing at his bookshelves, cheerfully unaware of my murderous dream-wish. I suppose he would not be surprised if he knew about it. After all, he dealt with such stuff all day long in his office. But would he care? I wonder. *Would you even care if I had a dream wishing you dead? Would it even matter to you?* I pull myself out of my contemplation to join the discussion.

"I certainly do. He is quite resistant. My question is whether I should continue working with him."

As is often the case, Freud is in no hurry to answer my question. He turns toward the bookshelves and starts thumbing through one of the volumes, apparently looking for something specific. The books are so impressive looking, especially the hardcover books, some of them bound in leather. The bookshelves are of solid wood, naturally, stained deep and dark. In my time, people can view a page of print on the screen of a handheld electronic device. The letters on the screen can be anything from a great novel to an advertisement for toothpaste. In Freud's day, great ideas arrived with a bit of style and fanfare, outfitted with the kind of regal apparel that announced their worth.

"Resistance was a force that I became aware of early in my career, you know. I even wrote about it in the *Studies*, my book with Breuer." The good Dr. Breuer, Freud's older friend and mentor. I can see his long beard and kindly eyes from the photographs in my books at home. I still wonder what happened between them. I wonder if the benevolent Dr. Breuer had murderous dreams about Freud.

"Oh, I see. I thought that the concept of resistance was something that you discovered later."

Freud has found his page. "Here it is: *I had to overcome a psychical force in the patients which was opposed to the pathogenic ideas becoming conscious.* Even then, back in 1895, it occurred to me that something was getting in the way. There was some obstruction to the analytic process. All these people were coming to me, eagerly looking for relief of their symptoms, but they were also fighting against my efforts to help them. At first, I thought that they simply could not remember certain ideas and memories; then I realized that they did not *want* to remember. So I coined the term *resistance.*"

The dream fades, and I am solidly in the room with him now, thinking about resistance. A psychological force opposing the process of analysis. I often hear resistance and defense used interchangeably. Are they different? I suppose that resistance implies a struggle to block the therapist from getting at one's deepest thoughts and feelings, whereas defenses are the particular ways in which one avoids those threatening thoughts and feelings, even when sitting alone at home. At any rate, it has always fascinated me that some patients show very little resistance, while others—like Tom—put up such a resistance that the therapist feels like he is swimming against a tidal wave.

"Right," I say. "Resistance. And that is one of your discoveries that has stood the test of time. Patients don't want to think of certain painful thoughts."

"Correct." He runs his eyes over the pages again. "And here is why they do not want to think of these ideas and memories: *They were all of a distressing nature, calculated to arouse the affects of shame, of self-reproach and of psychical pain, and the feeling of being harmed; they were all of a kind that one would prefer not to have experienced, that one would rather forget.*"

"And that certainly applies to my patient Tom."

"Absolutely." He looks pleased, satisfied with his teaching and with my acceptance of it. He is the master, I am the student, and the universe is an orderly arrangement again. I suppose neither one of us wants a repeat performance of the discord we experienced last time we met.

When Gretchen appears with her serving tray of tea, Freud makes a magnanimous sweeping gesture with his hand to indicate that she should serve me first, even though she routinely does so anyway. She serves and departs as quickly as she can.

"My concern," I say, "is that Tom is so resistant, so determined to stay depressed and miserable, that I may not be able to help him. This last session certainly ended on a better note, but we have had these positive interactions before, and he just comes in next time feeling miserable. And he tells me that the previous session was no help to him."

Freud puts his book back on the shelf, pausing for a moment to look over some of the other titles. What would it feel like to peruse a long shelf of books and know that you had written every one of them? I can only imagine the sense of satisfaction he must have, looking back at his career. "Well," he says, "you must remember that there are different reasons for resistance. Every patient resists therapy, to a greater or lesser degree, in order to avoid the uncomfortable emotions associated with unbearable ideas, but there are other factors at work. In this case, his *superego* is your biggest problem."

"Yes, he feels very guilty."

"Terrible guilt," Freud says. "His superego—his conscience, in plain language—is punishing him, as you pointed out to him. He cannot allow himself to enjoy anything pleasant in life, and he cannot enjoy his successes."

"Right," I say.

"So he cannot allow himself to be successful in psychotherapy, either. When he tells you that your efforts are not helping him, you must understand that he does not *want* the sessions to be helpful. This is all unconscious, naturally. He might tell you, speaking the contents of his conscious mind, how much he wants this to work; but no matter how good the session was, he will go home and convince himself that it was of no use."

"Oh, right. That makes sense. Successful therapy is just one more thing that he doesn't deserve." This is such a helpful insight!

"Absolutely," says Freud. "He is driven by his superego to destroy it."

"Because he feels guilty about wishing his father dead," I say. My dream drifts across my mind again, but only for a moment, and then it evaporates.

"Quite right. He feels guilty about his Oedipal wishes. The universal Oedipus complex. One cannot avoid it." He sips his tea with a satisfied look.

I am reluctant to disagree about anything today, in light of our last visit, but I cannot simply let this pass. Does he really think that Tom wished his father dead solely because of an unconscious childhood wish to get rid of his father and have his mother all to himself? Surely, children have such fantasies, but does he think it has nothing to do with the father's obvious cruelty? Does he really see this exclusively as an Oedipal fantasy, with no importance attached to the reality of who this particular father was, and how he actually treated his son? What about reality?

"But I'm not sure the Oedipus complex is necessary to explain his ill will toward his father. He tells me that his father was quite mean to him. He apparently had a terrible temper and hit him with a belt."

Freud puts his teacup down into its saucer and draws in a big breath. He exhales slowly, as if he is struggling to maintain his composure. He quietly gets up and goes back to his bookshelf. He pulls down a fairly thick volume and pages through it for a couple of minutes without saying a word.

Finally, he turns to me and reads. "*It is the fate of all of us, perhaps, to direct our first sexual impulse towards our mother and our first hatred and our first murderous wish against our father. Our dreams convince us that this is so.* The Oedipal complex. From my book *The Interpretation of Dreams.*" He snaps the book shut and vigorously nods once at me to punctuate his statement.

The only thing that surprises me in the quote is the word *perhaps. It is the fate of all of us, perhaps.* Freud was not a man who was prone to being indecisive. On the contrary, he tended to declare his discoveries as inviolable laws of nature. Each and every man has struggled in his childhood with murderous wishes against his father. Each and every case of hysteria was due to child sexual abuse. Each and every dream is a disguised wish fulfillment. This each-and-every disease permeated his work throughout his lifetime. To be fair, he was honestly trying to discover a few general principles of nature that could be applied universally to the psyche. Perhaps he was trying to fill the existing vacuum and compensate for the lack of solid theories in his day; or perhaps he was primarily driven by an ambitious desire to make a name for himself in the world. Whatever his motivation, he did not hesitate to jump prematurely into broad, sweeping generalizations. This was the one major flaw in his otherwise agile intellect. He was a man with a penchant for the absolute; there could be no exceptions to his theories.

"Yes, of course, Professor." Sometimes it is wiser to choose one's battles, and this is not one that I will win. His work on the Oedipus conflict was one of his accomplishments that he valued most highly—along with his work on dreams—and I would be a fool to think he is going to put that on the table for re-examination. "I am only saying that there is the added factor of his father's cruel discipline style." *And by the way, I was not angry at my father for being married to my mother. I was angry at him for yelling at me about his stupid cucumber plants.*

"Yes, yes," he says. "I understand your point."

Actually, I am not sure that he does understand. Perhaps what my patient describes was normal discipline for the authoritarian, turn-of-the-century Austrian father. But never mind, we are both trying to avoid conflict and establish a better alliance today, and I do not want to spoil our efforts. Better to move along and talk about other aspects of the case.

"I find it interesting that Tom carries so much guilt," I say, "while Carla had such fierce anger toward her father, but none of this crippling guilt."

"Yes," says Freud, "but Carla's father did not die. You see, Tom saw his wish come true. He wished his father dead, and the man died."

"True, true. He feels guilty on two counts. He thinks that his murderous wish killed his father, and he thinks that it ruined his mother's life."

Freud nods. "Ah, but the guilt about Mother only came out at the end of your session. That was lurking in the unconscious all these years."

"Yes, and I'm glad that it came out. But how do I stop him from attacking himself? We have had several sessions that felt like important breakthroughs, but he just returns with the same terrible depression, berating himself at every chance."

Another trip to the bookshelf. I suppose Freud has adopted a new strategy, calculating that his opinion will carry more weight with me if it comes directly from the pages of his books. The power of the printed word. He takes his time browsing his collection again, until he finds the right spot in the right volume.

"*If one listens patiently to a melancholic's many and various self-accusations, one cannot in the end avoid the impression that often the most violent of them are hardly at all applicable to the patient himself, but that with significant modifications they do fit someone else, someone whom the patient loves or has loved or should love.* From my paper, 'Mourning and Melancholia,' 1917."

His reading has the desired effect on me. I am swayed not only by the wisdom of the passage, but also by the poetry of it. "You're saying that the self-recriminations are just a disguise for his anger at other people. He turns the anger on himself and spares others."

"Precisely," he replies.

"I will need to explore his anger, then."

"Yes, definitely. You will do it in your own way, of course." He says this with a momentary tensing of the jaw and darkening brow, but he recovers quickly. "But whatever method you choose, you must help him to find the unconscious hostile wishes that he redirects toward himself."

"But I think we have a lot of work to do before we are ready to explore the depth of his anger. We are still struggling to establish a good alliance. I also think he needs to feel a bit of compassion for himself. And before addressing the anger, I have to do something about this destructive belief that he ruined his mother's life."

"That is all true," he says. "Perhaps you are learning to be more patient before you go rushing into your imaginary scenes of dramatic violence."

For a second, I take this as a provocation, and I am ready to respond in kind, but his expression is benign, almost kindly. I decide to let it pass and continue thinking about my case. "I also think we still have work to do on his pathological self-reliance. He is starting to understand it, but I think it will be very difficult for him to give it up."

"Yes, he is conflicted about it, as you told him. If he trusts someone to help him, he expects to be disappointed again. But if he remains stubbornly self-reliant, then he is lonely and depressed. This is his central conflict, and you formulated the conflict very nicely for him."

"Thank you, Professor." It always amazes me how one kind word can dissolve the tension between two people almost instantly. "I learned that from you, naturally. People often feel conflicted about some important thought or feeling or behavior, whether or not they realize it." I can see that he accepts my compliment just as readily. I can feel the atmosphere in the room warming steadily.

"The mind in conflict. It was one of the building blocks of my psychoanalysis from the very beginning. I could see that the patients were caught in a conflict between unacceptable ideas and the defense mechanisms that were constructed to keep those ideas from emerging. They were conflicted about getting well versus resisting the treatment. Later on, I wrote about the *id* impulses, the sexual and aggressive impulses, coming into conflict with the ego. Still later, I described the conflict between ego and superego, like with your patient. Conflict, my friend, always look for the inner conflict. If you look at the surface of the patient, you will see someone who is suffering and asking for your help. You will offer compassion and comfort, but you will never effect a fundamental change until you look beneath the surface and see that the person sitting before you is in conflict with himself."

I know all this, of course, and it crosses my mind to tell him. *I already know this. Did you not just say that I explained his conflict to him?* But he needs to say it, and I suppose it is good to hear it and recognize this major contribution that he made. Sometimes I forget how much we owe to Freud.

He adds, "And Reich helped with this too, you know. His book called *Character Analysis* was quite useful."

I am pleased by Freud's generous mention of Reich, and relieved to see that our previous session together has had a lasting impact on our dialogue. I reach into my briefcase. "It's funny that you mention that, Professor. I have brought Reich's book today, just to help me think about this case. I thought of Reich sometimes when I looked at Tom in my office. He would sit there saying nothing, but something about his general demeanor spoke of self-reliance. Even if he had never told me how hard he tries to be self-reliant, I could have guessed by his behavior in the office. He looked like he just didn't need me at all. May I read something to you?"

"Of course."

I am frustrated when I realize that my bookmark has fallen out of the book, and I cannot quickly find my place. Then I realize that I know the section well enough to put down the book and just paraphrase it. "The way the patient talks is just as important as what he says. The way he looks at the therapist—the analyst—is also important. The tone of voice and all the nonverbal behaviors are critical 'material' for us to understand. This is what Reich says, and it has helped me so much in my work. The basic character style of the patient is often the biggest problem needing attention."

"True, true. As I mentioned at our last meeting, my daughter Anna credited Reich for his work in the book she wrote. She liked his term *character armor*, the idea that people develop a personality style that functions to protect them." We talk about Reich a bit more, and then he talks at length about Anna, with great pride, of course. It is certainly the most cordial and collegial discussion we have had in quite a while. Returning to my case, Freud strikes a cautionary note. "No doubt, his self-reliance is an issue between you two, in the transference. Don't neglect the transference."

"Oh, I don't think there is much to worry about there, at least not yet. He is often so disconnected that I doubt there is much of a transference reaction at this point."

Freud says nothing, but smiles a knowing, kindly smile. It seems that he is entirely on my side now, wanting me to succeed, even if I do not use his methods. The adversarial struggle is gone, at least for now. He is my biggest backer today. The dream I had seems like it was years ago, a dream about someone else.

I am not sure I understand the transformation in him, really. I suppose I am riding on Reich's coattails since our last meeting; he had second thoughts about rejecting Reich, and I am reaping the benefits of his newfound remorseful attitude about the early days of psychoanalysis. But that cannot be the full explanation. Thinking of his daughter Anna might put him in a good mood, but even that does not quite explain it. I look over at Freud, who sits smiling at me. He offers to pour me another cup of tea, and then I have an epiphany: it is more than just the reparation of his guilt about Reich, and more than just taking pride in Anna. It is about me. *You need me. You need me as much as I need you. You ex-communicated Reich and countless others, and you isolated yourself. And now you are realizing that you need somebody—that you need me. After all, the teacher is not a teacher if he has no student. The master needs the apprentice, the prophet needs the disciple, and the father needs the son. You need me, and you need my approval, just as I need yours.* Freud pours my tea, which I accept with a gracious smile. Whether or not he can accept the fact, I know that we are not driven by sexual and aggressive "drives." At the core of human nature, we are driven by a need for attachment. We need each other.

10. The Last Season of Basketball

"Good morning," Tom says at the beginning of our seventh session.

"Good morning," I say.

And then we sit in silence for a minute or so. I have explained to him that I typically try to be quiet after greeting him, lest I pick a random topic that is not what he really needs to talk about. In this regard, I follow Freud by letting the patient lead, even though I often interrupt and redirect once the session gets started. He seemed comfortable when I first made that explanation, but the silence is a bit long today. After a minute or two, I decide that I should jump in and get things rolling. I ask him how he felt about last session. His answer is not very specific, and he quickly shifts the conversation to a relatively minor problem he is having at work. This is not something that will lead to any major results, but I suppose I have nearly given up again, so I let him talk about work. He always goes back to his very resistant stance, although we have had a breakthrough here and there.

In our past sessions, he has occasionally spoken of emotionally charged subjects and allowed himself to cross the border into the forbidden territory of his disavowed memories. If we string these moments together, they begin to look like a successful case of psychotherapy. Here is a fellow who can talk about the fact that his father died, and he can acknowledge his guilt for wishing him dead. He can remember that his mother became badly depressed, and that life became strangely quiet and lonely in the house. He can see now that he felt guilty about ruining his mother's life, even though he was never consciously aware of that guilt before our sessions began. He can tell me that he is always afraid that he is ruining his wife's life, and at moments he seems to see the connection between this fear and his feelings about his mother. It all sounds like a perfect case of dynamic psychotherapy.

Unfortunately, these important moments of insight and emotion are brief. They are always followed by an intense resistance and a refusal to explore any further. Sadly, I think the end is inevitable here. Perhaps I keep meeting with him because I just cannot say no. I do not like admitting defeat, and I do not like sending patients away, even when it is obvious that dynamic psychotherapy is not the right approach for them. This time it should be easier, of course, because he will not care anyway. The toughest patient is the one who quickly forms an attachment to me but simply cannot do the therapy. This fellow will not care. I will check one last time, but I can predict the answer.

"So how did you feel about coming to therapy this morning?"

"I don't look forward to coming here." He says this quite bluntly.

Case closed. It makes no sense to continue with him, because there is simply too much resistance. I have often wondered why some people are more resistant than others, and I just cannot make any sense of it. It certainly does not seem to correlate with a person's history. Some people with a very traumatic background have a high level of resistance, to be sure, but others show very little resistance; they seem to jump right in and do the hard work of looking at what happened to them. Likewise, people with relatively minor disturbances in their developmental years have a wide range of resistance, some low and some surprisingly high. Is the difference due to some kind of inborn temperamental trait? In one system of classifying temperament, the trait of *harm avoidance* has been proposed to describe people who naturally have a strong predisposition toward being anxious and avoidant; they fear uncertainty. (*What will I discover about myself if I pursue this strange conversation called psychotherapy?*) But the "harm avoidant" person is said to be a shy introvert, and that is not true for some people who are very resistant. It is certainly not true for Tom. It just seems that highly resistant patients are people who cannot tolerate the painful feelings of looking at negative memories. They might glance over their shoulders for a moment, but they cannot bear a sustained confrontation with their own life histories. They will not—perhaps *cannot*—look back at those disturbing memories because it is just too frightening to do so. No matter how gently I approach the subject, no matter how hard I work to show them the negative consequences of maintaining their current defenses, no matter how much I try to form an alliance and help soften their fears, they will not stay with the process long enough to open up and get some relief.

Seen from another perspective, I suppose the highly resistant patient is essentially resistant to forming a working bond with the therapist, and without that bond, the act of looking back in time is a lonely, frightening experience. This definitely applies to Tom. Without a strong therapeutic alliance, he has no one with whom he can share the journey. If only he had less resistance, he could perhaps find a way to talk about painful past experiences while simultaneously maintaining a connection to me in the present moment. He would be able to relive the past, while still maintaining the awareness that it is *only* the past; the present reality offers the safety of this office and the reassurance of a trusted other person. But why do some people take a risk and trust the therapist, even though they have been badly hurt in their earliest trusting relationships? And why do other people find it impossible to take a chance and trust again? A total mystery. Well, whatever the answer may be, the trusting bond is simply not happening here today.

"You don't look forward to coming here?"

He shakes his head in the negative. "Like I've said before, I don't see the point."

"So you don't look forward to coming here."

"Right. I feel the same way as if I'm going into a meeting I don't want to go to. Apprehensive. Anxious." This surprises me a bit. He doesn't look anxious. He looks bored and uninterested.

"Oh. Anxious. Apprehensive. About what?" I ask.

"I don't know. It's the unknown. I don't like the unknown. I'm not in control, that's the feeling. It's like a work meeting where I feel like I'm going to be pinned up against the wall about something. Or my boss is going to yell at me. Or ask me to do something that I know I don't want to do."

"Do you feel that I pin you against the wall or ask you to do things you don't want to do?"

"Sometimes," he says.

"How so?"

"I don't know." He pauses briefly, and then shifts topics. "You know, I haven't thought about my parents all week."

Yes, it is time that I just admit defeat already. This man is not interested in doing psychotherapy. He does not think about our sessions once he goes out the door, and he does not want to come back the following week to continue. Indeed, what is the point?

"What do you make of that?" I ask.

"I was busy." A hint of defiance, perhaps? He seems to be saying, *I refuse to think about my parents, and you can't force me!*

I have an urge to bring things to a head and ask him if he wants to continue therapy or just quit now, but something stops me. I do not know if I am just being stubborn and refusing to give up, or if there is something about him that keeps me interested. We sit for a moment in silence as I try to gather my thoughts and move forward. He looks quite hopeless. *Hopeless.* Yes, he looks totally hopeless. "I think you're afraid to hope," I say.

Surprisingly, he nods agreement. "Okay. I'll agree with that." I am always surprised at how quickly he can shift from conflict to cooperation.

"I think you're afraid to look at the fact that we have had a couple of good sessions, as well as a few frustrating ones. You're afraid to look at those two sessions and say, *This could really go someplace. There's hope for me. I could get better if I keep doing this.*" I am a bit surprised to hear myself still trying to engage him in therapy.

"That sounds like me."

"Yeah. So why are you so afraid to have a little hope?"

"Because I don't want to be disappointed again." The fear of disappointment again. Well, this is why it is so hard to give up on him. Every now and then, he opens the door a crack and reveals a bit of himself.

"That's a quick answer and a good one," I say. "That's a good one. That fits."

"I've been there before. I've gotten my hopes up before."

"You're so afraid even to hope that I could help you. You're afraid to be disappointed. So you shut your hopes down and discount anything good that happens here, which gets you exactly what you don't want. You're stuck in this endless suffering, wishing you were an old man ready to die."

"Right." He nods quietly, looking a bit sad. "I do wish I were old already. I don't much like myself."

"I know you've got some very negative feelings about yourself."

"Yeah. I hate myself. I would not be my friend. Other people would be surprised. My wife says that our friends would be astonished if they knew that I feel this way."

"Well, maybe this is what has been blocking all these therapy trials. That you hate yourself."

"Right," he says.

"Maybe you just brought up a really key point. If you hate yourself, then you wouldn't want to give yourself too much pleasure and relief."

"I want to get away from that person."

"You want to get away from yourself. Maybe that's a key point."

"Yeah." He nods sadly. It is not just my stubborn refusal to give up; there is something about him that draws me in. I want to help him. Most of the time, I am pretty sure that I *cannot* help him, but there is something about him that makes it hard to give up.

He is looking at me now, and he looks more open, more innocent than usual. "But I'm here," he adds.

"Yes, you are here. Which is kind of remarkable, if you think about it. Your wife called to make the first appointment, and you say that you don't like coming here. But you do come."

"Yeah. Well, should I wait till I'm seventy?" He even laughs a bit, a rare event for him.

"I hope not."

He jokes about coming to therapy at the age of seventy. He talks about his past trials of therapy and medications. As we talk, I get the impression that he is more open and receptive than usual. We are not talking about painful memories or difficult emotions, but I get the sense that he is more receptive toward me. I need to find out what is going on.

"How do you feel right now? Emotionally."

"I feel relaxed." He is smiling a bit.

"You look relaxed. And you look. … I don't know if I'm accurate in saying this, but you look more connected to me. And less like you're in the mode of fighting me off. In other sessions, I'd say something and you'd say, *I already knew that.* You know, you got sarcastic. Right now, you look friendlier, more relaxed, and more connected. Do you feel that way?"

"Yeah. I do," he admits.

"So what is it that's allowing you to feel more connected to me?"

"I don't know what causes this. This is the up-and-down of my moods that I struggle with all the time."

I find his answer completely unsatisfying. There is something going on between us, and I need to understand it. Never mind his moods, or what happened when he was twelve years old; something in the here-and-now relationship has changed. "But I'm not sure it's just you," I say. "There are two people in this room. Maybe I'm doing something that's allowing you to relax more."

"You're communicating more with me," he says. "We're talking."

"We're talking," I repeat. "But we talk at every session."

"Well, true. But maybe I just wasn't in the right mood."

"I was talking last week," I say, "and none of my ideas seemed acceptable to you."

"Yeah, I know." He shrugs.

"I'd say something and you'd say *No*, or you'd say *Yes, but I knew that.* Or I'd say something about you resisting the process, and you'd say *Well, that's obvious!*"

"Well, but I'm here, and that is a big step." He is actually smiling at me.

"Yes, it is a big step."

"It's the opening of the door, right? I might be resisting in here sometimes, but it would be a lot easier to resist out there." He points to the door.

"And not come."

"Right. I could just say that I won't come to therapy."

"But I wonder if you're just in a better mood right now, or if the way I'm talking to you feels different. And allows you to open up a little."

"I think it has everything to do with me. My moods just go up and down."

"But again, I want to look at myself too. Maybe sometimes I'm talking to you in a way that triggers the bristly defense and the sarcasm. And maybe sometimes I talk to you in a way that allows you to open up. I don't know."

He thinks for a minute. "Well, I guess one of the differences is … you started talking to me today. You asked me how I felt about last session. And you asked me what's my fear of coming in here."

"Yes. So?"

"So there was a bit of conversation," he says. "More exploratory. A discovery thing. As opposed to … sometimes you just wait for me to initiate."

"Right," I say. "I try to let you start."

"And I don't know what to initiate."

"Oh. Got it."

"And I sit here feeling lost. I don't know what you want me to say. It's kind of like this is a quiz with the teacher. What's the right answer? I don't know."

"Maybe that makes you angry," I say.

"Yeah, that makes me angry, sure."

"Well, that's very interesting. This is why I asked, because there are two of us in the room, and I assume that some things I say help, and some things I say don't help. So for me to sit here and say, *Start wherever you want*, that makes you mad." I begin to understand now: This is transference! I have to point out the transference to him.

"Yeah, it makes me mad because I don't know where to start."

I think I see where this is coming from, and I need to offer him an interpretation so he sees it too. "I wonder if it makes you feel like I'm not giving you support, either. Like you didn't get from your dad …"

"Yeah."

"… and you didn't get enough from your mom. So here I am saying, *Go ahead*."

He is looking directly at me, and he leans forward to make his point. "You know what happens when you start the session by just sitting quietly? You're just another person waiting for me to do something. On my own."

"Oh." Oh! This is transference! Just as Freud said in his books. Tom has transferred onto me his experiences of the past, and he expects me to behave the way his parents behaved toward him. His father died and left him alone; his mother took to her bed depressed and left him to fend for himself. So when I sit quietly at the beginning of the session, he feels that I am repeating what they did, waiting for him to function on his own, totally without support or encouragement from others.

But who would have thought that he had some transference feelings about me? I did not think that he was connected enough to have *any* thoughts about me. But that is foolish, of course. His emotional distancing left me with the sense that nothing I do matters to him. But how could it *not* matter? I have invited him to explore his deepest feelings about his parents, and we have done this several times. How could I believe that he has no connection with me at all?

I wonder about his explanation of our improving alliance, though. Is it really just because I asked a few more questions at the beginning of the hour? I am not really sure that I have been so much more active today. Perhaps it was something else in one of our sessions, something that made him see that I actually want to help him. Maybe he just feels better today because he senses that I am not giving up on him. Whatever it is, I hope it will allow him to stop viewing me through the distorted lens of his transference expectations, and see me in a more realistic light. Now perhaps we can make some steady progress. And perhaps I can strengthen our alliance a bit.

"So what are your impressions of me so far?" I ask.

His answer is slow and halting. "I don't know … I'm not … I'm not getting anything …" Not surprisingly, the question stumps him. He simply has no answer.

"Maybe you don't *let* yourself get anything."

"Right. That sounds right," he says.

"We've been sitting together for a while, and we all have first impressions of other people. Even if you see someone on a train for a minute, there is still a first impression."

"Um-hmm." He nods.

"Maybe this is one of the ways you disconnect from people. You don't actually let yourself register your impressions of them."

"Yeah."

He is not fighting me about this, so I will press my case. "So what are your impressions of me?" There is a long pause. "You already have some. It's impossible that you have no impressions of me." We sit together in silence for a long minute or two. This is a very confrontational approach that I am taking, of course, but he seems to be tolerating it. Besides, I doubt that we will make any progress unless I address his barriers against human connectedness. I think many a therapy case has failed because the therapist tried to help the patient with relationship problems, but never dealt with the actual here-and-now relationship in the room.

"Impressions of you?" he asks. "I don't know if I have any. Except that you're direct. Insistent. Insistent to the point of being *brutal.*" He smiles a bit saying this, but that last word certainly says something about his experience of other people.

"Brutal?"

"Yeah. That's what comes up. And then, just even thinking about having to say my impressions of you is making me feel pretty annoyed."

"Oh really?"

"Yeah."

"And what do you suppose that's about?" I ask. Another pause. Interestingly, he does not look terribly annoyed. And he is able to say that he feels annoyed without acting it out by becoming rude and impatient. We are still working together, even if my questions are a bit irritating to him. I press forward. "You have some negative impressions of me?"

"Not really."

"Positive impressions?"

He makes no answer to this. I am not sure if he is thinking or just stalling. "I just don't even *want* to have thoughts about you. I'll tell you this: I never thought much about my other therapists. They were there to do a job, and they did it, and that's that."

"So you didn't think about your therapists, even after long periods of time in therapy with them."

"Right."

"You didn't let yourself reflect on what these people meant to you, or what your impressions of them were …"

"Yeah. Right."

… or what your feelings were about them."

"Yes."

"And we already have the same issue here. Somehow you are excluding me from your mind."

"Well, you're implying that this is supposed to be a relationship. I don't have many of those. Not *real* relationships."

"But then much of the time here, we're not really connecting. It's been a bit better today because I asked you more questions at the beginning of the session, but generally you're not really letting me have a place in your brain where you would think about me after the session. You've already got me excluded."

"Yeah," he says.

"This worries me a bit. How can I be helpful under those circumstances?"

"Well, this is what I'm like. It's just the way I am."

"I see this, but I'm challenging you."

"Okay." He still seems to be tolerating my approach.

"I suppose this is the part that you call 'brutal.' I'm challenging you to look at this. If you shut me out entirely, and you never let yourself reflect on who is sitting in front of you, I can't see how I'm going to be very helpful to you. And then you are destined to live as you are, even though you say that you are terribly unhappy with your life right now. But I don't see how I could help you change your life if I don't exist in your mind."

No answer. He sits looking at me. I cannot tell if my words are having an effect or not.

"If you're shutting me out so thoroughly, I can't imagine how I could be of help."

He says nothing and looks to one side. A bit wistful, perhaps?

"Where are you right now?" I ask. "You look thoughtful."

"I'm just thinking that I don't ..." His voice trails off.

"Your eyes change," I say.

"Hmm?"

"Your eyes change a little bit."

"Change? How?"

"Do you have feelings coming up?" I ask.

"Yeah."

"You do?"

"Yeah."

"Can we look at those feelings?"

"Well, just sadness."

"*Just* sadness," I repeat.

"Yeah."

"I thought there was a sad look in your eyes. You looked reflective, as if you suddenly looked inside."

"Yeah. And what I get when I look inside ..." He falters here, trying to put his thoughts into words. "This thing that people call connection or relationship or whatever . ... I don't understand it.... I don't really know what it's like to .... depend on another person."

"And that makes you sad?"

"Yeah." And he really looks sad. We sit together for a short while. I try to encourage him to allow himself the feeling of sadness, but I can see that the experience is short-lived. It does not take long for him to bottle it up again. But it was there, and it was genuine.

We talk for a while about our handful of sessions so far. I try to point out to him his tendency to open up his emotions briefly and then close up again. If he continues to do this, he will not get any lasting relief, and he will inevitably conclude that this emotional stuff is both painful and useless.

"You don't quite let yourself finish a topic emotionally," I say. "You don't really let the feelings flow and understand what a person means to you—your wife, your son, your past therapists—and complete the discussion about that issue."

"Yeah, but I got emotional the other night. I went to my son's basketball game. For me, you know, emotional is two seconds." He smiles. How nice that he can make a joke about it now. And he does it without launching into a vitriolic attack upon himself. "My son has always played basketball, and we have always gone to his games. Now he's a senior in high school." He starts to give me too many unnecessary details about the basketball team. I am not sure if this is another defense against getting to the heart of the matter, or if he just the kind of person who is compelled to add all the details to a story. Either way, he quickly gets back to the point. "I started to get upset. No, not upset. I started to get *emotional.*" I think he gets it. I think he is beginning to understand the difference between emotions of expansion and emotions of contraction, calling the latter by the term *upset.* "My wife and I were sitting there in the bleachers with other parents. So I was just sitting there and I leaned over and I said, *I remember bringing him to basketball in fourth grade.* And now it's like, you know, it's almost done. I was there years ago when he started playing. And now here he is, a senior on the court. This is the last season we're going to see."

"So see if you can let yourself have your feelings right now, and not talk over them."

"I miss it! I don't get that back." He turns quiet now, sad and pensive. "He's our oldest child. And we don't get to do it again."

"When he goes to college next fall, it's over."

"Yeah. It's November already. College will come fast now, and that part will be over."

"The child-rearing years will be over," I say.

"Right."

"Before you know it, you'll be dropping him off at college next fall."

"Oh, that's not going to be fun. I'm going to be a mess, for sure." He reaches for a tissue, becoming a "mess" right now. "But it's exciting for him. And he doesn't see this." He points to his eyes and the tissue. "He doesn't feel this way. Kids don't."

"No. But you do. Do you have more feelings?"

"This whole basketball thing. It's just ..."

"What about it? It really meant something to you, obviously."

"Yeah! Well, I played basketball when I was a kid." His voice quivers with this.

"Oh, I didn't know that."

"Yeah, I think he picked basketball because it's something that I did."

"So, what was so intense about that basketball game?"

"I don't know. It's just the thought of fleeting childhood." He is tearful again. "I wanted ... I don't know what I wanted. ... I mean, I've been a part of his life.... I've been there for everything. Maybe I miss my *own* childhood. I don't know."

"Oh!"

"Because I look back and I remember ..."

"So basketball is ending for him, childhood is ending, and there's a sense of how you lost your childhood."

"Yeah. I just don't know how to process this."

"What do you mean, process?"

"I don't know. He's getting older. I don't really want him to move out. I like having him there."

"So, you don't know how to let him go."

"Yeah. I guess that's it."

It seems that he is actually in therapy now. I suppose we will have our tough moments, but I think we have gotten past a huge barrier. As we talk, I get the sense that he has allowed me to enter the world of his private thoughts, and I doubt that he will turn back now that he has begun to have the experience of letting another person in. I may be wrong, but I do not think he will choose to go back to the isolated fortress he has been living in.

It occurs to me that his isolation is largely related to his emotional reserve. How could anyone get close to him if they can never figure out what he feels about anything? Why would anyone offer sympathy if they have no idea that he is feeling sad? Emotion is such a powerful means of communication, and when he blocks it, he finds himself essentially cut off from the rest of the world. However, when he speaks emotionally about his son, I feel more connected to him. I can see why I did not want to give up on him. He has been isolated and depressed, but it is clear that he pushed himself beyond his depression to be the best father he could be. He went to his son's games. He went to parent-teacher conferences at the school. He knows the names of his son's friends. He has worked hard to be engaged as a father.

After talking for a while about the details of his relationship with his son, he falls silent for a minute or two.

"I don't know what I'm feeling." He looks very close to tears again.

"Right now?"

"Yeah."

"Well, just sit with it and you'll see if—"

"I don't know if I'm sad about my own life ... or the anticipation of him leaving."

"Or both," I suggest. "It's like we're in a movie theatre. On one side of the screen, we see you and your son. On the other side, we see you as a child with your parents. We are looking at both images. Childhood coming to an end, but in different ways. One from a death, and one from a great kid going to college."

"Yeah." He nods agreement.

So at the moment, the process of dynamic psychotherapy for this man demands of him that he must look back at painful memories of the past, look at the current reality of his life, and simultaneously maintain the connection to me in the safety of the present moment. It occurs to me now that it is not enough just to talk about these relationships; he must live in all three realms. He must see and experience the parallel themes of past and current life, while also having the sense of connection to me so that I can guide him through the process. And he seems to be doing it all quite well at the moment.

"You know," he adds, "my father never saw that. Never saw me go through school. Never saw me graduate from college."

"He wasn't there cheering you on."

"And I hope he would have."

"Not sure?" I ask.

"I don't know. Knowing the little that I know about him, I don't know how supportive he would have been. Had he never died, had he not died when I was so young, I don't know if he would have been a good father." He talks about his father, probably more than he has ever talked about his father. Not only the father who yelled at him and hit him, but also the father who put up a basketball net on the garage and showed him how to dribble the ball; the father who died after the son wished him dead; the imagined father, the longed-for father, the father who should have been. When he is done, we both sit quietly for a minute or two.

I ask him how he feels about the session.

"Okay, I guess. I guess it's all right." He looks a bit skeptical. "It has never served me well to dwell on the past, even though everything I am today is all history. It's how I got here." One would think he had read Freud, who taught us that our past has an enormous effect on our present. I think Tom is starting to understand that looking at his history might be helpful.

"Well, maybe dwelling on the past might actually help you. I suspect that you were dwelling on your mistakes of the past, rather than the full picture of what happened to you in the past. Maybe the kind of discussion that we had today could help you." And maybe we are building a therapeutic alliance here today. *Therapeutic alliance*: I have heard it defined as the sharing of goals, tasks, and a bond. Do we share the same goals? Well sure, I suppose so; we both want him to get free of his depression. Do we agree on the same tasks? We have not agreed, until today, but I think he is beginning to see that our task consists of Freud's early challenge: remembering with emotion. He must look back and face the most emotional—the most meaningful—events of his life. Is there a bond between us? Perhaps we have made a step forward in that process today, having explored the transference distortion and cleared the air, so he can start to see me as an ally, not an enemy.

"I guess I can imagine that this might help," he says. "Maybe."

We make our next appointment, and he leaves for the day. At the door, he quietly thanks me and walks out without looking at me. But I am pretty sure that he will return next week.

Freud's Study

Etching of Freud by Max Pollak

11. Doubt and Disillusionment

*A*t the door to the consulting room, Gretchen knocks gently as always, but today she opens the door without waiting for a response. She nods to me, and I enter an empty room with the shy girl just behind me. I am stamping my feet, both to shake off the snow and to bring some feeling back into my toes after walking in the bitter cold weather outside. There is a tall wood stove made of porcelain at the foot of Freud's couch, a *Kachelofen*—tiled stove— and the heat it generates is a welcome relief from the February chill. But where is Freud? I give Gretchen an exaggeratedly puzzled look, but she is obviously unable to explain anything to me in words. She shrugs her shoulders, giving up on the idea of communicating with me.

"But where is the Professor? Herr Professor?" She swings her head in the direction of a doorway leading into an adjacent room.

"Oh, here you are, my American friend." Freud appears in the doorway and invites me into the other room. "Gretchen is cleaning the consulting room today, so I thought we might meet in my study." As I follow him into his study, I look back over my shoulder, and I see Gretchen leaving his consulting room. She is not cleaning there today; Freud has just decided to invite me into his study. I have been invited into the inner sanctum.

He takes his seat at a writing desk and offers me a comfortable chair. To the left of the desk is a large bank of windows. The winter sun, reflected from the snow outside, finds its way in through the glass to illuminate yet another gathering of his little antiques. They inhabit the desk itself, a small table next to the desk, and every other available bit of space in the room. As in the consulting room, there is even a glass-enclosed display case for some of the antiques, adding to the museum atmosphere of the place.

And there are books, of course, just as there are books in his consulting room. Row after row of handsome, hardbound books sitting on his shelves. The titles that strike my eye reveal a reader who was interested in far more than psychology. I see an English language copy of *Diseases of the Nervous System*, no doubt from his early years as a neuropathologist, and some psychological volumes, to be sure. But I also see a book about Leonardo DaVinci, one called *The Riddle of the Sphinx*, and one simply called *Paris*, the title writ in large bold letters. Goethe's works are given a place in the collection, as well as *An Outline of History*. It seems that Freud was interested in everything, absolutely everything.

On the desk in front of him, there is a sheaf of papers that could only be a book in progress. The papers are much larger than our standard 8 ½ by 11-inch size. They are of a more generous cut, several inches added in both width and length. There is some writing on the top sheet, but there are no preprinted lines on the sheets, nothing that could constrain the size of the writer's pen strokes or the size of his ideas. It is less a sheet of paper than an unlined canvas for the intellectual arts. Yes, this must be one of his manuscripts in progress, an idea he is working on.

Books and ideas. Ideas and books. At this moment, it seems perfectly obvious to me that there is nothing else needed to sustain life, and nothing else truly worth living for. Such is the intellectual life, and I am refreshing myself at one of its most hallowed wellsprings. To me, this study is holy ground, even more inspiring than the consulting room with its famous couch. This desk is where he sat, night after night, wrestling with his theories and putting them on paper. This is where he tried to make sense of the outwardly meaningless symptoms of his patients. I have been admitted into his rarefied world of books and ideas, the kind of world that has always been a refuge for me from the noisy chaos of human behavior outside.

"How are you today, my friend?" Freud is in a particularly good mood. He pushes the stack of books farther back on his desk, as if he is clearing the space for our work this afternoon.

"Fine, Professor, and how are you?" I am surprised to see the photo of Lou von Salomé sitting on his desk. Apparently, he has moved it from the consulting room. What was the connection between these two intellectual souls? I know from her letters that she would visit with Freud and talk about psychoanalytic theory. I would love to be able to sit here and listen to one of those conversations. Did he find someone who understood him better than his other colleagues did? Did she make the emotional connection here that she could not make with other men? Not far from Lou's photo is the figure of Athena, Freud's favorite antique statue. Athena, goddess of reason and intellect, goddess of literature and the arts. He has his human intellectual companion and his divine Olympian Muse, and both are close at hand.

"Some tea?" he asks. He is looking at me with a curious look. There is the customary pot of tea already waiting, and I accept his offer to serve myself. I can sense that he is watching me, studying me. I engage him in a bit of small talk: the cold weather in Vienna, the difference in men's clothing between his era and mine. My attention is drawn—not for the first time—to the bow tie he wears, a black bow tie worn differently than in my era. The points of his white shirt collar are folded down over the tie, covering the top half of it. The outer edges of the tie are concealed beneath his "waistcoat"—his vest—so only the center of the tie is visible. A perfect model for the Freudian mind: partly visible, partly hidden from view.

"You look like there is something bothering you," he says.

"No, I'm really quite fine. It's good to see you, Professor." I know he does not believe me, but I do not really want to get into the little nagging doubts that have been in my head this morning. I would much rather talk about my recent sessions with Tom. "My case is moving along very well now. And you were right about transference." I explain what happened with Tom, and how he had seen me as just another person who was not supportive of him.

Freud smiles. "Transference. If you miss it, it becomes your greatest adversary. If you see it and address it, it becomes your greatest ally in the analysis."

"Yes, I can see that now. Ever since that session, we are progressing more steadily. Psychotherapy is not easy for him, and he still gets resistant at times, but we are moving along. He is starting to grieve over his losses. He even came in the other day and said that he didn't ruin his mother's life. So his entire understanding of his life story is changing. And the turning point was our discussion about transference."

"Wonderful, wonderful," Freud says, pouring himself a cup of tea. "I suppose that in your day everyone knows about transference, so there is less chance that it is ignored."

"Well, that may be true among us dynamic psychotherapists, but there are other models of treatment that do not take transference into account at all."

"Really? What do they do instead?" he asks.

"Well, many patients receive medications for common problems like anxiety and depression. I prescribe them myself."

"Medications? Instead of helping the patient to explore his psychological life, you give him medications? And what is the underlying rationale for that?"

"The theory is that anxiety and depression are genetic conditions. They are viewed as medical diseases, just like diabetes is a disease." I have to explain genes and genetics to Freud. He listens carefully, and I can see him becoming increasingly skeptical and disapproving.

"So your colleagues say that there is something wrong with the 'genes' of all their patients? But this is just like the *degeneracy* theory of nineteenth-century France. In those days, everyone with hysteria was thought to be suffering from a constitutional degeneracy, as if they had no lives, as if actual experience has no effect on a person's psychological health. The entire problem was simply due to a flaw in the patient's inborn constitution. I'm afraid that your colleagues are turning the clock back to a theory that was soundly rejected at the end of the nineteenth century." Freud is shaking his head in disapproval.

I am ambivalent in my reactions to his comments. On the one hand, I agree with him. The latest research on emotional problems does not support a simple genetic explanation. Instead, it shows that some people are more prone to anxiety or depression *if* they are exposed to a stressor, but somehow these findings have been oversimplified and misrepresented to the public. Only the genetic contribution to the problem seems to be discussed in the media. On the other hand, I feel obliged to defend myself and my generation of mental health clinicians.

"The medicines do help some people, Professor. I have used them with Tom, although I am tapering him off the meds now. And to be fair, I'm sure that the genetic element is more prominent is some cases. In others, there may be depression due to a neurological illness or a head injury, and certainly the medications might be more helpful than psychotherapy for them."

"Helping people is fine," he says, "but we need to have an intelligent theory to guide our practice."

"Yes, of course," I say.

Freud is up and standing by his bookshelves. Not finding what he wants, he disappears into the consulting room for a minute or two. When he returns, he has one of his books in hand. He has the stern look that he gets when he thinks that my contemporaries have dismissed his work. He reads aloud from his book.

"Transferences ... *replace some earlier person by the person of the physician....To put it another way, a whole series of psychological experiences is revived, not as belonging to the past, but as applying to the person of the physician at the present moment.* You see, the patient looks at the physician and imagines that he is in the same unhappy situation that he experienced in the past. He expects the physician to mistreat him, abandon him, or humiliate him, just as it happened so in the past. Just like your patient Tom. If we do not explore the transference in the moment, as it unfolds in the office, how are we going to help the patient? With a little pill?" He is holding his thumb and forefinger slightly apart, displaying the imaginary object of his contempt.

"You are preaching to the choir, Professor. My colleagues and I are promoting short-term dynamic psychotherapy. We are working hard to preserve your ideas, including the concept of transference."

"Well, good!" He puts his book down on the desk and takes his seat again. It seems that it only takes a sip or two of his tea—and my words of reassurance—for him to recover the good mood he was in before. I think he has finally come to see me as an ally, rather than a detractor. We talk a bit more about transference, and how he first discovered the idea. He mentions his case of Dora, which was a failed case, but the pivotal case that brought him to the concept of transference. His mention of an unsuccessful case reminds me of some troubling thoughts I had early this morning on my way to his office. During a pause in conversation, he looks at me with a bit of concern.

"I hope my comments about your medications did not offend you." I am caught off guard by his concern for my feelings. This is a relatively new element in our relationship, and I am not yet accustomed to it.

"Not at all, Professor. As I said, I too have problems with the genetic theory of my day."

Freud reaches for a cigar and spends a long moment examining it before lighting it. "But you looked troubled when you first arrived today. Something is bothering you, yes?"

"No, no, not at all. I am enjoying our visit as always." I find myself avoiding his gaze, but I know he is watching me. It is an odd talent we humans have, to know when someone is staring at us even if we are not looking in that person's direction. We can feel it. When I finally look up at him, prepared to distract him by asking another question about transference, he is indeed looking at me. He is like a hawk that has spotted something moving in the grass below, and he is not likely to take his eyes off me until he can get close enough to see what drew his attention in the first place.

"Well, to be honest with you, I do have something on my mind lately. A problem with psychotherapy."

"And what might that problem be?" he asks.

I struggle for a moment to put it into words. "Some of my patients seem to become a bit symptomatic again after the treatment ends."

"A bit symptomatic," he repeats.

He has caught me trying to minimize the problem. Clearly, I am apprehensive about exposing my vulnerable side to him. *Never mind,* I say to myself. *Maybe he can help. Tell him.*

"They relapse," I say plainly.

Freud smiles. "Did you think that all of your cases would be successful?"

"No, of course not. I realize that no therapy can be a panacea. But I have treated some cases in which the patient seems to get well, and then he returns six months later with a recurrence—a relapse—of the same symptoms. It troubles me."

"You mean the true believer is losing his faith?" he asks. I look up again to check his expression, half expecting that he is being critical. He is still smiling, though, and clearly speaking in good humor and with benign intentions. "So let us have a look and see what the problem might be. Are these particular patients more difficult in some way? Perhaps they are simply not analyzable."

I have told him many times that I am not practicing strict psychoanalysis, and I do not use the word *analyzable*. Never mind. He is trying to help me, and I need to overlook the choice of words. Besides, I can see how much he enjoys engaging himself in the pursuit of an answer. The hunt has just begun.

"No, they are wonderful patients. These people—I am just talking about a few of them, a small percentage of my practice—tend to be bright, highly motivated people who really work hard in therapy. Any therapist would be happy to have them. They seem to have a successful outcome in treatment, and then, as I said, they call me after a while and report the same symptoms. Anxiety, depression, irritability, relationship problems. I feel so puzzled when they call. But the problem is not that they are difficult patients."

"How about the analyst?" he asks. "Perhaps there is a problem with the analyst." He arches his brow and narrows his eyes, his face assuming the appearance of the stern interrogator: a courtroom lawyer or a police detective. Yet the human face is capable of conveying the most subtle nuances of emotional expression. In this case, he simultaneously gives two signals. The first message: *I am angry and aggressive and ready to attack you;* the second: *I am only pretending to be hostile; you are safe with me.* How can the facial muscles accomplish such a feat of communication? I study his features for a moment. The eyes and brow convey the threat, while the part of his face below the eyes conveys safety and kindliness. His eyes are narrowed as if to signal anger, but the skin below the eyes is relaxed, as it is when the eyes are trying to receive a smile from the mouth below. The mouth is not actually smiling, but the jaw is relaxed, not clenched in anger. Is there any other animal that can convey such a complex message? "You do not answer me, sir." He drums his fingers on his leg, feigning impatience. "Is it possible that you are having some problematic reaction to these few patients?"

"Not that I know," I say.

"Not consciously, you mean. But we shall see. Are they all men of your age who stir up competitive feelings?"

"No, not all men."

"Then perhaps they are women whom you find attractive? Many a case has foundered because the male analyst was too charmed by a young lady, and he failed to maintain the proper attitude necessary to confront the patient with the painful realities of her unconscious mind."

"No, no," I answer. "Just a mix of different ages, men and women. No particular pattern."

"Or perhaps these are patients who remind you of someone in your own past? Are you having your own transference feelings— counter-transference feelings—that are obscuring your vision?" All of these are good questions, of course, and he is only demanding of me the kind of honesty that he expected of himself. I can easily call to mind his own candor in reporting his psychoanalytic cases. It was one of the ironic complexities of his personality: in spite of his intolerance of criticism from others, he was often quite willing to criticize his own work and report his mistakes and oversights. I pause for a moment to consider my answer; I feel a responsibility to meet his standard for self-reflection.

"No, I can see no particular pattern to the patients. And I don't think I am having a reaction to them that interferes with my work."

Freud presses further. "Perhaps you are missing something. A subtle resistance in an otherwise pleasant patient who consciously wants to get well but unconsciously fights to maintain the status quo. Or perhaps these patients are making valiant efforts to look well in order to please the analyst."

Again, I take a minute to think about a few of my cases. "All good theories, Professor, but none of them quite seems to fit. I certainly miss things now and then. I realize that I'm not perfect. But I think I use the tools of dynamic psychotherapy pretty well, and these folks keep returning with the same problems. I have seen some of them for two or three rounds of therapy, and they still keep returning. It's discouraging."

"Well, then, perhaps your tools are not perfect. No such perfect tools are available to us, you know. With my psychoanalysis, I established some basic techniques. My student Willie Reich made his attempts at innovations, although I cannot condone them all. And your man Davanloo has developed some interventions that you find useful. But we always need to keep working to improve what we do." I appreciate his open attitude about the discussion, but I am still disturbed by the problem at hand. As we sit together talking about it, I realize how much it has been troubling me.

"Yes, of course," I say. "I never thought that Davanloo's ideas were the be-all and end-all of psychotherapy." Or did I? I suppose that Davanloo is part of my problem. He was so confident in his technique that he seemed to be promising a successful outcome for every patient in a short amount of time. At least, this was the intoxicating impression I had after attending his conferences. Certainly, I had moments of healthy skepticism, but I brushed them aside in my need to have an effective technique to follow. I remember sitting at one of his conferences when someone in the audience asked him how many of his patients dropped out of treatment after the first confrontational session. His answer was telling: Why would anyone drop out after he had shown the patient the psychological core of his neurotic problems? Yes, he had promised too much in his enthusiasm for his new approach, and my expectations have been a bit unrealistic.

Realizing that I have been brooding and ignoring my companion, I emerge from my ruminations to find Freud still looking at me. There is a kindly concern in his eyes instead of the playful aggression. I think he feels sorry for me. He opens his mouth to speak, but stops himself. He puts down his teacup and sits quietly for a moment, gazing toward some of his little antiques, as if he is consulting with them about whether or not to say what is on his mind. Finally, he makes his decision and looks back at me again.

"I had my doubts too, you know."

"Yes, you told me. You had doubts about whether your work would be remembered by future generations."

"No," he says seriously, "I mean I had doubts about the work itself. Sometimes I would hear reports of a former patient who was not doing well, and I would wonder about my effectiveness as an analyst. And I changed my technique a number of times. Did you think I changed because my approach was working perfectly? Not at all! I started out using hypnosis, as I was influenced by my friend Breuer's case of Anna O. But I soon found that many patients were not easily hypnotized, and I came upon the technique of free association. That was a significant advance, but far from perfect. As I continued in my career, I discovered that many patients were harboring an invisible opposition to getting well, and this *resistance* had to be addressed. Then I discovered the problems that I labeled as *transference*, and this too demanded changes in our technical approach. I had many moments of doubt along the way."

"Yes, I suppose I have never appreciated how hard it must have been for you. I remember when I was a resident and I read your first book, the one you wrote with Breuer, and I only imagined how exciting it must have been to make those early discoveries."

Now it is Freud who looks a bit distant and brooding, as I must have looked at the beginning of this discussion. "There was trouble with Breuer's case too," he says.

"Anna O.?"

"Yes, yes. Anna O."

"What kind of trouble?" I ask.

He draws in a long breath and lets it out slowly, deliberately. He shifts his position is his chair, as if he is about to stand up, but then he settles back into his seat. "In the years following her treatment with Breuer, the patient he called Anna O. did not fare so well. She had, as you put it, a relapse. His successful outcome was short-lived, you see."

"I never knew about this aspect of her story, Professor, but that is just one case."

"Just one case?" He looks a bit agitated. "It was a pivotal case, a case that influenced my entire career."

In my memory, I see the old photo of Dr. Breuer, his kind, patient eyes looking directly at the camera. I suppose I feel a bit sorry for Breuer, as Freud feels sorry for me.

"Of course," I say. "I realize that the case was an important one. But she did get some relief from that treatment, even if the gains did not last over time. And besides, Breuer discovered some very important principles that helped you build your system of psychoanalysis."

"Nonetheless, it was a failed case." Freud's mood is darkening rapidly. A few minutes ago, he was trying to help me with my professional struggles, but now he seems to be slipping into his own unhappy ruminations. Now he stands up as if to fetch another book, but then sits back down. Maybe he realizes that there is no book that will help him now. He suddenly looks tired and defeated. "I even had my doubts about Charcot."

"Charcot?" I exclaim. At that moment, Gretchen quietly appears in the doorway, presumably to check if we need anything. She tidies up the tea service on a small table, taking care not to disturb the little antique figures that sit there. Freud speaks to her briefly and then sits silently. She turns to leave, but then she notices that one corner of the Oriental rug on the floor has been kicked up upon itself. She pauses to bend down and straighten it. It is clear that he will not speak until she leaves, as if he dare not continue the subject in front of Gretchen, who speaks no English.

"There were rumors," he says very quietly. "I heard them after I had studied with him in Paris and returned home to Vienna. I tried not to pay any attention. People were saying it was all a fraud."

"Charcot was a fraud?" I am startled. Charcot, the mesmerizing showman-neurologist-hypnotist-teacher? After listening to Freud talk about him during our discussions, I have come to see Charcot through his eyes, as a hero of mythical proportions in the history of medicine. The Napoleon of the Neuroses, as he was called. In my mind, listening to one of Charcot's morning lectures must have been like listening to Mozart performing at the Hofberg Palace here in Vienna.

"No, not him," Freud says. "No one accused Charcot of being a fraud. It was about his patients. It was rumored that some of the female patients at the Salpêtrière Hospital were intentionally acting out the symptoms he lectured about. I even heard that some of his students were coaching these women on how to display the symptoms of hysteria. Why in the world would his own students do such a detestable thing?"

"So that doesn't make Charcot a fraud," I say.

"No, but it makes him look like a fool. He had described four stages of hysteria, but what if these unethical students were simply training the patients to put on a good show and imitate these stages? What would this say about the great Charcot?"

"Well, that would be embarrassing, of course, but it would not detract from his overall greatness and his other contributions to neurology. Besides, is there any solid evidence to support these rumors?"

Freud is starting to look more annoyed and irritable. He clenches his jaw tightly. "Have you ever heard colleagues talk about the four stages of hysteria?" he asks.

"Well, no, but we never use the word *hysteria* at all anymore."

He looks impatient, determined to make his case, as painful as it is for him. "But you know what I am asking. Whatever word you choose, did you ever see the four stages?"

"No. I never saw such a thing," I say.

"Nor did I, except for my time with Charcot. There are no such stages of hysteria! They never existed! It was all a sham!" Now he does stand up to pace the room. He picks up the statue of Athena, his literary Muse, his inspiration in battle. Her left arm is raised over her head, her hand empty of the spear that she originally carried. She is eternally ready for battle, but the ravages of time have deprived her of her weapon. "I was inspired by two mentors early in my career: Breuer and Charcot. Breuer's famous case turned out to be a failure. Charcot was deceived. So these are the twin pillars of psychoanalysis: a failed case and a phony hysteria. Quite a foundation, yes?"

I try to comfort him. "But even if Charcot was deceived, that is not what we should remember. We should remember the good in him. He was still making a heroic effort to understand hysteria. You told me that he was called the Napoleon of the Neuroses. These rumors cannot change the fact that he was a brilliant speaker. And he still contributed to our understanding of multiple sclerosis and other neurological diseases."

Freud pauses in his pacing and shrugs. Here we are, mired in the heavy mud of doubt and disillusionment, taking turns trying unsuccessfully to pull the other out of it. My attempt to reassure him has obviously done nothing for either one of us. "You are right, of course," he says, but without any enthusiasm. I feel sad and disturbed by what I am hearing. I want him to have Charcot for his hero, just as I want Freud to be *my* hero. Who else would serve that purpose in my day? Who are the heroes of my era? Narcissistic movie stars? Sports celebrities who abuse drugs to win their competitions? Maybe we have no heroes. Maybe I am living in an empty culture. But such negative thoughts I am having! It seems that one depressing thought just leads to another.

I get up to pour myself more tea, just to give myself something to do. I have no real desire for another cup of tea, but I cannot sit there feeling so gloomy any longer. I place the tea strainer over my cup and start pouring, watching the bits of tea leaves that stay back in the strainer. At first, I am barely paying any attention to what I am doing, still trying to digest the disconcerting news about Breuer and Charcot. By the time I have finished pouring, though, my attention has shifted to the tea set in front of me. Compared to our timesaving, efficient twenty-first-century tea bag, this fin-de-siècle tea set in Vienna seems to counsel leisure and quiet contemplation. The tea strainer itself is a work of art: a tiny silver bowl with a perforated bottom, balanced on the brim of my cup by three delicate silver struts, the metalwork structure complemented with a handle made of ivory. Just holding the handle leads me to imagine the slow, deliberate pace of the craftsman who carved it.

Have a cup of tea with me. The words drift into my mind. *Come sit down and have a cup of tea with me.* They are my mother's words that I am hearing, and I recognize them as a memory of my childhood. I am hearing the words as a teenager, but I am sure that this invitation was offered—and accepted—many times, at many ages. My mother is sitting down at the kitchen table on a Saturday afternoon, perhaps on a cold winter's day like this one, and she invites me to sit down and have a chat with her. It is a lovely memory, and it quickly lifts my spirits.

"You should remember the good in Charcot," I repeat to Freud, but this time I say it with more conviction. "There is good and bad in everybody. You should choose to remember the good." Freud stops pacing in the middle of the room and looks at me. I can see that he senses the shift in my attitude. *Come sit with me. The tea is ready.* "Maybe this would be good advice for our patients, too," I add. "Maybe they should learn to remember the good in their past, as well as remembering and working through the bad memories." I return to my seat. The tea is stronger now, having sat longer in the pot, and I have added more milk and sugar to balance the strong flavor. It tastes better than the first cup I had, better than tea has tasted to me in quite a while. The extra sweetness reminds me of the tea I drank with my mother when I was young, because I would use more milk and sugar as a boy. "In fact," I continue, "I wonder how often we even ask our patients about good memories from childhood. I suspect it is a rare event in therapy, but certainly most of us have had good experiences as well as bad ones. It is certainly true in my life. Maybe this is what I should do with my relapsing patients. Maybe I should ask them about positive memories."

Freud gives me a look that is both curious and skeptical. "You think you will cure these returning patients by asking them about pleasant memories? I think that would only be a nice distraction from the therapeutic work, with no real benefit to them."

"Perhaps," I say. "Perhaps." *Come sit down with me. Come talk to me.* I can see the old kitchen table with two teacups and two saucers set out. There is my mother, a quiet, gentle soul, but a woman who was generally a bit distant. Now she looks warmer and more engaged. My thoughts then jump inexplicably to images of my office and the faces of patients I have treated. It feels as though my mind is trying to remember something from my office, trying to make a connection. "But perhaps it might be helpful in some way. After all, with these returning patients, I have certainly worked with them on resolving their negative memories. Maybe positive ones would help somehow."

"You have some evidence for this?" Freud asks. "Or are you just speculating?"

"I know I must have heard patients mention positive memories in passing, but I can't say that it ever helped any of them definitively. At least, not that I can remember." On the small table just to the right of Freud's desk, there is a figure of an old Chinese man, a scholar perhaps, or maybe a spiritual sage. He looks wise and peaceful. I look at him for a moment, and then I think back to my office and I can see a patient: the engineer sitting across from me, reminiscing about being with his mother in church. "But wait," I say to Freud. "Maybe there was a time when a positive memory helped. Let me tell you about a patient I saw several years ago.

"It happened at the end of a lengthy treatment, after an engineer and I had spent many sessions talking about his mother's alcohol problem and how it had left him with a burdensome legacy of chronic anxiety and relationship problems. Once we got past his initial defenses, we discovered that his mind was filled with terrible memories of his mother

Freud's Chinese Sage

getting drunk. Every time there was a family reunion or any type of social gathering at their home, she would drink too much. Her speech would become slurred, and she would say embarrassing things. More than once, she stumbled or fell down right in front of family and friends. His father, a successful businessman and a prominent member of local community organizations, would make preposterous excuses for his wife: she was just tired, or she had a migraine headache. When Mother was not drinking, she was tense, anxious, and distant from everyone around her, including her youngest son, my patient.

"The engineer and I talked about what it was like to grow up with his mother's alcoholism and his father's excuses. He felt like his family life had been a lie, a myth of the happy, thriving upper-middle-class family. As a boy, he had naturally tried to believe in the lie that his father had invented, but the sense of pretense had plagued him throughout his adult life. In fact, he had actually been deceptive in numerous ways that he had never before understood. He didn't tell his wife about some of his financial investments, even though she was listed as a beneficiary of each investment. He lied to the partners in his engineering firm about where he was taking his family on vacation. He always needed to hide something, lest people find out who he really was. Not surprisingly, he just never felt that he could connect well with other people. Gradually, he understood himself better and confronted the painful feelings about his parents. His own anxiety diminished, and he began to feel more relaxed in his relationships with others.

"He came in one day for his session and spoke about how much better he was feeling. After saying this, he just fell silent and sat gazing at me. It was a bit unnerving at first, as this was one of the first patients I treated after I graduated my residency, and I wasn't sure what to do. I had a growing repertoire of things to say in reply to patients' words, but what could I say in response to silence? He just continued to look at me. He seemed unusually calm, and his gaze was more open compared to the fleeting, guarded glances of our earlier sessions. At a loss for anything else to say, I simply mentioned that I noticed he was quieter than usual. And

I commented on the fact that he was looking at me. He nodded agreement and kept looking at me in silence for another minute or two.

"Finally he spoke. He told me that it was almost a spiritual feeling he was having, just looking at me. I was not surprised by his remark. In that moment, he seemed to have transcended his normal persona, and he seemed like your little Chinese sage here, a spiritually evolved person who had made peace with his Universe.

"It was then that he told me about a memory of his mother. They were sitting together in church. It was the one place where he could see her looking calm and composed, instead of tense and apprehensive, or drunk and foolish. She loved going to church, and he loved sitting there next to her. He could finally feel connected to her, and he reported the same feeling of connection while gazing at me."

"And then?" Freud asks.

"That's the whole story. He remembered those times of sitting with his mother in church. After another session or two, he said he felt no further need for treatment and he left therapy."

"And you think that this memory helped him?"

"I do. I'm not sure that I can explain *how* it helped, but I know it helped. It helped him to remember the good." *And my mother and I drank tea together*, I think to myself, *so I remember the good in her, too.* Freud has been listening to my story from where he stands in the middle of the room. Now he comes back and takes his seat, looking deep in thought. He repositions his Athena and straightens up the stack of large writing sheets. *And this is what I will take with me from our meetings, Professor. I will remember the good about you.*

12. "Yesterday"

"*I* know I asked you this last session, Gabby, but I want to ask again: Do you have any *positive* memories of your mother?"

"No, I really don't think so," she says. "I thought about your question during the week, but there wasn't really much positive about her."

"Nothing? Not a single positive memory?"

"Not really."

I suppose I should just accept her answer and proceed to do another round of dynamic psychotherapy, but we have done this three times already, over a period of several years. At the end of each round of therapy, she reports that her anxiety is virtually gone, and she leaves the office feeling relaxed, happy, and optimistic about her future. After several months go by, she comes back. She always comes back, and always with the same complaint of anxiety and an occasional panic attack. Each time, she tells me that she is worried again—worried about her grown children, worried about money, worried that she is not doing a good job as an English professor, worried about everything.

She has been living with this anxiety for most of her fifty years, and I cannot seem to provide her with a lasting solution for it. Sometimes I wonder why she keeps coming back to see me. Maybe she should see another therapist, someone who knows how to fix her problem once and for all. But I am also glad that she comes back. In spite of a family background that might easily have made her a mean-spirited person, she is immensely likable. She has a quick intellect and a lively sense of humor. In fact, she has all the ingredients that occasionally come together in just the right proportions to create the inexplicable quality that we call "charisma."

Also, I am glad to have another opportunity to search for a solution to her problems. Maybe I can learn something from another trial of therapy with her, and I know I can count on her to help with the process. In addition to being intelligent in the field of English literature, she is also "psychologically minded." She can think about the workings of her own mind and the minds of others, and she is curious about what makes her tick. From our past sessions, she was quickly able to derive general rules of psychology from our exploration of individual moments in her life. Often, she would anticipate my next move: *You're probably going to tell me that my reaction to the dean of my department is a replay of my reactions to my mother.* More often than not, she was right.

That being said, she was not the first patient who came to mind when I began to think about exploring positive memories in psychotherapy. Her mother was so consistently negative toward her, albeit in subtle ways, that I cannot be too confident about finding a secret stash of fond memories here. Most of our past sessions have been spent talking about unhappy memories and the difficult relationship she has with her mother. She has come face to face with the painful reality that her mother never seemed to like her very much, preferring her younger sister instead. Mother was sometimes overtly critical of Gabby; at other times, she just seemed a bit irritable and distant. When there was a problem at home (*Who left the door open and let flies in?*), somehow it was always Gabby's fault. On the face of it, this does not sound like major psychological trauma. No one died during her childhood. There was no blatant child abuse. No one hit her, and no one abandoned her, at least not in the literal sense. Still, the daily exposure to this quiet rejection was hard to bear. I suppose many people would have trouble believing that such a subtle problem in childhood could result in decades of exhausting anxiety. But such is the lasting effect of childhood experience.

When she reached her teens and started to defend herself, things only got worse. Mother would get upset and accuse her of being ungrateful and mean-spirited. In fact, once Gabby was a teen, mother seemed to complain more loudly, and she complained about everyone around her. Her husband was not attentive enough, her children were inconsiderate, and her in-laws never cared about her. Somehow, someone was always ignoring her needs. (*My mother was narcissistic,* Gabby told me.

I am always amazed at how much of Freud's lexicon is common knowledge.)

For the most part, family life was quiet, if not very happy, but the situation became decidedly miserable every time there was a Jewish holiday. Gabby's father would invite his parents to join them for the occasion, and her mother could barely hide her disdain. Before the grandparents would arrive, there would always be an argument between the parents. It would be a quiet argument, to be sure, the whole of it consisting of a few terse words passing between them. There was no yelling, no cursing, no throwing plates. As Gabby told it, only one person spoke at a time, like an old-fashioned duel with pistols. There were unwritten rules for the exchange, including a requirement binding both parties to allow one person at a time to fire off a volley, while the opponent stood perfectly still and allowed the bullet to complete its trajectory. When several such rounds had been fired, and no one was mortally wounded, the duel was officially ended without a declared winner, and normal life resumed.

The consequences of the duel were nonetheless significant. Mother went back to her preparations in the kitchen, but her demeanor was dark and brooding. During the holiday meal, it became clear that she had indeed incurred wounds, and she was determined to let everyone know it. It always seemed worse on Passover, perhaps because there was such a long prayer service that accompanied the meal. When the prayers and songs recounted the suffering of the Jewish people, she ladled out chicken soup with the air of someone who had not yet been released from slavery in Egypt. Gabby and her sister would jokingly refer to this sad occasion as the Passover Plague. One year, though, the joke concealed a very serious fear for the two sisters: Would Mom leave? Would she just walk out and leave the family? Did she not say something to Dad about her family in Chicago, and how they would be happy to have her back in town?

In therapy, we have talked at length about all of these memories in the long process of this "short-term" dynamic psychotherapy case. We have also become very well acquainted with Gabby's defense mechanisms. Aside from using humor (the Passover Plague), she has shown a tendency to dodge the forbidden feelings of anger, pain, and grief by covering them with compassion for her mother. *I feel so sad for her. She had such a tough childhood, you know. I feel that I need to take care of her now that she is so old and lonely.* This is no surprise; when a defense is needed, we use what we have at our disposal. She has her humor and her gift of empathy, and she uses both to the best of her ability. She also uses the defense of the gentle people: *Oh, I can't even imagine hitting her. I'm just not a violent person.* I have done my best to convince her that if the meek are going to inherit the earth, as the Bible promises, they will have to fight to stake their claim.

Her defenses are tricky. In previous sessions, I sometimes accepted her compassion at face value, and I failed to recognize it as a veil that concealed less charitable impulses. This is the paradox of the healthy defenses. The more mature defense mechanisms—including intellectualization, humor, and compassion—are also perfectly normal, healthy behaviors. Even when they are used as defenses, they are useful coping mechanisms that help her regulate her emotions in a constructive fashion. In therapy, though, these high-level defenses get in the way, no less than unhealthy defenses like turning anger against oneself with bitter self-recrimination, or denying the reality of what happened in one's life, or turning to drugs and alcohol.

Nevertheless, we did get past her defenses, and we looked at the terrible rage she had harbored toward her mother, a rage that was fully justified. As she told me more about her mother, it became clear that her mother really did see Gabby through a dark lens. This was often made more obvious by the perspective of other people. Other kids were drawn to be friends with her, and other adults saw the kindness in her. "Gabby is such a nice girl," a neighbor would say. "Gabrielle is the sweetest kid in my class," a teacher told Mom. Everybody seemed to love her, except the woman who gave birth to her. Her mother would dutifully smile and beam at these compliments when they were offered, but back at home she would turn cold and critical, finding fault with the neighbor, mocking the teacher, belittling Gabby's friends, and discrediting all their kind words.

All this took its toll on Gabby, of course, although she never let it destroy her. In fact, she went out into the world with a fierce determination to prove her mother wrong and win the recognition that she did not get at home. The secret self-doubt and the invisible (but virulent) self-hated—not all of her defenses were healthy ones—were well hidden from most who knew her. Her friends probably knew that she was always a little too anxious about the welfare of her children, but they probably did not know her darkest fear: that her kids would suffer as she suffers, and it would be her fault because she was such a terrible mother. We have worked our way through these problems, and she left the last round of therapy in great shape.

Now she is back again and anxious again. We have done a couple sessions already, we are halfway through with this one, and I am not sure what to do. I have tried to explore my idea of working on positive memories, but without success. I have mixed feelings about pursuing this idea any further. I want it to work so badly that I keep hoping that she has a pleasant memory or two hidden away someplace from her early years. I want this to be true, and I want such a memory to be helpful in resolving her anxiety. But maybe I am fooling myself; maybe I should drop the whole idea and admit that I have been infatuated with a useless hypothesis of my own making. But I am pretty sure that she did tell me once that things were not so bad with her mother when she was very young. Would that not suggest that there might have been a kind maternal moment at some point? Besides, my theory *feels* right, based on my own memories of childhood. In any case, we have certainly devoted plenty of time to her negative memories, so what is the harm in trying something new?

Still, I suppose that this may not be the case for such an approach. Perhaps her mother was so consistently rejecting toward her that she has no positive memories of the woman. I do want to explore the realm of positive memories, though, and if I have learned anything as a therapist, it is that people are very complicated. There are no perfect angels in this world, and rarely is someone a two-dimensional villain. I have met very likable people who have done mean, cruel things to those they loved, and I have met very nasty, irritable people who have a secret vein of kindness and caring that would surprise the recipients of their malevolence. Her mother may have been mean to her quite often, but I still cannot accept the possibility that Gabby has no positive attachment memories of her.

"So you can't remember a single positive memory of your mother," I say. "This means one of two things: either you have no such memory, not a single one, or these memories exist but you somehow refuse to let yourself remember them." Having said this, I sit quietly and wait, hoping that my words will travel deep into her unconscious and dislodge some artifact of buried history from a time long past. She fusses with a silk scarf around her neck as if to loosen it, or perhaps tighten it. She unties it, then reties it, then smoothes it with her hands again and again. It occurs to me that she is doing for herself what a mother would do for her little girl before sending her off to a party: dressing her, but also caressing her. "So what do you think?" I ask. "What is going through your mind as you fix your scarf?"

She looks down at her scarf, as if she is just noticing what she is doing. She puts her hands in her lap and looks out the window. We are in the middle of March. There are still islands of ice and snow on the lawn, remnants from our most recent storm, and the temperature is just beginning to warm slowly. Spring is a still a thought in one's mind, more a hope than a certainty. Following her gaze out the window for a moment, I have a flicker of impatience; I need to see leaves on the trees. I need to see something green.

"I got out my flute a few days ago and played the Beatles' song 'Yesterday.'" Is this just a defensive non sequitur, or is it actually an answer to my question?

"You did?"

"Yeah."

"And why did you do that?"

"Because when I was a kid—and I didn't even realize I did this at the time—when I got really, really lonesome, I would go to my room and close the door and play the flute for hours. And now I don't play very often at all."

I wonder if she is heading toward another session of feeling sad for herself and then feeling sad for Mom. I doubt any of that would be helpful; we have been there so many times. I decide to explore it a bit, without much enthusiasm, but then I sense something different about her facial expression. "So you played 'Yesterday.'"

"Yeah. Right."

"But your eyes change just a bit. Is there some feeling coming up?"

She says nothing and holds my gaze for a long moment as if to show me that she is not feeling anything at all, but now it is clear that something is stirring. Is her forehead starting to wrinkle as the eyebrows rise up in grief? Not really. I do sense a wave of emotion coming over her, although it only affects her eyes. Her mouth does not move a millimeter in any direction, not toward a frown, a scowl, or an angry grimace. The message is only delivered through those eyes. They suddenly look fuller, bigger, and brighter, a bit moist, as if they have been pushed wide open by a surge of primitive oceanic salt water that fills them from behind. She says nothing, so I do not know what moves her. Is she sad about being lonely as a kid? Surely, we have explored that before. I suspect something else this time.

"You played the flute," I say, repeating her thought to her, to see if this is the one that triggered the opening of her emotions. She is silent, although her eyes are full and reaching out to me to say something. I send out another test by paraphrasing her words: "Alone in your room." Is she sad that she was alone? She is looking at me, but still remains silent. "But now you rarely play the flute, you say."

She sits quietly for another minute. When she speaks, her voice is barely more than a pinched whisper. "I think she liked it when I played the flute."

"Oh!" I say.

And then she cries. She cries hard, just as she cried in the past when she talked about the painful memories of mother. This memory is just as emotionally charged, and obviously she has put up defenses against this positive memory, just as she did against the negative ones. I find it fascinating that she would keep such a simple, sweet, positive memory behind a wall of defenses. Did Freud not say that we construct defenses to ward off the negative memories and painful emotions? Why would she fight so hard against *positive* memories?

I think of all the sessions we have had, spread out over several years, and I am astonished that this never surfaced before. But I never asked. Now I have asked, and now I see before me a whole new side of her and a whole new side of psychotherapy. After a long minute or two, she settles down and wipes her eyes.

"I played that song in a solo one time when I was in high school. A little talent show. And whenever I got out the flute at home, she would say, *Play that one.* She liked it the best."

"So you would play 'Yesterday' for your mom."

"Yeah."

"Well, isn't that curious."

"It's the only song I played when I took out my flute this week."

"I wonder why you did that," I say.

She looks at me with a knowing smile. "You know. And so do I."

"What do we know?"

"You asked me about a positive connection last week, and I wanted to find that connection to her. I wanted her to notice me. I wanted her to ... I just wanted her to be close to me. For a really long time."

"So let yourself imagine being close to her."

"Yeah, I just wanted to come home from school when I was little and be close to her. Maybe I can imagine sitting in her lap."

"That sounds nice."

"And she would ask me about school."

"She would be interested," I say.

"Yeah. *Interested.*"

"This is not an unreasonable fantasy. This is just the basics of what a kid should get."

"I want to be there every day," she says. I hear her shift into the present tense, as if she is back in her childhood. Such a sad, wistful look on her face.

"Just to be with her."

"Yeah. I want to sit on her lap every single day, for as long as she'll let me sit there."

"As long as she'll let you," I repeat.

"I just want that closeness." She is rocking back and forth in the rocker in my office.

"Right. So just sit with your mother. Rock if you like. Just imagine you're sitting there in her lap. Day after day."

"It's very peaceful. It's very peaceful."

"You're finally at peace. And that's what's been missing from your life. You're never at peace. You're always worrying about something. Now you have peace because you're getting what you want in this image."

"I want it for a long time," she says.

"For life, right? Forever. You want something that will last. The bond that will last." I stop myself from saying anything more. She is not actively crying, but I can see by her face that more feeling is moving through her, and I do not want to dampen it with too much talking on my part. There is a time for silence in psychotherapy, and this is it. She has found one good memory of her mother, and from this slender thread, she is weaving together a vision of what her childhood should have looked like. The longer she dwells on this image of sitting on her mother's lap, the better. It does not matter that it never really happened. Research tells us that if we vividly imagine a scene, we are activating parts of the brain as if we are actually seeing the scene. Perhaps this fantasy will take on the power of an actual memory and help to counter all the negative memories in her head.

She says, "The interesting thing is that for years and years, I've rarely played the flute. Usually, I would play if one of my kids asked me to. It's kind of a real breakthrough to want to play it by myself. And when I play the flute, I get close to some kind of feeling. I really play it with some kind of passion."

"I see."

"And I never even thought about the connection between playing the flute and my mother, even though she would often say, *Play 'Yesterday.'* When I was a kid, I had a tape recording of it, and she would play that tape sometimes." Now she struggles to speak again. "I suppose that when I came home from school and saw her listening to that tape, I knew that she loved me."

"You were making that music and she loved it."

"Yeah."

"So she loved you," I say. "What a discovery!"

And what a messy, complicated truth this reveals about human beings. This mother, who could be so relentlessly mean and destructive to her daughter, might have actually loved her. Yet the devil's advocate in my head says that maybe she just liked that song and she selfishly wanted to hear it, without any real appreciation of her daughter. Would it not be better to explore Gabby's positive memories about her father? Certainly, he was the more affectionate of her parents. But I have to monitor my own reactions to this mother whom I have never met. After listening to all the depressing stories about her, I have undoubtedly come to share Gabby's negative view of her. I remind myself that even if she was relentlessly vicious, I need to follow Gabby's lead and let her try to reconnect with her mother, no matter what I think. Otherwise, I will fall into the therapist trap of identifying with the wounded child and hating the parent so much that I cannot let Gabby feel what she needs to feel about her. If she needs to find some bond with this mother, it is not my place to prevent her from doing so. Besides, I am the one who pursued this positive memory in the first place.

"You know what else is interesting?" she says. "My husband was working in his study, and I asked him if my playing would bother him. He said it would be fine. But I came out of our bedroom several times and waited for him to tell me how beautiful it was, and he totally ignored it!" She laughs at herself. "I know he enjoys it, and you don't play for other people anyway unless you're a performer. But it was a way that I used to get attention."

"Oh, I think you got much more than attention. This is something that your mother asked for, some part of *you*, and when you put it out there, she was pleased."

"And the musical connection between us was so strong."

"Yes?"

"Oh, yeah. And I repressed it for so long. There is a bit of musical talent on both sides of my family. My mother played the piano." Then she falls quiet, and I can see she is searching her thoughts for something. She sits perfectly still, waiting for the answer to arrive. Then she nods slightly, confirming that whatever has occurred to her mind feels genuine. "We played together. When I was young. I played the flute and she played piano."

"Really?"

"Yes. We did. We played together. I don't think it happened very often, but we did."

"Are you just remembering this now? Just recovering the memory now?"

"No, I knew it happened, but I don't usually let myself think about it. It's almost like I've ignored the memories just to spite her." She looks sad. "That's not very nice, is it?"

"No, but it makes sense."

Gabby is not listening to me. She obviously needs to sit for a minute with her last thought. How ironic that she is sitting here feeling guilty about mistreating her mother—or the memory of the woman—when her mother was the real aggressor. But she feels what she feels, and this does not seem to be the unhealthy, neurotic guilt that she has felt in the past, the guilt that was associated with turning anger against herself to spare her mother. This is genuine guilt stemming from the realization that she has withheld affection from her mother—and probably from others—out of spite. Never mind that her mother could be so rejecting; that has nothing to do with this feeling.

She sits quietly, absorbing what has happened here, and it gives me time to think. She has some terrible memories of her mother, and then she has a few really beautiful ones. Like playing the song "Yesterday." And there is the memory of her mother playing along with her on the piano. Abandoned and ignored for all these years, these pleasant memories have been waiting to be found, like Hansel and Gretel lost in the woods. During the past week, one of them began to surface, unconsciously at first, as she picked up the flute without understanding why. Now she gets a clear view of this part of her childhood, and she begins to realize what it means to her. She looks sad, but so much more at peace than when she walked in. She looks up at me now, emerging from her private reverie.

"I guess I do have some nice memories of my mother, after all."

"I guess you do."

She nods quietly. I feel the need to slow the pace of my comments, as if I am talking to someone who has just finished a deep meditation practice. She rests her hands in her lap now, and there is no fidgeting with her scarf.

I say, "It might do you good to think of these memories at home during the week."

She nods. "And I could think about sitting on her lap."

"Right. You have an image of sitting on her lap. A created memory, perhaps, but areas of your brain are lighting up when you create an image like that, as if you are recalling a true memory."

"Okay, I see." Yes, she looks calmer now. Of course, she looks calmer. She has reconnected with her mother, after decades of conflict and bitter separation. "I guess I have another mother lurking in my memories." She glances out the window again, in preparation for her voyage back into the world outside.

We have time left, though, and we talk further. I learn that her mother was the one who took her for the first flute lesson in the fourth grade. Her father was out of town on business, and she went with Mom to the music studio where Mom told her she could choose any musical instrument she wanted. She thought the flute looked beautiful, and she remembers feeling surprised that her mother did not argue with her choice. She then reflects a bit on her mother's life growing up and tells me more specifics of how Mom was terribly mistreated by *her* mother.

"She was just passing on to me what she learned, I guess. It's all she knew." We have discussed this before, in previous sessions, but now her compassion feels more genuine to me, less like a sophisticated defense mechanism. We talk about this until I notice the clock bringing us to the end of the session. We exchange a few more words, make our next appointment, and she thanks me as she leaves.

I stand up to stretch after she leaves. So she has positive memories and she has negative memories. *So what?* says a skeptical voice in my head. *We all do.* I suppose that most people can easily remember both the good and the bad from childhood. For Gabby, the access to the good memories has been blocked for years, leaving her with only the bad ones. And what I have read recently in the latest memory research leads me to believe that awakening the dormant positive memories might just be helpful in psychotherapy. When something happens that activates a negative memory, consciously or unconsciously, it will stir up all the old emotions attached to that memory. When the dean of Gabby's college blows up in a meeting and criticizes the faculty, the upsetting early memories are reignited: her mother preferring her older sister, her mother spoiling Passover, her mother threatening to leave the family. All of this leaves her feeling that *she* is no good, that Mom does not love her, and that she must be unlovable. (After all, if her own mother does not love her, there must be something essentially defective about *her*. What other conclusion could a child reach?) So certain thoughts, emotions, and behaviors will emanate from these old memories, even if the memories are totally unconscious at the moment of the dean's tirade. She looks at the dean and experiences her mother. She feels anxious. She has a vague stirring of rage that feels out of proportion to the situation, and this only makes her more anxious. She has a wish to placate the dean, as she tried (unsuccessfully) to do with her mother. Perhaps she has a powerful urge to leave the dean's conference room and hide, just as she isolated herself in her bedroom as a teenager.

However, if she remembers Mom saying *Play that song called "Yesterday,"* then other feelings and behaviors will follow. Judging by the way she looked at the end of our session, I would guess that they include kindness, compassion, and forgiveness. And equanimity. A total sense of being at peace with the world. Such a feeling is contagious; I feel it myself now that she has found her flute again. But why would she put up such a resistance to this positive memory? I suppose she blocked the positive memory because it would just lead to an emotional expansion—opening up to Mom—and a fear of being vulnerable to getting hurt again. Besides, if Mom loved her, as it now appears she did, it was a sad waste that she showed it so rarely. Better to believe that Mom was just a nasty witch who did not care. Then there is nothing to grieve over and nothing to rage about.

Grief and anger. We must help our patients get in touch with their grief and anger, as Davanloo demonstrated in his Montreal lectures. He did well to follow Freud, who blazed the first trail to help us reach the unconscious hostile feelings. But what about love, attachment, and reconnection? Surely, this must be the endpoint of psychotherapy. And perhaps the memory of playing the flute could help us get there.

13. Writing with Chalk

"It's working. At least, I think it's working." I am talking with Freud about my latest sessions with Gabby, and I can barely talk fast enough to keep up with my thoughts. "We have been doing a lot of work with her positive memories during the last few sessions, and I think it's really having a strong therapeutic effect."

"Work? What kind of work do you refer to?" Freud has a certain expression on his face that he gets when I am particularly excited about a subject and he is feeling completely relaxed and secure about his status as the senior member of our little two-person psychotherapy society. His look is a combination of interest, amusement, and fatherly indulgence. If I am straying too far from the official doctrine of psychoanalysis, he seems willing to attribute it to the foolish extravagances of the younger generation.

"We are strengthening the positive memories," I say. "As we talk about them, and she mulls them over at home between sessions, she seems to be getting better."

"Wonderful," says Freud. "Very good, indeed." He is clearly in a good mood. Perhaps it is due to the fine April weather outside. Who could be in a bad mood on a day like this?

"Thank you, Professor. But I need to understand more about memory. I have been reading some papers on the topic. I need to understand the role of memory in psychotherapy, and I have some ideas."

"I should like very much to hear these ideas."

"All right, then. Let me back up and talk about *bad* memories before we move to the good ones. And let me pose a question: How does psychotherapy work? If we think about memory, how does psychotherapy do anything to help a patient who has bad memories?"

Freud is pouring me a cup of tea. When he finishes, he smiles and makes an exaggerated gesture of turning his palms upward and shrugging his shoulders to signify his humble inability to answer the question I have posed.

"So let's consider Gabby," I say. "In an earlier round of therapy, several years ago, she told me a very disturbing story. When she was young, her parents would always argue just before the traditional family Passover dinner. Gabby's father would invite his parents to join them, and her mother resented it. So Mother would be sulky and miserable, and the family gathering was ruined. Now imagine the first time in therapy when Gabby tells me about the memory. She makes a joke of it—she calls it the Passover Plague—but it still affects her. At the time, she was afraid that Mom would somehow blame her for a miserable evening, or worse, that Mom would just walk out and abandon the family. The memory, as you said in *Studies on Hysteria*, is acting like a foreign body in her mind, and it continues to influence her life. Such a memory, sitting in the mind, occasionally gets activated by something in her immediate environment, and this triggers an emotional reaction—an emotional *contraction*, to use Reich's term. So when her boss, the department dean, is irritable and mean, she gets anxious as she did around her mother."

"Quite right," he says.

"She is not actually thinking of her mother at the moment. The memory is *activated*, but she is not consciously remembering anything at all about her mother. She is only looking at her dean and feeling anxious."

Freud smiles the satisfied smile of an experienced teacher who has the pleasure of seeing his pupil learn a critical lesson. "Quite right. A memory trace of a negative experience can be aroused without becoming conscious. Thus it can activate the emotion without activating the unconscious thoughts and images of the original events."

"Yes, yes," I say. "The thoughts and the remembered images remain unconscious."

"When a patient is anxiously expecting some terrible event," he adds, "she may be responding, without consciously realizing it, to the memory of something terrifying that actually happened to her in the past. We can assume that your Gabby was terrified at the thought of her mother leaving the home. She feels the emotion of the memory without identifying the other elements of memory."

"Of course, of course," I say. "So this happens to Gabby. The meeting with her dean triggers an anxious state of pulling away from the world, even though she does not know why. In fact, she often feels anxious and helpless, like she is still a little girl. She is living as if the Passover Plague could happen again at any moment. This state of affairs will continue until the memory can be *processed*, as we say today. But what does *that* mean?"

"All right, tell me, sir," Freud says. "What does it mean?"

"She comes to therapy. What happens in the office? We start to look back at the memory, and she mobilizes her defenses against the painful thoughts and feelings that accompany the memory."

"Naturally," Freud proclaims.

"After some initial difficulty, we breach the defenses, and she remembers what happened. She remembers *with emotion*. She cries over the loss of family happiness and the loss of the bond with her mother. When she was young, the fear of Mother leaving the family shattered her sense of a safe, secure family life. In one of our sessions, she experiences the long-buried rage at her mother and imagines an act of vengeful justice: she throws a Passover plate at Mom, the plate hits Mom in the head, and Mom dies."

"I see." Obviously, Freud is still uncomfortable with this visual imagery of Davanloo the Warrior, but he seems willing to sit back and let me make my own errors.

"So why does this help?" I ask. "I know you don't like the angry imagery, Professor, but why would it help to remember such memories and experience the emotion, with or without the aggressive imagery?"

"Because she is facing the incompatible *idea*: she has unconscious hostile wishes against her mother. You have broken through the resistance, and you have made the unconscious conscious."

"That is true, certainly. But according to modern memory theory, her memory can also change."

Freud looks at me skeptically. "Modern memory theory?" he asks.

"Yes. There is good evidence from our latest research that memories can change."

"I am not arguing with the theory," he says. "I am only surprised that you think this is modern. I said this repeatedly in my writing."

"You did?"

"Absolutely. Obviously memories can change! Let me demonstrate. Tell me one of your own childhood memories." Sigmund Freud is asking me to recall a childhood memory. I feel a twinge of nervousness. What will he surmise about my character from my answer?

"Well, all right" I say. "I have a very fond memory of sitting and drinking tea with my mother."

"And what do you see in this memory?"

"I see the old kitchen and the kitchen table. I see the teacups. And I see the two of us sitting there in the afternoon drinking tea. I am about ten or twelve years old."

"You can see yourself there?" he asks.

"Definitely. I can see myself sitting near the window that looks out over the backyard."

"But in the original scene, you would not have seen yourself. You would see everything else, but not yourself."

"That's true!"

"So this memory trace of yours is not an exact repetition of the original scene. You are seeing it from a different perspective, from outside yourself. This is a *revision* of the memory."

"You are right, Professor. You are obviously right." I never knew that Freud had written about the nature of memory. Is there anything he did *not* write about?

He adds, "I am not the only one who knew that memories can undergo revision and remodeling. Your American psychologist William James suggested that a memory can change when we retrieve it at a later time in a situation that is different from the original one."

"He did?"

"Yes, he did. I met him, you know, when I lectured in your country."

"Oh, I see." I can tell that he is getting ready to settle into a long reminiscence, so I pick up the pace of my speech slightly to forestall a lengthy digression. "So here is an example of how memory can change. When Gabby first revisits the Passover Plague, she sees it through the eyes of a helpless little girl."

"Undoubtedly," he says.

"She looks back in a state of emotional contraction. But when she looks back with different emotions, when she re-expands with anger and sadness, the memory is different, too. Her memory of herself as a helpless child, which has left her with a sense of helplessness ever since, changes into a memory of herself as a powerful person, someone unwilling to be treated poorly."

"That makes sense. One's character is, after all, based on a collection of memory traces from one's life."

"Right." Again, I am surprised that he knows all this. I have prepared a whole lecture to give him about modern memory theory, but I never expected that he would know so much about it before I even speak. I decide to proceed anyway. "We can explain this change in her self-image using memory theory. There are different forms of memory that have been identified. One is called *episodic* memory, the memory of a specific episode. The Passover Plague is an episodic memory. Another type is called *semantic* memory, a factual memory: Vienna is the capital of Austria. But we also have semantic memories of ourselves and others. Her view of herself as a helpless person is based upon childhood memories of actually being helpless. From these negative episodic memories, she develops a semantic memory—a piece of semantic knowledge about who she is: *I am a helpless person*. As you say, this becomes part of her basic personality, her basic character. And, if I understand memory theory correctly, this memory of herself as a helpless person can change in therapy."

Freud reaches for a cigar and a match. "You have some old wine in new bottles, my friend. But the wine is still good." He lights his cigar. "Proceed."

"As her memory of herself changes in therapy, her memory of Mother changes, too. Mother is no longer remembered as the all-powerful moody oppressor, but as a woman with serious emotional problems. That is, there is a change in the semantic memory of Mom, and a change in Gabby's attitude toward all women of authority."

"Which means that she would no longer have a negative *transference* toward other women," Freud adds.

"True, Professor, that's so true."

He smiles knowingly at me, amused that with all my twenty-first-century knowledge, I am still a step behind him. As I am thinking about this, Gretchen enters to check on our tea supplies. We are in Freud's study again, and the picture of Lou von Salomé sits on Freud's desk, rather too close to the edge. Gretchen gingerly moves it back a few inches away from danger. I have often looked at this photo and wondered about the subject's mental state at the time of the shooting. What was she thinking? What was she feeling? I have never been able to come to a conclusion, but it occurs to me today that she definitely does *not* look very happy. I have looked at other photos of her in books since I started meeting with Freud, and she does not look happy in any of them. I suppose she might have simply assumed the serious, formal pose that was expected by the photographers of her day, but I wonder: Did she ever look happy? Did she have any happy memories? Childhood in Russia? Talking philosophy with Nietzsche? Her love affair with Rilke? She looks at me with her not-very-happy eyes. I wonder: *Were you happy when Freud accepted you into his Wednesday evening discussion group? Or were you just pleased to have a forum in which to explore the general unhappiness of other people?* Athena is standing close to the photo of Lou on Freud's desk. Athena, who sprang fully formed from the head of Zeus, having no mother. *Where was your mother, Lou von Salomé? Do you have any happy memories of your mother? Did you even have a mother?*

"So your patient's memory changes," Freud says, bringing us back to my case. "There is a new memory of herself."

"Yes, she has a new memory of herself, because all these types of memory can change. And even the visual impression of episodic memories can change, as you pointed out. Although I suppose that this might be truer for some people than for others. Some people are just more visual."

"Absolutely. Charcot spoke about that in his lectures."

"Oh, really? I didn't know that." I am a bit surprised to find that I am getting a little irritated with him. I suppose I came here today with the idea that I would be the teacher and I would present him with the latest in modern memory theory and its implications for psychotherapy (as well as my own attempts at innovations in therapy), and he would be impressed. I quickly decide to suppress this feeling and carry on. There is a time and a place for normal, healthy defenses, and this is not the time to get angry. "When Gabby remembers her mom's behavior and gets in touch with her anger and grief, her visual memory of the event changes. She suddenly remembers seeing her little sister crying in the corner. Before therapy, she had seen herself and her mother in the picture. Now she sees her sister and feels compassion for her."

"Just as you have revised your memory of drinking tea with your mother," he adds.

"Right, right." I struggle not to feel annoyed. Does he have to keep reminding me that he knew everything before I started talking? Well, I have more to say, and I decide to finish my train of thought. "Until fairly recently, we believed that a memory that is preserved in the mind is stored in its original form, like a photograph. Like your photo of Lou von Salomé here. According to this outdated theory, the memory undergoes the process of *memory consolidation*. It is permanently stored. When we reflect on the memory, we pull it out and it looks just the same as when we first stored it.

"Like writing in permanent ink," he says.

"Right. But as you have pointed out, memory can undergo a change. So the newer view of memory is that memory can change."

"Like writing in chalk."

"Yes, that's a good analogy, Professor. Like writing in chalk. But there is more. *Every time* we retrieve a memory, it can be altered a bit, and a new version of the memory can be filed away in the mind. This theory is called *memory reconsolidation*."

Freud pauses to mull this over. "Every time?" he asks. "Every time we activate a memory we can change it? Well, I suppose that is what William James was saying."

"Every time," I say. "We even have evidence that the hippocampus is reactivated when we recall a memory. The hippocampus is—" I catch myself as I remember that he started his career as a neuropathologist, studying anatomical sections of the brain. He surely needs no definition of the brain structure called the hippocampus.

"The hippocampus is active? How would one know this?" he asks.

"Using the MRI scanner." I cannot suppress a feeling of elation as I explain our modern technology for obtaining images of the brain. I am stepping out of his shadow again, and he is the one who can learn from me. He is predictably interested and attentive as I talk. He abandons his burning cigar to an ashtray and becomes wholly focused on grasping the new concepts that I am describing. "The hippocampus becomes active when we take in a new event and record it as a new memory. With the passage of time, any memory worth keeping will be transferred to other areas of the brain. But when we activate an old memory, the hippocampus again lights up on the MRI scan, as if to prepare for the creation of a new, revised version of the original memory."

"This MRI of yours can actually take a picture of the living brain and tell you which areas are most active at a given moment?"

"Exactly."

"This is quite amazing. Truly amazing." He is mulling this over, piece by piece. "And the hippocampus is active in recording a new memory."

"Right," I explain. "One might say that it is the chalkboard where we draw the new memory."

"And it becomes active again when we reflect on an old memory?" he asks.

"Yes."

"So you are saying that the old memory is available for remodeling in the hippocampus. It is sent back to the chalkboard for revisions. It can be revised to form a *new* version of an *old* memory."

"Quite right," I say.

Freud is fascinated, and I am delighted. He picks up his cigar to puff on it and think for a while. I pour myself another cup of tea, feeling like a young college instructor who has just been promoted to the rank of full professor. "Can I pour you another cup of tea?" I ask graciously.

Freud nods without really paying any attention to me. He is clearly lost in thought, totally engrossed in the intellectual work of absorbing the new bits of information, laying them out alongside the massive store of information already in his head, and looking for ways to integrate the new data with the old. "That would imply that every time a patient thinks of a memory in a psychoanalytic session, there is the possibility for this reconsolidation process involving the hippocampus."

"Right, Professor. Exactly right! And this is one way to explain how psychotherapy works—when it works. The patient walks in with negative memories. Gabby remembers a specific incident, like the Passover Plague, as a moment of helplessness and fear. By the end of the session, she remembers it as a sad moment, but not a traumatic one. In the larger perspective of her mental life, she first remembers her mother as a monster and she remembers herself as a helpless, unlovable child. At the end of therapy, she remembers her mother as a troubled soul, and she remembers herself as a nice kid who had a troubled childhood."

"Well, there is some sense to all this," he acknowledges.

"Yes, definitely. So after an earlier round of therapy is concluded and something activates the memories of her mother, she might remember the new version of the memory, the version that is more emotionally neutral. And then she would not react with all the anxiety that was driven by the original memory.

"A most interesting theory," Freud says. "So we bring the old memory into consciousness, and we expose the unconscious ideas related to the memory."

"And we help the patient express all the buried *emotion*," I interject pointedly.

"And we also change the nature of the memory in the process of exploring it."

"Right," I say.

Freud gets up and goes into his consulting room for a moment. He returns with a book in his hand, and sets it down on his desk. He does not open it, but I can see the cover. It is his *Studies on Hysteria*, the book he wrote with Breuer. He drums his fingers on the book. "You know, in Breuer's pioneering case of Anna O., he was determined to help with her bad memories. I wonder if this memory theory can help us understand her case. And the other cases in our book."

"It might."

"So according to your modern memory theory, Anna must have created new versions of the frightening memories she had."

"Yes, I would assume so," I say.

Freud nods. "But even if that helped her to get well," he adds, "we would still have to explain her relapse after the treatment. As I told you, we later learned that she became quite ill again."

"Right. Just like my patient Gabby keeps relapsing with her anxiety. And perhaps memory theory can explain this, too. Perhaps it can explain how psychotherapy fails."

"I should like very much to hear your thoughts about this."

"Well," I continue, "there is a new version of the memory, the therapy version, if you will. But what has happened to the old memory? Is it still lurking in the mind alongside the new version? Or have we transformed it into the new memory, so it no longer exists in its original form?" Freud shrugs to signal that he does not have an answer to the question. "Let's assume that we have permanently changed the old memory. And in the process, we hope that we have helped the patient to change her core beliefs related to the memory, like Gabby's belief that she was an unlovable child."

"But then why would the patient relapse?" asks Freud.

"Exactly the problem," I say. I am about to continue, but I feel the need to pause in my arguments and collect my thoughts. Something tells me to slow down and take a break. The sunlight is resting comfortably on Freud's little collection of antiques, including the Chinese sage sitting on the small table next to his desk. The stillness and tranquility of this little figure invite me to linger in the moment without lurching ahead to my next thought.

I do have some ideas about this relapse problem, but I am not sure about how to put them together. I remind myself, as I do in the middle of a tough therapy session, that I do not have to know everything at the moment. It is all right not to know. It is all right to sit with the uncertainty until things become clear. In fact, there is something to be savored in these moments of not knowing. Freud is sitting patiently, clearly in no rush to proceed. Certainly, he has no problem accepting my need to slow down and gather my thoughts. He does not live in my hurried world where people expect quick solutions to complex psychological problems. His is a world that allows for the leisurely process of contemplation. He is in no hurry. He neatens up a stack of the large papers on his desk and draws in a big breath of the fresh spring air. I resume my thesis.

"Maybe we change a particular memory—Gabby's Passover Plague, let's say—but what about all the other similar memories of her mother? If we change this one memory, will the effect somehow spread to other similar memories? If we rewrite one memory in chalk, will the other bad memories of her mother automatically be rewritten in a similar fashion? Or will they remain in their original versions, with all the negative thoughts and feelings attached to them?"

"Excellent question," says Freud. "Certainly, we cannot explore each and every negative memory she has of this mother."

"Right. There must be thousands of them. So the problem is that we don't know if the effect of changing one memory will generalize to other similar memories. We just don't know." It is all right not to know, I remind myself. "But since Gabby relapses with anxiety, I suspect that the effect of changing one memory, or even several memories, has not spread to other similar ones in her mind."

"And perhaps patients vary in this regard," Freud says. "Perhaps for one patient this rewriting effect will indeed spread to similar memories, while for another patient the effect is more limited."

"That makes sense, Professor. And it might explain why some patients relapse while others maintain their gains after therapy."

"Quite so," Freud says. He picks up his little Chinese sage and holds him up in the sunlight. He turns him in his hand as if looking for some bit of wisdom to guide us.

"So," I say, "let's assume that there are still negative memories in Gabby's mind. We have successfully transformed one particular memory, but the rewriting effect has not spread, and other bad memories of her mother still linger. So what will happen when Gabby has to meet with the dean of her college and the dean is angry and disrespectful? She is confronted with a woman in a position of authority, a woman who can be kind and supportive at times, but mean and critical at other times. Let's assume that the dean is quiet at the beginning of their meeting, and Gabby can't quite read her. Which memory of mother will be activated? The bad memories of mother as oppressor? Or a revised therapy version of mother as troubled soul?"

Freud shrugs. "How could anyone know the answer to your question?"

"Exactly, Professor. That is exactly the problem. We have no way of knowing. Both memories are there: the original memories of Mother as monster, and the revised therapy memory of Mother as a sad and troubled person. Memory research with animals suggests that this is like a coin toss. We just don't know which way the coin will land."

"So if a negative memory is activated ..."

"The patient will have a relapse of symptoms," I say. "Only one memory—either an original negative memory or the revised therapy memory—will be dominant in her mind at any one moment. Whichever it is, this will be the dominant memory trace at that instant.

It will have *trace dominance*, in the language of memory researchers, and it will drive her emotions and behavior."

"I see. But what is your solution to this problem?"

"Well, it occurred to me one day—actually it occurred to me at our last visit—that we pay very little attention to positive memories, such as Gabby's memory of playing the flute for her mother. Perhaps if we could help the patient to activate those positive memories of early attachment experiences, they might have trace dominance over all the other memories, both the original negative memories and the more neutral versions of the memories created during the therapy sessions. And perhaps this might prevent a relapse."

Freud suddenly looks skeptical, as if I have just proposed raw carrots as a treatment for the prevention of tuberculosis. "You want the patient to talk about pleasant memories of childhood, and this will cure her of her neurosis? This will replace the hard work of psychoanalysis?"

"No, of course not, Professor. First, we must work on the negative memories, as we have always done. I think it would be a terrible mistake to bypass that work. We definitely have to explore the bad memories and help the patient realize what happened to her, what it all means to her, how she feels about it, and so on. But in addition to that work, I think we should include an examination of the positive memories." I pause for a moment as a problem surfaces in my mind. "Of course, this assumes that she *has* a few positive memories. Some of my patients had such horrible childhoods that I would not even search for such memories." I wonder to myself, *what would I do with these patients if the traditional work on negative memories is not enough?*

Freud answers me as if he heard me thinking. "But perhaps these patients with traumatic childhoods have happier memories of another adult. A favorite uncle or a grandmother."

"Well, yes, that might do." I am surprised and grateful for his help in thinking this through. "But getting back to Gabby, I think that positive memories of the early attachment to a parent—or another caring adult—are very powerful, very emotional, and perhaps these memories could help her repair the negative images she carries of both her mother and herself. Of course, we must also work on the patient's defenses against recalling these positive memories. Patients fight against bringing these memories to light."

"But here you ignore one of the most basic principles of psycho-analysis," he says. "When we forget something, the forgetting is based on a wish to avoid something unpleasant. This is the nature of the dynamic conflict in the mind. Here you say the patient tries to avoid *pleasurable* memories. This makes no sense."

"It certainly does make sense, though. I am following your concept of signal anxiety. If Gabby remembers playing the flute for her mother, she will begin to experience love for her mother, and that is a dangerous emotion. It could motivate her to open up to her mother and try to get close to her, and this could lead to more emotional abuse and rejection. So the ego sends out a signal of anxiety: If you experience this love, you will only be hurt again. Gabby avoids the positive memory because it can lead to more hurt and suffering."

Freud nods slowly and thoughtfully. "But still this seems like a strange turn to take in your psychotherapy. This emphasis on the positive memories." He picks up his copy of *Studies on Hysteria*, peers at the cover with narrowed eyes, and then gazes off to one side. "Or perhaps not so strange." He begins to thumb through the pages at the beginning of the book, scanning the lines in search of something. "Wait, here it is. We wrote about abreaction of the emotion."

"Abreaction. You mean, catharsis."

"Precisely. First we wrote that the traumatic memory must be abre-acted. That is, the patient must experience the buried emotions. She must have the catharsis. That was our original theory, before I developed the technique of free association. But here is what we wrote next: *Abreaction, however, is not the only method of dealing with the situation that is open to a nor-mal person who has experienced a psychical trauma. A memory of such a trauma, even if it has not been abreacted, enters the great complex of associations, it comes alongside other experiences, which may contradict it, and is subjected to rectifica-tion by other ideas.*"

"The memory comes alongside of other experiences? Did you mean positive experiences? Positive memories?"

"Apparently so. Listen further: *After an accident, for instance, the memory of the danger... becomes associated with the memory of what happened afterwards—rescue and the consciousness of present safety.*"

We look at each other, both of us surprised. "You said this in your first book?" I ask.

"I did. *We* did. Breuer and I. But I had forgotten about those remarks until now." He laughs, amused that he had forgotten, or perhaps pleased that he and Breuer had come upon this insight so many years ago.

"That fits perfectly," I say. "So the memory of a trauma can be detoxified by the subsequent memory of rescue and safety."

"Yes. That is what we wrote in 1895."

"Well, that is what I am saying now, but I am adding a specific corollary: negative memories of a parent can be overcome by reactivating positive memories of that parent. Early attachment memories, such as Gabby's memories of playing the flute for her mother. And if we work on them, we can give trace dominance to those attachment memories."

"Um-hm," he says. "In a sense, the positive memories will become dominant over the negative ones."

"Yes, I think so."

"The negative memories will be there in the mind," he continues, "but they are less likely to be activated when someone reminds Gabby of her mother. The bad memory will lie alongside the good, but the good will prevail."

"Right," I say. "The flute memory will prevail. And I am hoping that the semantic memory of Mom—the 'factual' memory—will be more likely to change, too. This semantic memory has to be constructed from all the individual episodic memories encoded in Gabby's brain. It is a process of selecting and emphasizing some memories and de-emphasizing others. The result is a composite memory of Mother, the internalized essence of Mother. Maybe a focus on these positive attachment memories will help transform this internalized model. All the individual good and bad memories will be there in her mind, but maybe Gabby's *essential* image of her mother will shift, and she will carry with her a new image: neither a monster nor a troubled soul, but a woman who loved her. That is what I hope to accomplish."

"Well, that is fine then," he says. "If you are helping your patient, then it is fine."

But something is *not* fine in my thinking about all this. It occurs to me that there is an aspect of all this memory theory that I have never considered before. "But wait," I say. "Wait, wait, wait. There is something I am overlooking here."

"And what might that be?" he asks.

"Well, suppose there are two contradictory memories in one's mind. Gabby remembers the negative memories of her mother rejecting her, and she also remembers the flute memory. If the flute memory becomes dominant after our work in therapy, then we must ask *why* it would become dominant."

"Why?" he asks.

"Yes, why? Why would she not just stick with the negative memory? Such a negative memory serves a purpose, you know. It reminds her not to trust again and not to get hurt again. That would make sense in terms of protecting herself, even though this self-protection causes her problems. If we say that psychotherapy can help a patient rewrite a memory—via memory reconsolidation—there is an implicit assumption that the mind will prefer the positive memory to the negative one.

"I suppose so," Freud says.

I get up to pace back and forth in his study, trying to bring my thoughts together. "There must be some sort of psychological homeostasis in the nature of the mind," I say.

"Homeostasis?" He is obviously unfamiliar with the term.

"Yes, homeostasis," I explain. "The body has mechanisms to maintain stability. When the blood sugar goes too low, the liver releases stores of sugar to bring the level back up. When the sympathetic nervous system makes the heart rate go up, the parasympathetic nervous system will eventually bring it back down. So there must be a built-in tendency of the mind to overcome stressful experiences and negative memories and return to a resting state of happiness and relaxation. Otherwise, the mind would not necessarily choose the positive memory over the negative."

Freud smiles at me with that knowing smile he gets when he already has the answer to my question. "Well, certainly. It is my *pleasure principle.*" He pauses to give me a minute to think about this.

"Oh, right. I had forgotten about that."

"The mind needs to maintain a state of equilibrium," he continues. "I wrote about this in physiological terms. When energy builds up past a certain level, it becomes uncomfortable. The energy must be discharged and kept at a constant level so we can experience pleasure. In terms of energy, I called it the *principle of constancy.* From a psychological point of view, it is my pleasure principle. We naturally strive to experience pleasure and avoid pain."

"Yes, of course." Of course! There is a natural tendency in us to seek pleasure, to be happy. Never mind that no one in psychoanalysis knew quite what to do with Freud's attempts to relate psychology to ideas about a physical energy—no one except Reich, whom Freud rejected. But none of that matters right now. Freud is answering my question.

"That fills in the gap in my thinking, Professor. If Gabby benefits from the flute memory, it implies that there is a natural tendency to recover from bad experiences by remembering good ones."

"Of course," he says. "We all experience Shakespeare's 'slings and arrows of outrageous fortune,' but we are driven to seek more pleasurable experiences and recover from unpleasant ones."

"Yes, of course. Otherwise, the concept of memory reconsolidation is not likely to help us in psychotherapy. Why would we reshape a negative memory into a positive one unless we have a built-in need to have positive memories and pleasant experiences?"

How odd that we remember Freud for talking about resistance, the patient's unconscious need to cling to his symptoms and stay ill, yet we forget that he also described an opposing force. He built a theory about an innate need to recover from stress and tension, a need to stay calm and happy. The pleasure principle. Sitting across from me now, he looks like a man who is basking in the pleasures of conversation and the fine spring weather, without a care in the world or a negative memory in his head.

14. Going Up in Smoke

*G*abby has positive memories of her mother now, and she has done a bit of the "homework" I assigned her. She reflected on these memories during the week. She also took the project one step further by going through boxes of old photographs until she found what she was looking for. A smiling little girl, maybe five years old, is sitting on her mother's lap in a beach chair. Mother is wearing a broad-brimmed straw hat, and she is also smiling a big smile that has recruited every muscle in her face to participate in a moment of unfettered relaxation and pleasure. She has her arms around the little girl's waist. The smiles on their faces are easy, natural, and perfectly matched; they are smiling the same wide-mouthed toothy smile. To complete the impression that the two figures in the photo belong to each other, there is a striking resemblance in their overall appearance: the same high forehead, the same straight, thin nose, the same ears that are cupped slightly forward, just enough to appear cute rather than outlandish.

It may have been only for that moment that they looked so happy with each other while someone snapped the camera shutter, but there is something timeless about the image. (It makes me think of great paintings that have the power to stop the clock. Vermeer's *Girl with the Pearl Earring*. Could anyone imagine the girl in the painting *not* turning to look at us with her innocent, wistful eyes? Could we imagine her turning away and mopping the floor? Never.) The still image of them sitting together seems like more than a one-time event, more than a transient moment in the temporal world of moments. It is hard to believe that this was not the constant state of their lives together, a perfect synchrony between mother and child. The anonymous photographer has accidentally captured the timeless essence of all human relationships.

"I keep it on my bedside table now," she says, as I hand the photo back to her. She looks at it again, allowing another few seconds for this positive image to take its place in her brain alongside all the negative ones. "I feel like I have a new mother now. Or maybe I'm building a new mother in my mind."

"This is certainly a different mother than the one you have described in the past."

"Yeah."

She puts the photo away in her purse, handling it very gently, as one might handle a treasured family document that traces one's ancestry back to a noble line of benevolent kings and queens. She sets her purse on the floor by her chair, and we talk for a while. The pace of our conversation is slow and leisurely, much slower that it was when we first met several years ago. In our early sessions, she spoke quickly, nervously, and she was always trying to please me by saying the "right thing," just as she had tried in vain to please her mother. Now she makes a statement and then sits quietly and comfortably. There are brief silences between our words, moments when we just look at each other without speaking. This is such a rare encounter in this hurried world. When do two people just sit together, even for a few seconds, and just look at each other without generating strings of words to distract each other from seeing and being seen? How ironic that the end result of all this "talk therapy" is the capacity to sit together without talking.

I suppose we are done with therapy and it is time to say good-bye, but I have been waiting for the right time to explore one more avenue with her.

"I would like to ask you a question."

"Sure," she says.

"It's not the typical psychotherapy question."

"Go ahead. I can handle it." She smiles playfully. She has never looked so calm, so at ease with herself.

"What is your spiritual life like these days?"

She seems not the least surprised by the question. "My spiritual life? Well, there isn't much of it. The Jewish holidays didn't mean much to me this year. I went to synagogue, but I didn't feel much about it. It just doesn't feel ... I'm too much of a doubter, I guess. But there are other avenues of spirituality that I'd like to pursue."

"For instance?"

"Meditation. Buddhism. Stuff like that. When I was doing yoga, I felt better."

This sounds perfect. If anyone would be receptive to my idea, she would be.

"I have less interest in the Judeo-Christian traditions," she says. "I was watching the sun set the other day, and I came to the conclusion.... I accepted the fact that I don't believe in God. At least not the Judeo-Christian God. The God who is supposed to answer my prayers and get me a raise at work. And I was okay with that. I don't think I'm ever going to believe in God the way a lot of people believe in God."

Yes, it is time to introduce my idea. "The reason I ask is because over the past few weeks, I have come to think that if therapy can help you to reconnect successfully with your parents, it could also be a springboard for spiritual connection."

"Um-hm. I see."

"I think it could lead to a greater sense of feeling spiritually connected. So that's why I'm asking."

"All right," she says.

Can it be this easy? Does she understand me already? It seems sensible to me, but I have been brooding over this idea for weeks. For me, it adds a last step to the process of psychotherapy. First, she had to open up emotionally and get reconnected to her own feelings, thoughts, and memories. She had to face her emotions, particularly feelings of anger and grief related to the adverse events of her past. This led to a significant decrease in her anxiety, albeit a temporary decrease. And it led to definite changes in the way Gabby relates to other people. When I first met her, she was typically self-sacrificing, always tuned in to the needs of others, always neglecting her own needs. Now she can speak up for her own needs and wishes. So this would suggest that therapy has led to a change in her personality, a *character change*. (Without Reich's work on character analysis and Davanloo's active approach to the defenses, I never would have thought such things possible in therapy.) With the added work on positive memories, she can now reconnect to her mother and recapture the feeling of early attachment experiences. The positive memories will begin to have trace dominance over the negative ones and—I hope—will protect her against another relapse into anxiety. Finally, as the last step in therapy, this connection to her mother could be used as a pathway to a spiritual experience. I will find out soon enough if this is true.

I notice that she is sitting with her hands loosely clasped in her lap. To my surprise, I realize that my hands are together in exactly the same way. Is she copying me? Or vice versa? The *chameleon effect*, as it is called in the research world. We have a wired-in tendency to copy each other's behavior. One of us does something—clasps hands together—and the other one registers this activity in the *mirror neurons* of the brain. The one who observes is preparing to copy the other person's behavior in an automatic game of monkey-see, monkey-do.

"After my dad died a few years ago," she says, "I went to synagogue a lot and felt very connected. But then I stopped going." Her father comes to mind. That makes sense. He did not protect her from her mother's rejecting attitude, but he was certainly the benign parent, the one who obviously loved her. True, she had distanced herself from him, and she carried great anger and disappointment about him, but that was easy to work through, compared to her feelings about her mother.

"Well, if you are interested," I say, "I think there's a way to meditate on the memory of your father—or your mother—that could lead to some spiritual growth coming directly out of this therapy. If you want, I can walk you through that now. We don't have to try this, of course. It's up to you." I can hear myself hesitating a little bit. I have the urge to reassure her again that she can decline the offer. Why so tentative? I feel a bit presumptuous offering her a guided meditation. What do I know about meditation? Also, I suppose I am a bit concerned about what colleagues will think when they start hearing that I ask my patients to meditate. This is provincial Albany, jokingly dubbed Smallbany, not New York City or Berkeley. Maybe they will think I have lost my senses.

"Oh, it definitely appeals to me," she says.

Well, let people think what they will. I have to try this. "You've meditated before a bit?"

"Um-hm."

"And what kind of meditation did you do?"

"It was in a yoga class."

"And were you focusing on your breath? Did you have a mantra?"

"Both," she says. "It was a mix of things. And they lit a candle." Well, there will not be a candle in this office. There is a limit to how far I will go.

"Okay. This is a meditation exercise based on your attachment to your father."

She has unclasped her hands and has them resting separately on her thighs. To my amazement, I have done the same thing. But who shifted posture first? I was going to monitor this, but I forgot about it as we talked. Oh well, I suppose it makes no difference who did it first. We are in synch with each other. Somebody's mirror neurons decided to get in synch with the other person.

"I'm going to ask you to pick a positive image of being with your father, and then I'll invite you to meditate on that."

It does not take her a second to produce a good memory of him. "Well, there's a memory of my dad and me in the ocean. Where we have gone on many vacations."

"Oh, that's great. So let's get started."

I tell her to close her eyes and focus on her breath. I tell her to take a few breaths in and out, and just empty her mind of whatever might be going on in there. It strikes me that I sound surprisingly confidant in my instructions, as if I know what I am doing. Why in the world do I think I know how to teach meditation? I have listened to a few meditation tapes, but that hardly makes me an expert. I have tried a few meditation groups over the years, but I felt disappointed in them. All I can rely upon is my own home-brewed concoction: one part self-analysis, one part positive attachment memories, one part meditation. That plus a head full of books I have been reading. Is that enough?

Yet I do feel confident as I instruct her to focus on the image of Dad and her in the ocean, in the waves. I suppose I am assuming that my own personal experience with this kind of thing will translate into effective practice with my patients. That is a big leap. True, I have seen the memory of drinking tea with my mother, and at moments it felt like she was a presence in the room. (No, that is not quite right. I did not actually feel her presence in the room. It was not like a séance run by a medium. I focused on the memory and felt a connection to her *as if* she were in the room.) That does not mean that anyone else will have that kind of experience. However, I am working on the premise that we are all pretty similar, despite our competitive insistence on being unique and special. So why would my patients *not* have a similar experience, given the opportunity? Besides, this just feels right, and I keep going with a few more instructions, paced at increasing intervals, until I am silent and she is sitting in front of me, also silent. I begin to feel as peaceful as she looks. I let her sit quietly for a few minutes, and I wait for her to open her eyes.

I am waiting for her to connect with her father via meditation and perhaps make a spiritual connection. Psychotherapy leading to spiritual growth. Why not? I wonder how therapy and spirituality ever became separate endeavors in the first place. I suppose Freud is partly to blame. After all, he failed to distinguish between organized religion and true spirituality, and he rejected the whole enterprise. Besides, it is not obvious that the two realms—psychotherapy and spirituality—are even remotely related. What is the connection between this woman's anxiety and the notions of the great spiritual traditions? How is a panic attack related to the concept of an eternal reality that transcends this temporal life?

On my desk, sitting under a stack of psychiatry journals, is a translation of the Upanishads, the Hindu scriptures. The spiritual problem, according to the translator's introduction, is the widespread illusion that each of us is a separate being, separate from each other and separate from the greater Source of our being. In the Hindu tradition, this is called *maya*, the illusion of separateness that causes so much confusion and suffering. But is it not obvious that a sense of separation is also the underlying problem behind many psychological problems? There is something that goes wrong in the early attachment to the mother (or father, grandparent, etc.) that leaves the child feeling separated, isolated, and lonely. The child has to construct defenses against positive, loving feelings toward the mother in order to avoid more pain and disappointment, and these defenses against closeness are employed, to a greater or lesser degree, in other relationships as well. At the root of things, the psychological problem and the spiritual problem are one and the same. There is a psychological separation and a spiritual separation. It seems to me that the remedy should be some kind of integration of therapy and spiritual practice. There have been many books about an attempted integration, of course, but I have never read of a method that begins with a positive connection to a parent. There ought to be a reunion with a parent followed by a reunion with the Universe.

It occurs to me that Gabby's memory is not only a positive memory about her father, but also a memory of the two of them together. I should probably change the way I ask my questions about positive attachment memories. *Do you have a positive memory of your father?* That is what I have been asking, but that could draw a memory of Dad cutting the lawn or Dad drinking his coffee. It might be a pleasant image, but it could leave the patient still feeling quite separate. A good image of Dad and a good image of oneself, but still no connection. *Do you have a positive memory of a shared moment with your father?* That is better. Emphasize the togetherness. Help the patient build a lasting internal image of *us.*

"Hello." She opens her eyes and smiles, pulling me out of my thoughts.

"Hello."

"That was nice," she says. "Nice and interesting, because I am thinking about the memorial prayer they say in synagogue during the

High Holy Days in the fall every year. When I'm sitting there before the prayers begin, I sit and I imagine my mom and my dad, one on each side of me." She gestures to her right shoulder, then to her left. "They're just sitting next to me. My mom is still alive, of course, and my dad is dead, but I imagine them both. I do exactly—this! I do what we're doing here today."

"It sounds like you're way ahead of me here. So what happened when you did this little meditation just now?"

"Oh, it was so nice. I was in the water with my dad, and he was behind me with his hands on my shoulders." She looks over her right shoulder.

"So there was the sense that he was with you."

"Um-hm. That's how I felt it."

"You look very peaceful. And happy."

"Yeah," she says. "It felt nice."

I find myself feeling particularly calm and relaxed, too. Mirror neurons at work again, I suppose. After all, we are wired to feel each other's emotions, not just to copy each other's postures. Somehow we have a built-in need to share each other's experiences and be part of each other's lives. So I am taking in the sensory information about her state of mind, and I begin to experience it myself. After a leisurely pause, she continues talking.

"There are definitely moments when this kind of thing happens to me. I'll be walking along and I'll see something that's just beautiful, and I'll just think *Universe*. So it's there in front of me, but I just don't ... I don't find myself seeking it as often as I would like. But it's there. It's everywhere. I think what you're saying is ... you're putting words to something I have felt before."

"Well, that's great," I say.

"I don't engage in the act of seeking it, though. I don't really know how. But I would like to have more of the feeling that I have with my dad. It's lovely. It's definitely what connects us."

"Well, this could be one step that would help you to have more of this experience."

Her eyes drift off to the right, and I can see that she is not listening to me right now. She looks lost in thought. "My dad is dead, but the whole idea of Heaven and Hell, it doesn't make any sense to me. Being raised Jewish, it's just not part of me. But I feel very strongly that the power, which is our consciousness, the power that is us—I don't want to say soul—doesn't just dissipate. So we become One with ... with whatever this is." (A line comes to mind from another one of the books I have been reading: *The universe is not a dead machine but a living presence.* I cannot remember who wrote that. Oh, Bucke. The Canadian psychiatrist Bucke.) "And it may not actually be my dad that I'm feeling, but just his part of the Universe, and ... and I don't know why I don't draw on that more often. I've always been a very frenetic person, but that doesn't give me an excuse ... You know, it's an excuse. I can say, *I'm always going, I'm always busy.*"

She does not look frenetic or busy now. She looks quite calm and centered. Meanwhile, I am busy theorizing about what is happening here today. She can expand—no, *we*, all of us—can expand emotionally, and then we can expand our consciousness until we merge with the greater Consciousness. There must be a therapy–spirituality continuum of expanding and opening up until we make the greater connection.

"So your father is part of the Universe now."

"Yeah." She is reflecting again. "There was another memory that surfaced. I don't know if you want to hear it."

"Sure. Why not?"

"Well, actually, I was thinking about how he would shave." She laughs. "Sometimes I would put the lid down on the toilet and sit on it. And he would shave. And he'd smoke a cigarette. Back then, no one knew about the risks of secondhand smoke. And obviously he wasn't worried that he would get cancer, even though he finally did. So he would smoke a cigarette and shave, and I would just sit there. It would be warm, and there was the smell of the shaving cream ... so it brings me feelings of warmth... It's very visual and tactile and ..."

"Olfactory."

"Yeah. That too."

"All right. So close your eyes and just picture that. You can rock in the rocker if you want, if it helps. Picture that you're back there. How old are you in this memory?"

"About six."

"A little girl sitting by Dad as he shaves. And smokes."

"I wish this chair was high enough so I could kick my legs like I did when I sat on the toilet seat." She laughs.

"So imagine you're sitting on the toilet seat, kicking your legs. And just let your mind be relaxed and empty of everything else, and be there with him." She closes her eyes and settles into it again. "Just focus on it for a minute or two. If anything else irrelevant comes into your mind, just gently push it out. Just focus on that experience. And since you spoke of a greater consciousness, see if you and your father are surrounded by that. See if you are part of that greater consciousness or greater awareness. Something that doesn't die when the body dies. Just think of that and see what happens. You might start by imagining that you are aware of your dad, and that he's very much aware of you, even though he's looking in the mirror shaving. He's conscious of your presence, he's aware of it. And vice versa. And then imagine that there's a greater awareness around both of you."

Consciousness. It occurs to me that I have not tried to integrate this notion of spiritual consciousness with Freud's views. Freud delineated the mind into separate realms: conscious and unconscious. He labeled the ways in which we defend ourselves from the more painful, frightening contents of the unconscious. He worked to develop a method to make the unconscious conscious. But this spiritual notion is different. The anonymous authors of the Upanishads were teaching their students about the greater Consciousness, the Self, a universal Awareness that is not bound up with the physical body. So Freud explored the nature of the unconscious thoughts and feelings within; the ancient Hindu masters were teaching about the nature of the eternal Consciousness all around us.

As she sits in meditation—or whatever you call this—I begin to feel more confident that my theory will actually bear fruit. My hypothesis: early attachment experiences between parent and child are the developmental precursors to the spiritual experience. The sense of oneness with a parent in early childhood sets the stage for the later experience of Oneness with All. I remember the child development theories I have read, all the theories about these early experiences and the various names for them: *affect attunement, symbiosis, synchrony, dyadic states*. And there are the names that spiritual teachers have coined to describe the experience of going beyond one's individual identity to reach a state of perfect union: *enlightenment, nirvana, satori*. It seems impossible to me that the childhood experience does not somehow create an early template for the later experience of unity.

She is opening her eyes again.

"I lost awareness."

Her comment confuses me. Is she not supposed to be *gaining* awareness?

"At least, I lost my normal awareness. It's hard to be aware when you're part of it."

That sounds better. That makes sense.

"So," she continues, "what happened in that moment was ... we became smoke. And the more I became part of the smoke, the less there was a separation between myself, my dad, the room, and everything. Everything merged into the smoke." She nods, affirming to herself that her words fit her experience. "And it wasn't uncomfortable at all. But when you asked me to take my time with it, I was already gone. Gone!" She laughs.

"It was hard to know how to pace my comments, because I didn't know where you were." We both laugh. "A pleasant experience, though?"

"Yeah! Yeah. It started off with the cigarette smoke, and then I became part of the smoke, and then as I became more a part of the smoke, he whirled and I whirled ..." She makes circular hand motions, both hands rotating around an invisible axis. It occurs to me that she is going beyond Freud's individual ego, taking a developmental step that so many therapists have discussed. I think of Jack Engler, who said, *You have to be somebody before you can be nobody.* You have to build a strong ego before you can transcend that ego and merge with the Universe. I think she is describing a transcendent experience, using the memory of her father as the starting point. "So we whirled until we were just ..." Her voice trails off without finishing the sentence, and then she stops. I am not surprised that she cannot finish the sentence. The American psychologist William James said that the religious experience cannot be put into words. It is *ineffable*. Gabby continues. "It's similar to what I feel like when I have dreams of dying. It's almost like a birth. Going through a physical falling ... into nothingness. You become part of nothingness. Whenever I've dreamt of dying, I was never scared. It was always like piercing a membrane. Going between atoms of reality."

"Piercing a membrane," I repeat.

"Yeah." Our conversation moves along in its own way now, at its own pace, alternating between her spontaneous experiences and our mutual intellectual analysis of those experiences. It feels like we are traveling in a canoe, sometimes gliding while the water carries us along effortlessly, sometimes paddling hard to get where we are going. I am a bit surprised when I become aware of the clock and realize that we will have to end the session soon. She has been sitting quietly for a moment, gazing at the floor.

"The other day I went for a run, and when I run in the early morning and there's no car traffic, I don't want to have my music headphones with me. I run and I look around, and I just feel like I'm a part of all of this." She gestures to the window and the pleasant April weather on the other side of it. "And my father as a body, a remembered physical body, isn't as important as feeling a part of it all. You know, he's just a part of all of it. So any time I want to tap into him, he's part of it, and I can." (The Upanishads: *See the divine in your mother, father, teacher and guest.*) "If I believe heartily that we don't ... that who we are doesn't disappear when we die, then he's there. He may not talk to me, but that's all right. When I'm out in nature and I'm a part of nature, it doesn't talk to me either. But I still feel connected to it. And that's the way I can feel with my dad." She has been looking back and forth from the window to me, and to the window again. Now she looks at me directly. "And apparently I'll be able to do that with *you*. Even though you're still alive."

Freud out for a stroll

15. A Fairy Tale Ending

"If you are leading your patient down the path of religion, I will not be following you on such a path." He speaks without rancor, as he cheerfully picks out a fresh cigar from his cigar box. Indeed, everyone seems cheerful today. It is a beautiful afternoon in May, the kind of day that makes everyone feel a bit lighter and happier than usual. On my way here, a workman walked past me carrying a shovel, sleeves rolled up, whistling as if he had just been promoted to the head of his company. "Religion is the universal obsessional neurosis of humanity. An illusion. It is simply an absurdity." Freud says this in an amused tone, not the least troubled by the subject, not the slightest bit malicious in his damning indictment of it.

"But Professor, I am not talking about organized religion. I am talking about an underlying spiritual experience. If you think I am encouraging my patient to accept the rules and rituals of religion, then you do not understand me."

He smiles and nods as he examines his cigar in anticipation of the pleasure it will soon bring him. I can feel the soft breeze blowing in through the windows by his desk.

"Well, you are not the first to tell me that I am missing the point with religious feelings. After I wrote my book on religion, *The Future of an Illusion*, I received a letter from a friend of mine, the French author Romain Rolland. He said that he did not disagree with my comments about religion, but he wrote that I was missing the true source of religious feelings. This source, he claimed, is a feeling of eternity, an *oceanic* feeling."

"Exactly. That's what I am talking about."

"I see this," he says. "I see this. But I have no personal experience of such a feeling, so there is really nothing I can add to such a discussion."

And that is that. There is no argument, no conflict, no animosity in his voice. He is simply done with the subject of spirituality. He does not seem troubled by the fact that he cannot have the experience of his friend Rolland, nor does he seem to be curious about the nature of this experience. He lights his cigar and looks out the window of his study. The ancient Chinese sage sitting on his desk seems unperturbed by this attitude; I suppose I will have to emulate the wise man's serenity and let Freud be Freud.

"It looks like we are having a beautiful day in Vienna," he says. "I think it is time for us to take that stroll along the Ringstrasse."

"Certainly. I would like that very much." Yes, I would like that, except for the nagging feeling that this walk will be the end of our visits. I have had this premonition all morning. Neither one of us has ever mentioned the possibility of ending our meetings, but I suppose it is inevitable that we will part ways soon. As he said, he just cannot follow me down the path I am on. It is not just religion; it is all this talk of positive memories and attachment experiences and spiritual moments. I have veered too far from the psychological territory that he mapped out in his work, and there is no way he can go any farther with me.

My thoughts shift to a preoccupation with the large Oriental rug on his floor. The reddish brown color in it draws my attention. It needs a name. It is certainly not burgundy, as that would have a more purple hue. Maroon? Not quite enough red in it. Russet brown? But perhaps I am just engaging in the same intellectual rumination that critics of classical psychoanalysis accuse the analysts of fostering. It is good to put words to our experience, but sometimes better just to have the experience. Perhaps I need to look at the rug, just to look at it, to see it without naming or analyzing. Besides, why am I ruminating over the color of his rug? Answer: I am avoiding the thought of not seeing him again. I need to face this good-bye. And it should be a happy ending. After all, I have said what I wanted to say to him. I have done what I wanted to do. I wanted to meet him and tell him about our new way of doing psychotherapy, and engage him in a discussion about it. Well, I have done it. It did not always go as I had expected, but I have done it. Still, I have a heavy feeling as we both stand up and walk to the entranceway where he chooses a hat and a walking stick.

I suddenly notice that Freud looks older today than he looked during our last visit. Still vigorous, but older. In fact, it now occurs to me that he has been aging with each successive visit. How could I notice this yet *not* notice it? I suppose I registered the changes in some unconscious part of my brain without actually acknowledging it to myself. We see only what we want to see.

He puts on his hat. "I have a favorite museum in the Inner Stadt—the old section of Vienna—that I often visit." When we get outside onto the cobblestone street, it is still a beautiful day in Vienna, although I can see some clouds off to the west. We start walking up Berggasse, which goes uphill. (*Berg* means mountain, as I have learned in my German dictionary.) I am surprised at the rapid pace that he keeps, considering his age and the rather sedentary life he lives.

"So how do you deal with termination of the treatment in your short-term dynamic psychotherapy?" he asks. He knows, too. We both know that this will be our last visit together. Our termination session.

"Well, the general principles are the same," I say. "We encourage the patient to experience and express his feelings, and when the therapy is ending, there are often feelings of loss. A sense of pride and celebration too, but certainly loss."

"Yes, yes, that makes sense." We are passing by the Hotel Regina, where I am staying, and he gives me a bit of history about the place. Strollers pass by, and I hear the sounds of a cosmopolitan city: German, French, Italian, English. As we walk farther along, he quickly returns to the topic of termination, and he has questions, as usual. How do we decide when to terminate? What if the patient does not feel ready to end the treatment? How many sessions do we spend on the termination? I answer him as best I can. *But are we not going to talk about our ending, too?* We are turning right onto the Ringstrasse (the Ring Road), and he points out another landmark. "And here is the University of Vienna. A very fine institution." He pauses in front of the university to tell me about its history, and I start to feel a little impatient, a little annoyed. *I did not come here today to go sightseeing in Vienna. I came here to say good-bye to you.* He offers a couple more facts about the university, and then he goes back to the subject of termination. He wants to know if my interest in exploring spirituality with patients has ever interfered with termination. "Is there perhaps a risk that you hold onto the patient because you want to explore this spiritual theory of yours?" A fair question, of course, but I reassure him that I am careful not to do that.

But what is he really saying? Is he implying that I am holding on to him? That I need to let him go? Or does he have a wish to hold on to me? *Why don't you just say what you are thinking? You have spent your entire life getting other people to open up and say what is on their minds, but you are so maddeningly opaque!* He is oblivious to my thoughts, of course, and strolls along quite cheerfully.

We are both surprised when it starts to rain, lightly at first, but I can see a dark cloud mass moving in over the Vienna sky. Freud grabs me by the arm and gives me a tug in the direction of a café across the street. It occurs to me that aside from the occasional handshake, firm and businesslike, this is the only time he has ever touched me.

"Come," he says. "We will avoid Nature's wrath." Once we are seated at one of the plush, comfortable booths at Café Landtmann, the rain begins in earnest, accompanied by loud bursts of thunder and brilliant lightning bolts. I can see one of the waiters startle involuntarily, hunching his shoulders in response to one of the loudest thunderclaps. "*This* is the source of religion," Freud says, pointing to the darkening sky outside the window. "People had to find some way to comfort themselves in the face of Nature's unpredictable behavior, so they created a God, a father figure, an all-powerful protector." A waiter nods recognition at Freud and heads our way. "I prefer a good cigar and a cup of Landtmann's coffee. Then Mother Nature can do as she pleases with me."

The waiter arrives at our table and addresses Freud by name. Obviously, the professor is a regular here at Landtmann's. They chat for a minute, and then Freud remembers that I cannot read the menu. When he explains some of the offerings, I tell him that I am not a big coffee drinker, and he suggests that I try the Wiener Melange, a half-and-half mixture of coffee and hot milk. I also ask him to order me a Sacher torte, the famous chocolate torte that has been known in Vienna since the 1830s. He orders for us, and the waiter nods his approval and disappears into the kitchen. Other people have come in from the rain: men taking off their hats, women closing their umbrellas, all of them settling into their seats with coffee and newspapers and leisurely conversation. We talk for a couple of minutes about the coffee houses of Vienna, but he soon returns to the topic of religion.

"It is an ambivalent relationship that people have with their God," he continues. "They see him as the great protector, but they also fear him, as the little boy fears the father in the Oedipal conflict."

I cannot resist the urge to argue with him. "But you know, Professor, the Oedipus story is not so widely accepted in my day, even by people who respect your work very much. Obviously, children have fantasies about the opposite-sex parent, but we just don't see it as the universal root of problems, the way you saw it."

"Well, do you have an alternative story to explain the neuroses? Do you have a myth that would capture your modern view of psychological problems?" he asks.

"Actually, I think I do." We are interrupted by the waiter, who is back already with our coffees and my torte. He talks with Freud for a minute. When he pauses, Freud breaks into laughter. I think of all the photographs of Sigmund Freud with a severe expression on his face. If only people could see him now, letting go with a good laugh at whatever the waiter said.

"This waiter knows that I like a good joke," he explains. "It is an old European joke about the mythical town of Chelm, a place inhabited by fools. I will translate into English for you. Two men from the town of Chelm go out for a walk when suddenly it begins to rain. 'Quick,' says one, 'open your umbrella.' 'It won't help,' says his friend. 'My umbrella is full of holes.' The first man asks, 'Then why did you bring it?' And his friend answers, 'I didn't think it would rain!'" He laughs again. "I am so fond of jokes that I wrote a book about jokes and the unconscious." He takes a sip of his coffee and winces.

"Too hot, Professor?" I take a sip of mine, but it does not seem unusually hot. Hot, but not burning hot.

"No, no. I have had a little sore in my mouth for the past few days, and it is making it difficult to eat and drink. How annoying such a little lesion can be!" I put my cup down on its saucer, fearing that I will spill it. I have a sudden sensation of feeling shaky and chilled, despite the hot coffee. I realize I am staring at him with a worried expression on my face, and I am glad that he has looked away for a moment. He does not appear to notice. But what is the difference if he does notice? We both know that it is not just a little sore in his mouth. It is the beginning of the oral cancer that will plague him for rest of his life. He will suffer years of pain and multiple operations, and then he will die. "So you have a myth to replace my Oedipus story?" he asks.

"Yes, yes I do." But I cannot really talk, and he hardly looks ready to listen. His expression is troubled now, his brow deeply furrowed, his jaw tightly clenched, his lips pressed shut to keep out all evil. There is another boom of thunder, the loudest yet of the storm. I think everyone in the place flinches a bit at this one. A few booths away, a young man puts his arm around his sweetheart to reassure her that he can protect her from thunder, lightning, and all the dangers of the world.

"I would like to hear your myth," Freud says, without yet meeting my gaze, but the waiter is back again. Judging by the playful look in his eyes, and the slightly dramatic rise and fall of his intonation, I surmise that he is telling another joke. As he talks, I can see Freud's face start to relax. His forehead becomes smoother, his eyes warmer, and a little smile breaks loose at the corners of his mouth. When the waiter finishes, Freud chuckles and nods his approval. "That was a good one," he says, as the waiter hurries off to another table. Then he turns to me with a translation. "A man is becoming impatient with his tailor. The tailor is making him a new pair of trousers, and the job is taking too long. Finally, the man confronts the tailor. 'Tailor, in the name of Heaven, it has already taken you six weeks!' 'So?' says the tailor. '*So*, you ask?' says the man. 'Six weeks for a pair of trousers? God in Heaven! It took Him only six days to create the whole world!' The tailor shrugs. 'So? Look how *that* job turned out!'" We both laugh, welcoming the distraction. I feel a debt of gratitude toward the waiter for his serendipitous interruption. Freud now looks at me expectantly. "So? You have a myth?"

I see he is still not drinking his coffee, but I force my mind to move away from that concern. I will use the defense mechanism of suppression; I just will not think about it. A little suppression and a little humor, and we will get through this.

"Yes, I think I have found a myth," I say. Freud nods, just as eager as I am to steer us away from the darkness. "A story that could be our Oedipus Rex myth. I do think I have found one."

"And what might that be?" he asks. I brace myself before speaking. It seemed easier when I imagined this conversation while getting ready this morning. Now I fear that what I am about to say will sound ridiculous.

"'Hansel and Gretel,'" I say.

He laughs out loud, long and hard, just as I feared. "Now *you* are making a joke!" he says.

"No, I'm quite serious."

"But this is no classical myth. It is only a little German fairy tale. A children's bedtime story."

"No, Professor, you are wrong about this. Listen to me. Just *listen* for a minute!" He is taken aback by the sharp edge in my voice. "It is not only a German story. When the Grimm brothers published it in their collection of folk tales in the early 1800s, they probably did not realize that many versions of the same story existed in other countries. In France, there is the story of a boy named Little Thumb, whose parents abandoned him and his brothers. In Russia, the story is about a brother and a sister thrown out by a wicked stepmother. In the Philippines, Juan and Maria are rejected by their cruel father. Always the story line is basically the same. The parents abandon the children in the forest, but the children somehow survive. In the end, they find their way back home. This is not just a German story called 'Hansel and Gretel.' It is the fable of the abandoned child." I can see that I have caught his interest already. A story that has been told in several different cultures might have a universal psychological meaning, and he is curious now to understand it.

"So what is the significance of this little story?" he asks. I reach into my book bag and pull out my copy of *Grimm's Fairy Tales*, feeling a bit embarrassed to show a children's book instead of a weighty tome on psychology. Still, if I am going to present my views to this giant of the printed word, I feel that I need a book in my hands.

"Well, first of all, the stepmother in the story urges her husband to leave the children in the woods because there is not enough food to feed them."

"Yes, I know the basic story, at least the general outline."

"It is a perfect allegory for the root of many psychological problems. The mother figure in the story is more concerned about herself than about her children. She tends to her own needs before their needs. Metaphorically, we are not talking about a shortage of food, but a shortage of love, nurturing, and compassion. She does not have enough to give to them. In therapy, many of my patients have told me how their parents could not meet their emotional needs. Sometimes the parent was cruel and violent; more often, though, the parent was well intentioned but unable to provide the emotional closeness that every child needs."

Freud is attentive. He nods a signal to continue.

"The children in the story are neglected and abandoned. My patients have not usually been abandoned literally, but they *feel* neglected and abandoned, and they do not understand why this happened to them. They were, after all, innocent children." I censor the rest of that thought: *They are not seething with sexual and aggressive drives, as in your view. They are innocent children. They do not spontaneously want to murder the parent of the opposite sex. They just want to be loved and protected.*

"I see," he says. "So the mother figure in 'Hansel and Gretel' is rejecting. She is not a compassionate mother. Proceed."

"So the father, a wood-cutter, does not agree with his wife's plan, but he submits. This part of the story varies in other cultures. Sometimes the father is the cruel one, and sometimes both parents are rejecting. In 'Hansel and Gretel,' the father is kindhearted but weak. In the office, I often meet patients who describe one parent as particularly difficult—cruel, angry, critical, or just distant—and the other parent is not so bad, but this 'good' parent does nothing to protect the child from the difficult parent. Just like in Gabby's case. So in the story of 'Hansel and Gretel,' the father, against his better judgment, agrees to take the children to the woods and abandon them there."

"So you see this as a parable, rather than a story of literally abandoning children."

"Yes, I do."

"But such a story may have evolved from actual events during times of famine. There was a great famine in Europe in 1315, and it is quite possible that some families might have abandoned an infant or young child to save resources."

"That may be true, but the story of 'Hansel and Gretel' endures because of our universal fear of being abandoned as young children. For a young child, when Mother is angry—when she gets intensely angry or stays angry for a long time—there is often a primal fear that she might leave. Just like Gabby felt when her mother became so miserable at the Passover dinner. The child fears the experience of being cut off. In many families, something goes wrong with the early attachment, and the child experiences a painful separation from the mother. For me, and for many of my colleagues, this is the root of the neuroses. It is not a chemical imbalance of the brain, nor is it the result of frustrated Oedipal longings. It is a failure in the early attachment. The problem is the *actual* failure of parenting, not the imagined threat of retaliation by the father in your Oedipus complex." I realize I am being uncharacteristically blunt with him, but why not? This is my last chance to tell him who I am and what I believe in.

"So the parents leave them in the woods," Freud says, staying with the story rather than arguing with me. "And this symbolizes the child's fear of abandonment. All right. Then, as I remember the story, Hansel leaves a trail of bread crumbs so they can find their way back home, but the birds eat the bread crumbs."

"Right."

"And the two children wander until they find a house made of cakes and sweets, and the old woman living there invites them to come in."

"Right," I say. "And she turns out to be a wicked witch."

"And what does the wicked witch represent in your psychological analysis?" he asks.

"She represents the children's stepmother, although in the original German version of the story they were abandoned by their biological mother. But the witch is not the actual mother or the actual stepmother. Instead, she is the *memory* of the mother." Freud nods his approval. "As you said, Professor, 'Hysterics suffer mainly from reminiscences.' They have bad memories. And the children in the story remember their mother as a wicked witch. To some of my patients, the lack of compassion on the part of the mother—or father—sometimes feels evil and malevolent, as though the mother is a witch who wants them dead. For others, it seems that mother didn't care enough to keep them safe from the evils of the forest."

"You make an interesting argument."

I notice that he sips his coffee now that it has cooled a bit. I am engrossed in our conversation, but my brain is able to spare a couple of neurons to notice this. I also briefly notice a sense of relief in my body. My shoulders relax from their slightly hunched posture. *He is drinking his coffee. He is all right.*

"Let us assume that this little fable holds such wisdom, and we shall continue with the plot," he says. "The witch traps the children and plans to cook them and eat them, as I recall."

"Right," I say. "She traps them in a cage. And they are frightened and helpless. As our patients often feel helpless, trapped in their child-hood memories of a parent who was critical, rejecting, detached, or cruel. So Hansel and Gretel are helpless, until Gretel can overcome her fears and take action."

"She pushes the witch into the oven, yes?" he adds.

"Exactly. And in my psychological interpretation, she overcomes her fear and gets in touch with her anger at the witch. Just as our patients must overcome their emotional contraction—fear and anxiety, depression, shame, and guilt—and face their feelings toward the offending parent. Including anger, Professor. And as soon as she does this, she and her brother are free. She has vanquished the evil mother—the distorted memory of the evil mother—and they are free."

He takes his time with this now, sipping his cooled coffee and thinking. The friendly waiter is coming our way again. *Not now,* I think to myself. *Not now. This is not the time for another joke.* Fortunately, he walks by on his way to another booth. Freud sits, quietly mulling things over, slowly pondering, moving at the leisurely turn-of-the-century pace of the Vienna coffee house. I take the opportunity to pick up my fork and dig into my Sacher torte, which is delicious.

I have come to enjoy this slow-paced style of talking and not talking. It gives us time: time for ideas to travel from one mind to another, like visiting ambassadors traveling abroad; time to meet their counterparts in the host country and cultivate relationships with them; time to compare their differing views of the world and time to debate, argue, clash, and reconcile; time for them to make the long journey back home, bringing with them a slightly changed *weltanschauung,* a perspective tempered by the intimate contact with foreigners. The whole process requires time; it is most likely to succeed under the conditions of comfortable seating and hot coffee or tea. It simply cannot be rushed.

I find myself feeling inexplicably happy. I suppose it has something to do with our conversation; I find it satisfying to put these ideas into words and have him listen. Is that why I feel so good? Maybe it has nothing to do with the conversation. Maybe it is just that we are not outside in the rain. Or it could be the simple pleasures of the Sacher torte and the Wiener Melange half-and-half coffee, which tastes good, even to a non–coffee drinker. Or perhaps it is none of that, but just the feeling I get sometimes that all is right with the world. The *oceanic feeling* that Freud's friend described in a letter to him.

"So this is your psychological parable for human emotional suffering."

"Right," I say. "We can read the story as a psychological journey, rather than a physical one."

"Your 'Hansel and Gretel' fable, as you employ it, carries with it a certain view of human nature, you know."

"Absolutely," I say. "Children are born good."

Freud's face turns a bit stern. Now he cannot resist an argument. "Children are born with powerful instinctual drives, sexual and aggressive drives that must be tamed by civilization. Years of psychoanalytic research has confirmed this to be true."

I pause a moment before speaking, but only for a moment. "I wish you no disrespect, Professor, but I must disagree completely. The anger we see in our patients is not an innate part of their constitution. The anger is a reaction to an environment that has become disappointing or menacing or frightening. Aggression is a secondary phenomenon."

"And where is your evidence for this?"

"I suppose I have no evidence for my view—no more than you have evidence for yours." He raises an eyebrow to warn me against becoming too bold, but I can see that there is no real anger here, only a facial display to preserve his role as the Master. "But I can see that once we get beneath the anger in a therapy session, there is always an underlying need for connection, a need to be part of a relationship, part of the whole. A need to love and be loved. This, for me, is the essence of human nature."

Freud tilts his head back slightly and exhales through his nose, a snort of disbelief, not quite derision. He gestures toward a table where two older men sit opposite each other reading newspapers. "I don't know about your era, but in my time the daily newspapers suggest quite another view of human nature."

"Oh, the news is no better for my generation. But all the irrational anger in the world does not convince me that this is our basic nature. Gretel does not kill the witch because she has lost control of her innate aggressive drives. She kills the witch to overcome a frightening old memory. Her goal in the story is not murder, but reunion. She needs to reunite with her parents. And when Gretel comes to psychotherapy as an adult, the goal is likewise reunion. She must reconnect—with herself; with her emotions and memories; with parents, if possible, or perhaps some other caretaker; with other people; and ultimately with the Universe."

Freud sits quietly for a long moment. Clearly, he does not agree with everything I say, but he does not argue either. He just looks pensive. "May I?" he asks, looking at the book on the table in front of me.

"Sure." I pass him the book of fairy tales. He turns the pages slowly until he settles on a spot, and then he sits reading. I happily return to my engagement with the Sacher torte.

"I could not remember the end of the story," he says, after reading a page or two. "Here it is. Hansel and Gretel have to cross a body of water, but there is no bridge. A white duck appears and caries the children over, one at a time."

"Right."

"A white duck crossing over the water," he says.

"Yes. Then they find their way back home and reunite with their father, who has been unhappy without them. The evil stepmother has died."

"Yes, yes." His eyes go back to the page and he reads aloud: "*Then all anxiety was at an end, and they all lived together in perfect happiness.*" Oddly enough, he is smiling at me. It is clearly not a sarcastic smile, but a smile of pleasure. I have the impression that he likes the ending. Perhaps he likes something about the entire story, or even my interpretation of it.

"So the story tells the origin of psychopathology and its cure," I say. "And it's almost a perfect story. If only there were a reunion with the mother, too. Not an evil mother or evil stepmother, but a real mother. The *good* mother."

"The mother?" he asks. "A reunion with the mother?" He looks back at the book and smiles, this time with a knowing smile. He hands the book back to me. "Look!" He points out the window. The rain has stopped as suddenly as it started, and the sky is starting to clear. "We can resume our walk."

When we get outside, a blue patch of sky widens itself and forces the remaining clouds into retreat. If we did not have to step around an occasional puddle, one would never think it had just rained. People seem to be appearing from nowhere as the fine weather returns. A little boy of four or five years runs away from his mother in a garden to our left, and he squeals with laughter when his mother catches him. Then he is off running again with his mother close behind. Freud redirects my attention to a man in a three-piece suit riding a bicycle; I need to step aside and let him pass. As we approach the Parliament, he points to a large statue of his goddess Athena in front of the building. Standing tall and proud, carved in stone, she wears a gilded helmet and holds a spear in her left hand, the spear that is missing from his miniature Athena who stands on his desk back in his study. While he is still admiring the statue, I am distracted by the sight of a young man nearby making an impassioned speech to a small gathering of spectators. He is gesturing wildly with his hands and speaking with an angry, indignant tone.

"What is he saying?" I ask.

"Politics," Freud answers with obvious disdain, and we pass by. Farther along, he points out the Hofburg Palace as it comes up on our left, but otherwise we walk along in silence now. Across from the Hofburg, we arrive at the Kunsthistorisches Museum, the art history museum. We stop together in front of the ornate edifice built by Emperor Franz Joseph to house the imperial family's collection of art. I am not sure whether he wants me to go in with him, or he wants to separate right here and say our good-byes.

"I had a friend at the museum here who would check on any antique I was interested in buying. He could verify the authenticity of the item before I bought it. I bought from a dealer I knew, Robert

Kunsthistorische Museum in Vienna

Lustig, and Herr Lustig would bring the piece to my friend here for inspection."

"A good policy, I'm sure."

"Oh, yes. There were many fakes in my time. One had to be careful not to be fooled." Does he think that I am a *fake*? Is this what he thinks, after all the time we have spent together talking about psychotherapy? Is this a conscious criticism? Or his unconscious mind leaking out his true thoughts about me? Well, conscious or unconscious, I need to say something. I need to confront him about this. "But our time grows short," he adds, interrupting my train of thought, "and I have been thinking about these modern ideas you and your colleagues have about psychotherapy." He pauses as a young woman, perhaps twenty, passes by and nods to him, looking a bit uncertain about how to greet him in public. A patient, perhaps? He nods slightly, discreetly, in her direction. Yes, it must be a patient. I wonder what she thinks of him, but she continues on her way with her back to us. Well, I am going to tell him what *I* think of him right now! I open my mouth to speak, but he speaks first. "While it is true that you have moved away from some of the core principles of psychoanalysis, it must be said that your work is not entirely without merit."

I am taken by surprise. I was overanalyzing his comment about fakes and working myself into a fit of righteous indignation. It never occurred to me that he was just talking about his antiques, and I certainly never suspected that he was about to compliment me.

"Well, thank you, Professor." I stand before him, waiting to hear what he is going to say. I pull myself up a bit straighter, like a good soldier standing ready to receive his medal. A full minute goes by in silence, and I realize that he has said it. That is it. That is all he is going to say. *It must be said that your work is not entirely without merit.* If I am waiting for more lavish praise, I will have a long wait, indeed. I suppose I should say something more. *Someone* should say something more. I should tell him how much he has meant to me, or how much his work has influenced me. I should say that no matter what changes we make in theory or technique, we are still carrying on his work; that the modern changes in psychotherapy do not in any way negate the greatness of his many discoveries; that we would not be where we are today if not for his pioneering work. I should say all of this, but nothing comes out of my mouth.

"Well," he says, "I will not keep you."

"Yes, Professor, I suppose it's time for me to be getting back."

He points to the large wooden doors of the museum. "And it is time for me to go visit my friends, the antiquities on display. Time for me to mingle with the other relics of ancient civilizations. I wish you a safe trip home." We shake hands one last time. We stand together for a long moment.

"Thank you, Professor. Thanks for everything." I would like to say something more eloquent, but now my mind is as silent as my tongue.

"And I thank you for your visits," he says. "Can you find your way back to your hotel?"

"Oh, yes. I left myself a trail of breadcrumbs."

He smiles and turns toward the museum steps, but then turns to face me again. "By the way," he adds, "you are wrong about your 'Hansel and Gretel' story."

"Oh, I didn't think you would agree with me. I just—"

"No, I am not disagreeing. I mean that you missed something in your analysis of the story."

"How so, Professor?"

"You said it would be better if the children could be reunited with the mother as well as the father."

"Yes, that would make it perfect," I say. "A reunion with both father and mother. That would be a perfect fable for the psychological reunion that ideally takes place in psychotherapy."

"But let us look at this story more carefully," he says. "When Hansel and Gretel escape from the witch, they encounter a body of water, yes?"

"Right."

"In my dream book, I pointed out that water often represents birth."

"Oh, I didn't think of that." Actually, I never gave much credence to the symbols he identified in *The Interpretation of Dreams*. Water means birth, small animals stand for siblings, and so on. None of that ever made much sense to me.

"So water represents birth," he says. "And a white duck carries them, one at a time, across the water. Correct?"

"Correct," I say.

"So let me ask you one question: Who is this white duck that carries the children across the water to see their father?" Without waiting for me to answer, he adds, "You have your perfect story, my friend." And with that, he turns and walks briskly up the first set of steps—I count eight of them—to arrive at the landing, then continues up the remaining five steps and abruptly disappears into the museum. I am left standing alone, here in the heart of Vienna, saying good-bye to the Kunsthistorisches Museum, a monumental nineteenth-century structure, almost excessive in size, perhaps overstated— even boastful—in its imperial grandiosity, but nonetheless of noble intent: to unearth the artistic expressions of our past, long ago buried and forgotten, and bring them into the light of day so we can clearly see where we come from—and who we really are.

AUG 0 0 2016

CPSIA information can be obtained at www.ICGtesting.com
Printed in the USA
LVOW10s1515170616

493067LV00001B/77/P

9 781457 544033